AGENDA
AN ANTHOLOGY

AGENDA

AN ANTHOLOGY

The First Four Decades

(1959-1993)

Edited, with an Introduction
by William Cookson

Foreword by Grey Gowrie

Agenda: London
Carcanet Press: Manchester

First published in Great Britain in 1994 by
Carcanet Press Limited
402-406 Corn Exchange Buildings
Manchester M4 3BY

Reprinted in paperback in Great Britain in 1996 by
Agenda, 5 Cranbourne Court,
Albert Bridge Road, London, SW11 4PE
and Carcanet Press Limited
402-406 Corn Exchange
Manchester M4 3BY

A CIP catalogue record for this book
is available from the British Library.
ISBN 1 85754 302 5
      0 902400 54 1

Carcanet Press acknowledges financial assistance
from the Arts Council of Great Britain

Set in Palatino by Bryan Williamson, Frome
Printed and bound in England by SRP Ltd, Exeter

For Margaret
and Emma

CONTENTS

Foreword: Forward for Agenda by Grey Gowrie   xi
Acknowledgements   xii
Introduction by William Cookson   xiii

1   The Founders
Ezra Pound   From *Canto* 115   3
          Canto 115   4
          Notes   6
David Jones   A, a, a, Domine Deus   8
          The Sleeping Lord   9
Basil Bunting   Six Poems   34
Hugh MacDiarmid   When the Birds Come Back to Rhiannon   38
          Bracken Hills in Autumn   42
          The Day before the Twelfth   43
William Carlos Williams   The Painting   45
          Iris   46
          Coda from *Asphodel,*
            That Greeny Flower   46
Extracts from 'Louis Zukofsky', a special issue
    of *Agenda*, edited by Charles Tomlinson   51

2   A Sheaf of Poems
Michael Alexander   Three Poems   65
William Bedford   Letter from Cumbria   67
Anne Beresford   Five Poems   68
Heather Buck   Three Poems   73
Stanley Burnshaw   'The house hollow . . .'   76
John Cayley   Two Poems   77
Humphrey Clucas   In Darkness   85
William Cookson   Spell: a Sequence   86
Peter Dale   Nine Poems   92
Donald Davie   In the Stopping Train   100
Peter Dent   Two Poems   108
Ronald Duncan   Two poems from 'The Solitudes'   109
Thom Gunn   Touch   111
Donald Hall   In the Kitchen of the Old House   113
Michael Hamburger   Two Poems   115
Ian Hamilton   Five Poems   118
Seamus Heaney   from *Station Island*   121

David Heidenstam 'The land stands silent...'   124
A.L. Hendricks The Tree-lady   125
Geoffrey Hill *Soliloquies*   126
     From the *Songbook* of Sebastian Arrurruz   128
     Lachrimae   130
     Terribilis est locus iste   137
     Five Sonnets from *An Apology for the Revival*
        of Christian Architecture in England   138
     Five Poems   143
Roland John Memory   150
Peter Levi Two Poems   151
Eddie Linden The Miner   157
Edward Lowbury Learning to Walk Again   158
Patricia McCarthy Three Poems   159
Jean MacVean Return   164
Eve Machin Two Poems   168
Sylvia Mann For Three Lords   169
Virginia Maskell Two Poems   170
Alan Massey Three extracts from *Leechcraft*   171
W.S. Milne Two Poems   181
George Oppen Psalm   183
Penelope Palmer Four Poems   184
Rachel Pelham Burn Fragment from Sleep   188
Kathleen Raine Two Poems   189
Theodore Roethke The Rose   192
Peter Russell Russell's Rest   196
N.K. Sandars S.F.   197
Tom Scott Five Poems   199
C.H. Sisson Three Poems   205
W.D. Snodgrass Owls   210
R.S. Thomas Two Versions of a Theme   211
Charles Tomlinson Winter Journey   213
Peter Whigham The Orchard Is Not Cut Down   216
Julie Whitby After 'The Road in Louveciennes'   217
Caroline Wright Three Poems   218

3   Translations
Peter Whigham Five Translations from Sappho   225
Peter Jay Three Translations from Ibycus   227
Basil Bunting A Version of Horace: 'Eheu Fugaces'   229
Peter Whigham from *The Poems of Catullus*   230

Arthur Cooper Three Poems translated from the Chinese   231
Michael Alexander The Ruin, from the Old English   233
Alan Massey From the Provençal of Arnaut Daniel   235
Peter Dale / Dante Sestina   237
W.D. Snodgrass Miorita, from the Romanian   239
Tom Scott and Peter Dale Three Versions of Villon   243
Michael Hamburger / Friedrich Hölderlin 'But when the
                                          heavenly...   247
Michael Hamburger / Georg Trakl De Profundis   251
Peter Russell Three Versions of Osip Mandelstam   252
Alan Neame / Jean Cocteau Leoun   254
Michael Hamburger Paul Celan 'Speak, you also'   278
Hugh MacDiarmid Two Poems by Giuseppe Ungaretti   279
David Rokeah / Ruth & Matthew Mead Two Poems   280
Ezra Pound L'Ultima Ora, from Montanari   281

4   Two Landmarks of Prose
T.S. Eliot Scylla and Charybdis   285
Donald Davie Can Literary History be Permitted?   300

5   Essays
Moelwyn Merchant The Coke Cantos   309
Tom Scott The Poet as Scapegoat (Pound and Politics)   318
Henry Swabey The Just Price (Pound and Economics)   328
Robert Lowell A Tribute (to Pound)   331
Marianne Moore A Note (on Pound)   331
Stuart Piggott David Jones and the Past of Man   332
Saunders Lewis A Note (on David Jones)   336
Kathleen Raine Tom Scott and the Bardic Lineage   338
Heather Buck on Geoffrey Hill   343
Alan Massey on Geoffrey Hill   345

6   A Reconsideration
Jonathan Barker on Swinburne   351

7   Two Memoirs
Basil Bunting Yeats Recollected   365
Norman Rea 9.9.42 Hill, Geoffrey W.   376

8   A Closing Miscellany
W.H. Auden On Technique   391
Basil Bunting Hugh MacDiarmid Lost (an obituary)   392
Geoffrey Hill 'The Age Demanded' (Again)   393
Peter Levi on Penelope Palmer   395
John Bayley 'Death and the Captain'   397
Ezra Pound Gists from Uncollected Prose   404

Sources   409
Index of Authors   417

FORWARD FOR *AGENDA*

To run a magazine for poetry for thirty-five years is a perverse and heroic undertaking. You cannot do it without passion and something of the loneliness of disciple or long-distance lover. William Cookson presents an amiable exterior to the world and to his friends he is an epitome of faithfulness, here for the duration. This rather medieval, knightly quality has delivered the steel he needs for his quest, but even more remarkable is the nature of the quest itself. As he tells us in his introduction, it started with an intellectual love affair with the work of Ezra Pound. A friendship with Pound followed. And so a little magazine, the kind of thing literary folk flirt with frequently in their lives, became a vessel for the exploration of excellence. A classical, not a romantic mind, Pound never believed in subjectivity. Standards existed. You just needed to track them down.

The hunt brought big game to *Agenda*. Think of publishing William Carlos Williams's *Asphodel, That Greeny Flower*, one of the greatest love poems ever written, in England for the first time. David Jones's *The Sleeping Lord* reminds us that there is more to poetry than a well-wrought urn engraved with linguistic wit. There are good poems by Bunting, MacDiarmid and Pound himself. Robert Lowell once said his favourite twentieth century poets were Hardy and Pound, 'because of the heartbreak'. I have always found 'from *Canto* 115' a great poem whose words have the translucence and consistency of tears.

Agenda's house poets have just one thing in common. Peter Dale, Cookson himself, Anne Beresford, Penelope Palmer and others have to make their poems ring. Belles-lettristic chattiness is barred. Dale is a wonderful poet, consistently championed here, inexplicably neglected elsewhere. This anthology would be worth buying for his poems as well as work by heavyweight elders like Geoffrey Hill, R.S. Thomas and Tom Scott. The important thing is for Cookson's Parsifal obsessiveness to continue. It brings to poetry, as no committees can, a passionate attention to the authentic. We need *Agenda*. As Williams wrote in *Asphodel*:

It is difficult
to get the news from poems
yet men die miserably every day
for lack
of what is found there.

Grey Gowrie

xi

Acknowledgements

With *Agenda*, copyright remains with the authors and most of the material in this anthology is reprinted with their permission. In the case of writers who are dead, while efforts have been made to secure permission, we may have failed in a few cases to trace the copyright holder. We apologize for any apparent negligence.

Material by Ezra Pound is reprinted by permission of The Trustees of the Ezra Pound Literary Property Trust and Faber and Faber Limited in Great Britain and New Directions in the United States.

'A, a, a, Domine Deus' and 'The Sleeping Lord' by David Jones are reprinted by permission of the Trustees of the Estate of David Jones and Faber and Faber Limited.

T.S. Eliot's 'Scylla and Charybdis' is reprinted by permission of Valerie Eliot.

Basil Bunting's poems and prose are reprinted by permission of the Estate of Basil Bunting and Oxford University Press.

Hugh MacDiarmid's poems are reprinted by permission of Carcanet Press Limited in Great Britain and New Directions in the United States.

William Carlos Williams's poems are reprinted by permission of Carcanet Press Limited.

Geoffrey Hill's 'Soliloquies' and 'The Songbook of Sebastian Arrurruz' from *King Log*; 'Lachrymae', 'Terribilis Est Locus Iste' and 'An Apology for the Revival of Christian Architecture in England' from *Tenebrae*, from *Collected Poems* by Geoffrey Hill (Penguin Books, 1985), copyright Geoffrey Hill, 1968, 1978, 1985. Reprinted by permission of the author, Penguin Books Limited in Great Britain and Houghton Mifflin Company in the United States. 'An Uncollected Copla' was first published in *Stand* 14/1 (1972). It is reprinted by permission of the author and Jon Silkin.

Poems by Thom Gunn, Ian Hamilton, Seamus Heaney and Theodore Roethke are reprinted by permission of Faber and Faber in Great Britain, and those by Peter Levi by permission of Anvil Press. Ian Hamilton's 'At Evening', 'Again', 'Soliloquy' and 'The Garden' first appeared in the *L.R.B.* In the United States permission to reproduce the poems by Thom Gunn and Seamus Heaney has been granted by the authors and Farrar Strauss and Giroux Inc, and 'The Rose' by Theodore Roethke by Doubleday.

INTRODUCTION

My aim in editing this anthology has been to gather a collection of good poems, and essays about poetry, that can be enjoyed as a book in its own right. I've prepared it as if I were editing a bumper issue of *Agenda* out of an unusually rich welter of submissions – not surprising after thirty-five years! My touchstone has been material that has stayed in my mind, so it is inevitably a very personal choice.

In order to give the reader some idea how *Agenda* began, a few autobiographical notes seem to be required.

Poems were with me from the beginning: my father, George Cookson (1870-1949), was the author of two books, both published in Swinburne's lifetime. They contain well-wrought poems, having qualities he had learnt from Wordsworth (an ancestor), Keats and the Classics. In 1936, three years before I was born, he founded *English*, the magazine of the English Association. Before the war, he edited it from the same mansion block, Cranbourne Court, that has always been *Agenda*'s H.Q. So for me, editing a poetry magazine was to continue a family tradition. My mother also wrote poems – a few were published in *Time and Tide*. She was a great support to me in the early days of *Agenda* and over twenty years later, shortly before her death in 1982, I published a late poem of hers under her maiden name, Rachel Pelham Burn. I've included it in the anthology.

The founder of *Agenda* was Ezra Pound. Probably early in 1955, when I was fifteen, in a bookshop in South Kensington, I bought a little book with a yellow dust-jacket: *A Selection of Poems*. I've no idea who was responsible for the choice, but it was a good introduction to Pound, and in its eighty pages, included a bit of everything, ending with a few Cantos. At first, I found the poems difficult – I'd already been reading Eliot and his impression had been more immediate – but I persevered and was soon buying every work by Pound that I could find. At first this was not good for my meagre poetic talent as I started to pick up Pound's mannerisms and tone of voice. It may be better for a young poet to learn the rudiments of his craft from a minor poet rather than a major one.

In the Spring of 1956 I got hold of the first, Scheiwiller edition of *Section Rock-Drill* (Cantos 85-95) that had appeared in Italy in

September 1955. I don't remember being so excited by a book before or since. The experience of reading the lyric, paradisal cantos 90-95 for the first time was akin to that of falling in love. There was a sense of great happiness – of light and air.

About this time I had met the English poet and editor, Peter Russell. He had recently published the final issue of his excellent magazine *Nine*, which I regard in many ways as a precursor of what I have attempted in *Agenda*. He was then a bookseller and he introduced me to the work of many writers who later were to become important to *Agenda*, among them Hugh MacDiarmid and Tom Scott. He also had the courage, when no one else would have touched them, to publish Pound's *Six Money Pamphlets* and *A.B.C. of Economics*. Reading these polemical writings was an enormous help to me in discovering what the *Cantos* are about.

In the same year (1956) I had my first experience as an editor when Edmund Gray, Howard Burns and myself decided to revive the Westminster School literary magazine, *The Trifler*, which had an intermittent history dating back to the eighteenth century. In the second issue (July 1957) I reviewed *Rock-Drill*. To my amazement, Pound liked what I had written, saying, 'Forget if I thanked you for best rev/ of Rock-Dr since Stock's'. He began writing to me regularly, and, with characteristic generosity, tried to educate me and put me in touch with people all over the world. He was pleased that I hoped to get to Oxford; he began a letter of 23 October 1957, 'Yes I think it an excellent idea that there shd/ be at least one y.m. at Oxon who knows the score, or at least wants to know it.'

I continued to correspond with Pound throughout 1958. These were the last years of his incarceration in 'the bug house', as he called St Elizabeth's Hospital where he had been held prisoner since 1946. He was particularly pleased that my school friend, Edmund Gray, was the grandson of Laurence Binyon. He named him 'Binbinides' after his nickname for Binyon which was 'Bin-Bin'. Edmund was to become *Agenda*'s associate editor at the beginning, and is now a trustee. Often Pound wrote about anything that happened to interest him at the moment; he asked me to find out what I could about Linnaeus at the Natural History Museum, 'I keep gittin round to second kindergarten studies'. The tone was usually affirmative, 'The enemy is IGGURUNCE, not jews or masons' . . . 'best defence is POSITIVE'. Also, 'Every man . . . has the right to have his ideas examined one at a time' and 'one shd/ not make the battle line on the edge of race'.

Pound was released in May, 1958. Soon after this event, he wrote to me, '25 Maggio/ Dear Cookson/ as you are the youngest I am writing to you for the others, as you have greatest interest in preserving the vestiges.' In the Autumn, my mother and I took a three-week holiday in Italy. Pound invited us to stay for a week in Brunnenburg, the castle in the Italian Tyrol belonging to his daughter and son-in-law where he had gone to live on leaving the USA.

Although he had warned me in a letter (12 September) 'I alternate short bursts of energy, with total exhaustion, dont expect me to function as dynamo, or diesel, when yu get here', Pound was in reasonable health. I remember how he rushed into the room to see us – there was no formality about his greeting. As Mary de Rachewiltz has written of her father, 'He brought with him a dimension of – no, not stillness, but magnitude, momentum'.

In the mornings Pound was putting the final touches to the *Thrones* cantos and every evening he read aloud to his family – his two grandchildren were particularly attentive listeners. He read some of the *Confucian Odes* and he also tried out poems from *Confucius to Cummings*, the anthology of poetry that he and his friend and assistant, Marcella Spann, had made together. There was some Browning and Hardy, but I chiefly remember how he read, with great delicacy, Ford Madox Ford's long love poem, 'On Heaven' which expressed Pound's innate gentleness and *humanitas* – a quality which the rage and fanaticism of some of his writing can never wipe out.

At this time I was a painfully shy and serious youth. My mother told me that he said to her on the stairs, 'Does he ever speak?' I wish I had met Pound a few years later when I could have talked to him more easily. However, he immediately set me to work, giving me a pile of notebooks of the *Cantos*. Most of these consisted of material he had rejected. He asked me to go through them, putting in white paper markers where I considered there were lines or passages worth rescuing. It was typical of his simplicity and openness that he should have entrusted such a daunting task to a young man who had just left school and about whose abilities and understanding he knew little. I assiduously tore up much white paper, inserting it throughout the twenty or so books, with, I hope, a little perception. Whether he found what I had done useful, I shall never know. I wish I could remember more of what was in those notebooks; I think they mostly concerned nineteenth-century European history; there was a good deal about Bismarck. There were also references to Hitler, 'Even Adolf was human/ playing Wagner on the piano to calm his nerves'... 'Adolf infected/ in Germany no free expression of opinion' are lines that have stuck in my memory, though I don't claim I've quoted them exactly.

The week passed rapidly. When we left, Pound climbed the steep salita from the castle and came with us in the car to Merano. He got it to stop to show us a fresco of a mermaid on the Duomo wall. What remains with me from our meeting was an electric energy, the Chaucerian robustness and humour which make the *Cantos* such an affirmative poem, 'holding that energy is near to benevolence' (Canto 93).

The idea of *Agenda* grew from this visit. Pound had a scheme that I should organize a four-page section in an existing publication, possibly *Time and Tide* – my mother was a friend of Theodora Bosanquet who was at one time literary editor of that paper. But after my return to London, this plan came to nothing. Then Peter Russell suggested I start my own publication, and thus *Agenda* was born. He introduced me to Czesław and Krystyna Bednarczyk of 'The Poets' and Painters' Press' and they were to remain *Agenda*'s printers until they retired in 1991. Without the high quality of their work (and at times generous credit) we would not have survived so long.

Pound wanted *Agenda* to be called *Four Pages* – a continuation of a periodical which he had similarly instigated. I avoided the name, because, although I was only groping my way at this time, I was vaguely aware that the title left no room for expansion!

I present here, on pages xvii and xviii, the first editorial as it was ghost-written by Pound, and the text, as it appeared in *Agenda*'s first issue.

When I inserted sentences drawing attention to the work of David Jones and Hugh MacDiarmid I had, of course, no idea that one day I would be in a position to produce substantial special issues devoted to these writers and a Ford Madox Ford number eventually followed. Our first number also included a translation of a poem by Osip Mandelstam by Peter Russell. This may have been the first English translation of that poet to be printed; we continued to publish translations of his work. Peter Russell has received inadequate recognition for his virtual discovery of Mandelstam and his translations are finer than those that have appeared subsequently. I reprint three in this anthology.

Pound liked the first issue and wrote, 'Pleased with Agenda. It

FOUR PAGES revives becqause its editors find themselves
faced with the almost total , and possibly criminal, demise
of cHHHHHHH curiosity on the part of nearly all our elders
who get into print ,the worst cases being the most celebrated ,
HHH most highly publiciçed and most highly remunerated.
     There is also a painful lack of communications between
isolated outposts , some of them possibly frivolous , some
eccentric .(An outpost cannot be central).HHHF ,

     London has no map of european thought
               at this moment,   , some
continental groups are to be regarded with deep suspicion.
Several are run by kindly (but wholly illiterate) old ladies
with money. There is a swiss gang labled   Eranos
which arouses our utmost mistrust.
     We hear that Martin Heidegger is a serious character
and that it would be worth our while to discuss ideas with him
or his acquaintance , if , as is unlikely , any of our
continental contemporaries will carry on a discussion. We are
also told that his " last phase " : " Aus der Erfahrung des Denkens"
is untranslatable. A pocket dictionary gives " Erfahrung :
experience.
          cf/ cummings on sadism.   (**)

(**) footnote at bottom of page.
We are creditably informed that the English translations of Heidegger
are so inaccurate that they make himwant to (textually) vomit.
No copy of"Holzwege " is available to us at this moment.

Dear C/n yes, I prefer title Four Pages, to estab/ continuity,
ultimately a reprint of usefulg parts of 4 P/ Strike and Edg
in some larger mag/ possibly Furop.
I dont thik it out to " coincide " , but to appear 2 weeks after
and before Europe giving greater possibility of quick news
. i.e. some outlet every fortnight. and to comment both on
Europ and Listen. favourably and unf-
ignoring in the main the schleimerei, save for ¼ page of occasionally
sottisier, ? mainly of TLS. ?

        The above is strictly ghost writ
as from editors.   not from E P

agenda

January 1959.   No. 1.

Ford Madox Ford in "Ancient Lights" wrote: "It is one of the saddening things about Anglo-Saxon life that any sort of union for an aesthetic or for an intellectual purpose seems to be almost an impossibility." This is still the case today.

We are faced with an appalling, almost criminal, lack of curiosity on the part of authors who get into print, and often the worst cases are the most celebrated, most highly publicised and most highly remunerated. All the active ideas in the many thousands of books published each year, could be expressed in a few pages.

There is a distressing lack of communications between isolated outposts. Some of these are no doubt frivolous, some eccentric—outposts cannot be central.

London at this moment has no map of European thought. We are all too ignorant of most Continental groups—a few it is difficult not to regard with suspicion, others are run by kindly (but wholly illiterate) old ladies with money. It seems to us that it is a Scottish Nationalist, Mr Hugh MacDiarmid, and a Welshman, Mr David Jones, whose writings are the most stimulating to thought and show a more lively curiosity than any of their English contemporaries at this moment. (That we disagree with Mr. MacDiarmid in many fundamental ways is immaterial as we believe his ultimate objective to be similar to our own: i.e. the furtherance of civilisation.)

"You damn sadist!" said mr cummings
"you try to make people think."

How much of Heidegger's thought can be grasped from the English translations? Is it true that "Aus der Erfahrung des Denkens" is untranslatable? Erfahrung = experience (pocket dictionary).

In the furtherance of civilisation, numbers are not of first importance, what matters is that those actively engaged in this task, should not become isolated, but communicate and keep curiosity alive in the differing fields of their activity.

A Poem by Osip Mandelshtam (1891-1941) adapted from the Russian by Peter Russell.

When the urban moon comes out on the squares
And slowly the teeming city shines with its light,
And night comes down, full of despair and darkness
And the melodious wax yields to harsh time:

don't look too Poundista. At least not too unadulteratedly.' He sent many lists of names and addresses, some of whom became the first subscribers. A year's subscription was five shillings!

Pound regularly sent in items for publication, many to be used anonymously, for about six months. After he had received a particularly boring issue (No. 5) he suggested I should stop, but he soon relented, sending £5 towards the printer's bill to help me to continue, writing, 'Oke Hay / Fluctuat, But get some GUTS into the next issue, and something that isn't watered down E.P. / and that shows desire to FOCUS various energies.' He was now tiring, but with what energy remained, he continued his 'struggle' (to quote his 1970 Preface to *Guide to Kulchur*) 'to preserve some of the values that make life worth living'. He had also begun to write some of his deepest poetry, *Drafts & Fragments*. I think it is fitting to open this Anthology with the two versions of Canto 115 that appeared in *Agenda*, the first as it was approved by Pound for the issue celebrating his eightieth birthday, the second, longer and earlier draft, which Mary de Rachewiltz sent us for our 21st Anniversary Issue (1979).

Pound was glad that *Agenda* had no affiliation with any political party and this remains a tradition of the magazine to this day. As he wrote to Moelwyn Merchant, 'Cookson and Binyon's grandson are reviving Four Pages, without connection with ANY political aroma'. Pound's political views have been more misinterpreted than any other aspect of his work. Tom Scott got to the truth when he wrote in *Agenda*, 'I have never known a poet whose politics are to be taken other than poetically, that is to say in terms of his vision of the coming of the kingdom of poetry on earth, the divine harmony, and not in terms of power politics. A poet's politics are visionary, not political.' I have thought it right to give Tom Scott's essay on Pound and politics a central place in the prose section of this anthology. Most poets now lack the courage to tackle major subjects. *Agenda* has always believed that Pound's ideas and beliefs are of vital importance, and that the passion with which he held them made him a great poet. There is no doubt that the Second World War engulfed part of Pound's mind in a kind of darkness ('That I lost my center / fighting the world' as he wrote near the end of the *Cantos*), but even his wartime broadcasts, despite their excesses, are essentially a document of anti-war literature. The vision at the core of the *Cantos* is right in its fight against the makers of war and 'Usura'; ultimately it is light that wins in the poem. It is also often forgotten that, to adapt Ben Jonson on Shakespeare, the *Cantos* was not written for 'an age, but for all time' – who now bothers about the immediate political turmoil in Dante's or Milton's life? On the subject of Pound, history and politics, it is appropriate to give the last words to Geoffrey Hill:

> Pound's vision of history in the *Cantos* focuses on heroic figures, heroic creators and patrons, snatching brief victory from a general context of defeat, their achievement all the more luminous and illuminating because of the darkness that surrounds and encroaches. His most powerful and cogent metaphors are of light shining all the more strongly, beautifully, because of the surrounding darkness. That Pound's own great intelligence itself sank into darkness for a time does not, for me, obscure the truth of much that he has to say about the tyranny of Mammon or diminish the noble beauty of his finest work.

Towards the end of 1960, Pound suffered increasing ill health and it was rare to hear from him, so he ceased to be actively involved in the editing. *Agenda* remained only a folded sheet until April 1960, when the actress Virginia Maskell gave me £10 for the first card cover. She was a poet, and a friend of Ronald Duncan – I printed a few of her poems in early issues; I have put two in the Anthology. When she committed suicide a few years later, 'a great matter went out of the universe', to use a line Peter Dale wrote about the death of his father.

In the Autumn of 1960, I went to New College, Oxford, to read English, taking *Agenda* with me. John Bayley, now one of the magazine's trustees, was my tutor. Here the periodical gradually grew in size and I started printing long poems – the first, Alan Neame's memorable translation of what is probably Jean Cocteau's greatest poem, *Léone*, which he wrote during the German occupation of Paris. It was Pound who suggested to Neame that he should translate this, and no one could have done it better – I think it is the single most important item in the translation section of this Anthology.

The next turning point occurred about a year after my arrival at Oxford. I had read a poem by Peter Dale, in the student magazine, *Oxford Opinion*, called 'Nearly Got the Moon In', which has not been collected. I was struck immediately that here was 'the true voice of feeling' – the sensation, which I remember vividly in connection with this poem (not one of Dale's best) is impatient of definition, but associated with a kind of electrical force; throughout my years of editing, this feeling has occurred rarely, but it is the only touchstone on which I can rely. At this period, I often saw an Irish poet called Michael O'Higgins; when I told him how much I thought of Dale's poem, he introduced us. Soon afterwards, Dale started to advise me, and persuaded me to publish a regular reviews section. He did not become officially associate editor until 1971 (and co-editor ten years later) but many of the most useful things we have done were instigated by him (Rhythm Issue, Rhyme, State of Poetry, etc.) I have not been able to represent this side of *Agenda* adequately in the Anthology as it is not easy to excerpt. Dale's deep knowledge of the craft of poetry and all matters of technique help to continue the Poundian tradition of the magazine. We also often disagree, which results in a creative tension that may make *Agenda* more living than if either of us had been editing it alone.

Our first special issue (1963) attempted to introduce William Carlos Williams to England by printing entire his long, moving love poem, *Asphodel, That Greeny Flower*, together with an introductory essay on his work by Peter Whigham. I've represented the poem by its 'Coda' in the 'Founders' part of this Anthology. A feature on Theodore Roethke followed, printing one of his last poems, 'The Rose', with essays by Ian Hamilton and Peter Levi and then, in 1964, Charles Tomlinson did the first of our guest-edited issues, which was devoted to introducing Louis Zukofsky. I close 'Founders' with an excerpt from this. In this first decade of *Agenda*, special numbers followed on Ezra Pound, Basil Bunting, Hugh MacDiarmid (edited with Tom Scott) and David Jones.

I consider David Jones, after Pound, to be the most important 'founder' of *Agenda*. Edmund Gray introduced me to him when I was sixteen, and, in 1961 he designed the lettering that has been used on the cover ever since. He read little Pound, apart from being interested in his writings on money and history. Nevertheless his poetry has qualities in common with the *Cantos*, which was something to do with the *Zeitgeist*, as he used to say. I believe Hugh MacDiarmid was right when he described him as 'the greatest living poet in the British Isles' and in 1967 I brought out a triple issue which included reproductions of his paintings and drawings, as well as new poems. As it is short, I place my editorial note here:

At a time when there seems danger that the world is losing its memory, and few poets possess the visionary imagination which lies at the root of all the permanent poetry of Europe, I think it is fitting that these three issues of *Agenda* should be devoted to different aspects of the work of David Jones. His poetry and his painting are both filled with a numinous material detail; they contain a particular beauty which, while gathering strength from many various sources, holds its own haecceity that has a certain kinship to *Sir Gawain and the Grene Knight*. He has drawn from 'the dark backward and abysm of time' radiant layers of past experience into a living cosmos – as Ezra Pound has written:

> There *is* the subtler music, the clear light
> Where time burns back about th' eternal embers.

This was the first really large number I produced and I like to think it was in part responsible for David Jones writing the longest of his later poems, *The Sleeping Lord*. I remember he read me about three pages of a poem he had begun in the late 1930s and asked me whether I thought anything could be made of it. I was deeply moved by the fragment and urged him to continue, and so *The Sleeping Lord* took shape; working often into the early hours, he just managed to complete it in time for our press date. It is the most important long poem that *Agenda* has published so it is fitting that it should form the core of the 'Founders' section of this book.

The next major issue was a triple one on Wyndham Lewis (1969/70). This was done at the instigation of Agnes Bedford, concert pianist and close friend of both Pound and Lewis. Without her help it would not have been possible, but sadly, she died before seeing it. I dedicated it to her memory. Unfortunately it has not been possible to excerpt from it and the same applies to other important issues: Thomas Hardy, edited by Donald Davie, and US Poetry, edited by Lord Gowrie to name but two.

I have divided this book into eight parts and I hope its shape will be clear without the need of much commentary. I have dated each item by the year of publication. I think I have already said enough about the 'Founders' section, but I'll add a few notes on the remaining parts.

In Part Two, I've arranged the poets alphabetically. They have been chosen from all periods of *Agenda*'s history. Considerations of space have forced me to omit many important poems and poets – in particular, Peter Russell is represented by only one lyric, when I would have liked to include at least one of his excellent and funny Quintilius monologues.

Part Three is devoted to foreign poetry because I believe that English poetry, since Chaucer, has been constantly enriched by the art of translation. *Agenda* has always encouraged this in all its variety. Where versions first appeared in the magazine and are now available in Penguin Classics (Peter Whigham's Catullus, Michael Alexander's Old English, Peter Dale's Villon and Michael Hamburger's Celan) I have chosen just one poem from each. I regret that space did not allow the inclusion of Desmond O'Grady's fine version of the sixth century Arab poem, 'The Wandering King'.

Part Four introduces the prose section of the book with two writings of wisdom, expressing central truths about poetry which in the present literary climate are often forgotten. The Eliot lecture, for which we are indebted to Valerie Eliot (it has only been published in *Agenda*'s T.S. Eliot Special Issue, 1985), shows how hard it is to write lasting poetry of any kind – as Randall Jarrell said, 'Writing good poetry is only occasionally difficult: usually it is impossible'. The Davie essay is equally pertinent:

> For literary history is, undeniably, threatening. It threatens vested interests in the book trade, in various Chambers of Commerce planning 'Poetry Festivals', in academic institutions, in journalism, in manipulation of the public. This is because it is, of its nature, inescapably *élitist*. It declares, necessarily and of its nature, that most of the words uttered from public platforms in verse or prose, in syndicated columns and on TV programmes, are *lies*. This is what everyone knows, but no one will say. Literary history, if it is undertaken in a Johnsonian spirit, must say the unsayable: that most literary reputations, promoted and sustained by *hype*, are bogus; that the persons promoted as articulating our deepest sentiments are in fact only articulating the shallowest; that the best and most truthful writers of our time have, almost without exception, been side-lined, accorded at most a perfunctory respect.

In Part Five, I've chosen a few articles about poets central to *Agenda*. On Pound, I've deliberately put in essays that stress the vitality of his ideas and content – most of his critics avoid these aspects. Moelwyn Merchant is particularly perceptive about the ethics of the *Cantos*, and Tom Scott writes with passion and clarity about Pound and politics. Finally, the Revd Henry Swabey deals with Pound and economics from the perspective of the many years' study he has made of the Church and Usury. It is good to have his piece as he was a contributor to the first issue of *Agenda*. Likewise, in Part Five, I've chosen a distinguished archaeologist's view of David Jones, rather than that of a literary critic, to stress the living nature ('nowness' to use a word he liked) of his vision. A recent letter from a subscriber who writes that he is not 'by profession involved in any way in the literary world...I am, I suppose, that rare beast the "common reader"' says, 'I find *Agenda*'s untheoretical approach to literature, that it is about our experience in the world and has a true value is very important'. I like to think this is true. I also put in two short notes on Geoffrey Hill to manifest the beauty of his poetry and its accessibility. They seek to counter the false belief that it is 'difficult'.

Part Six gives an example of an ongoing series of articles ('Reconsiderations') on dead poets. Jonathan Barker reveals forgotten qualities in Swinburne. *Agenda* believes past poetry is as living as that of the present.

Part Seven presents two memoirs both of which I hope make the Anthology more lively and humorous. The Norman Rea article is particularly interesting for its publication of Geoffrey Hill's juvenilia.

Finally, in Part Eight, I've put together a few important shorter writings. The one by Auden is the only thing he wrote for us, and as space prevented including much from issues on technique, it is probably the best piece of its kind to put in. I also include three significant reviews, and one obituary, and it seems fitting that the Anthology should close, as it opened, with some words of Pound.

No account of *Agenda* should fail to express our gratitude to the Arts Council for their twenty-seven years' unobtrusive support. This began in 1966. It is to end, at least on a basis of regular income support, at about the time of the publication of this book. Perhaps our inherent unfashionability, which has always been one of our strengths, in a worldly sense told against us, but the magazine is not bitter at the withdrawal of funding, nor do we have any intention of folding. This is not edited as a retrospective anthology – it merely marks a stage in *Agenda*'s development. Through the generosity of Valerie Eliot, J. Paul Getty and others, our future is assured for 1994/5, and we are actively seeking some kind of regular sponsorship for the years after this.

That *Agenda* will never be popular, with a large circulation, does not worry me, as I believe, with Pound and Machiavelli that 'L'Umanita vivè in pochi' (the life of the race is concentrated in a few individuals):

> in pochi,
> > causa motuum,
> > > pine seed splitting cliff's edge.
> > > > (Canto 87)

As I have reprinted *Agenda*'s first Editorial (January 1959) in these pages, it seems appropriate to close this Introduction with a few gists concerning the making of poetry, that I have put together, thirty-five years later, as the Editorial of our Autumn 1993 issue:

A great poem must remain a mystery. In every age, it is a rare event. To take a few random examples: it is impossible to say why, 'You do look, my son, in a mov'd sort...', 'As you came from the holy land of Walsingham', Landor's 'Dirce' or Pound's 'Canto 115' shake the reader to the roots on each rereading, but it is poetry of this voltage that we seek.

'No man can read Hardy's poems collected but that his own life, and forgotten moments of it, will come back to him, a flash here and an hour there. Have you a better test of true poetry?' (Pound). The Muses ' "are" as Uncle William said "the daughters of Memory"' (Pound quoting Yeats).

Imagination is the tap root, but, a poet's 'data' must be 'accurate, experiential and contactual...The imagination must work through what is known and known by a kind of touch. Like the Yggdrasil of northern myth, the roots must be in hard material though the leaves be conceptual and in the clouds; otherwise we can have fancy but hardly imagination' (David Jones).

The 'knowledge of contrast, feeling for light and shade, all that information (primitive sense) necessary for a poem...' (Keats).

'Writing poetry is like juggling with conflicting forces in a tiny unit' (Geoffrey Hill).

The 'workman must be dead to himself while engaged upon the work, otherwise we have that sort of "self-expression" which is as undesirable in the painter or the writer as in the carpenter, the cantor, the half-back, or the cook' (David Jones).

There are no rules that a genius cannot break, but 'originality precisely the *not* to be desired, unless it happens...' (Pound).

'*The Divine Comedy* is a constant reminder to the poet, of the obligation to explore, to find words for the inarticulate, to capture those feelings which people can hardly even feel, because they have no words for them' (Eliot).

One use of poetry is to enlarge our experience, 'if it...reveals to us something of which we are unconscious, it feeds us with its energy' (Pound). Rather than expressing the predictable, poems should 'seek to carve out a shape in the unknown' (Peter Dale on Geoffrey Hill).

Lasting poetry remains timeless and is therefore always contemporary – it does not date, like the ephemera – often the most popular in whatever era. 'There is really no modern poetry and ancient poetry only good poetry and bad' (Auden).

One of the aims of *Agenda* should be to take a stand against the trivia, cleverness, dull predictability – emotion without intellect, fancy without imagination – that pervades much widely praised, and award-winning, current poetry, both here and in the USA. Perhaps a new *Dunciad* is needed!

'However often philosophers and linguisticians may have declared it an impossibility, poetry's business is with telling the truth; and the truth in question is not restricted to the truth about its own workings and its own production. It seems incredible that this should need to be said; and that professors of literature should earn their salaries by denying it' (Donald Davie).

Poetry ought to be the most subtle and living form of language. That it really matters, and is somehow vital to human communication and to our perception of the universe, needs to be remembered.

William Cookson

PART ONE

The Founders

EZRA POUND

from Canto 115

The scientists are in terror
                and the European mind stops
Wyndham Lewis chose blindness
                rather than have his mind stop.

Night under wind mid garofani
                the petals are almost still.

Mozart, Linnaeus, Sulmona,

When one's friends hate each other
                how can there be peace in the world?
Their asperities diverted me in my green time.

A blown husk that is finished
                but the light sings eternal
a pale flare over marshes
                where the salt hay whispers to tide's change

Time, space,
                neither life nor death is the answer.

And of men seeking good,
                doing evil.

In meine Heimat
                where the dead walked
                and the living were made of cardboard.

                                                    (1965)

3

Canto 115

The scientists are in terror
                and the european mind stops.
                                Su! coraggio.
                                        Do not accept it.

                Tan   ☷   the dawn
                                        somewhere.
Wyndham taking blindness, rather than risk having his mind stop.
A bronze dawn, bright russet – but dawn of some sort
                                and some how.

There is so much beauty.
                How can we harden our hearts?
A beautiful night under wind mid garofani
                That wind wd be?
                                        Apeliota.
Do not move
                let the wind speak
                                        That is Paradise
The petals are almost still.

                        Απηλιώτης

The beauty of thought has not entered them.
                That is, it has as but a flash in far darkness –
I have tried to write Paradise –
                let the Gods forgive what I have made.
                Let those I love try to forgive what I have made.
Mozart, Linnaeus –
                        Sulmona
                out of dust –
                out of dust
                                The gold thread in dark pattern at Torcello.
The wall still stands.
                                There is a path by a field almost empty.
Great trees over an avenue
When one's friends hate each other
                                how can there be peace in the world?
Peccavi.
                Their asperities diverted me in my green time.

4

Their envies.
                    Their paradise?
                                        their best
for an instant.
? to all men for an instant?
                              Beati!
the sky leaded with elm boughs,
                    above the vision
                              the heart
"the flowers of the apricot blow from the East
                                        to the West.
I have tried to keep them from falling."

A blown husk that is finished
                              but the light sings eternal
a pale flare over marshes
                    where the salt hay whispers to tide's change.

Note. Another version, in place of the line, 'Great trees over an avenue'
has: Ub. '43: 'Damn it, your future utility I am thinking of.' '45: 'Fa un
affare', he said, 'chi muore oggi.' The Admiral Ubaldo degli Uberti helped
Pound to 'go North' in 1943, encouraged him to put himself into safety . . .
but in 1945 he wrote his son that death was a bonus – and was shot on the
very last day of the war, by mistake.

                                        Mary de Rachewiltz

                              (1979)

Notes

Parts of which have been used in later drafts.

La carence or damn slimness
des affaires characteristic, this week of La Bourse
           Le Journal 25 Juin mille neuf cent trente cinque
                      1935
or any time in the past 20 years
at any time during
      Informations little encouraging from New York
Whereas the rentes London and Paris
and a heavy tendency *au debut de la huitaine*
but on the other hand coal mines in Silesia
           the lady pianist is playing even scales
      "de fine amor vient science et beauté"   WITH expression
The sun, as Guinicelli says beats on the mud all day
and the mud stays vile
      Birds to the Wood, as of sleep in sapphire inherence
as the sun to the mortal eye or as Zeus remarked of ΟΥ ΤΙΣ
      the fellow is one of us.
A man with a mind like that
           the fellow is one of us
Shines in the mind of heaven, as I quoted in
                      Canto which was it?
God who made it, more than the sun in our eye
As says Pliny the younger
                 That one man help another. God is that
one man help another. In the time of the Emperor Titus
or Guinicelli about 1274
                      encircling all movement stillness
and the glaze of its own made light
      as time scuttles under the door jam
      as they say Omeros was lacking in purpose
because he had no need to dispute with the reader
                 Ἦρι μὲν αἵ τε
      as Ibycus in the spring time, or Roland
by god I have broken the olifans I have broken that
                      elephant horn
      and scattered all its encrustments
           "Bigod", he said, "that pagan is done for,"
Bigod, Barney is finished, is he indeed,

6

and the fighters were Gesell and Douglas and Fack
and Odon with diabetes, and Jeff Mark against usury
all very prosaic and Orage and Brenton and Woodward
    not to say Kitson and old T.C. back in the seventies
and said Mr Bryan to Kitson
        "of course Bimetalism isn't it,"
It's the national credit
                        control of the national credit
        there was and is no rest in this war
His phiz like an honest man's
            and his tail over hell pit
"Bigod I have broke the encrustment,
            that was the best horn in this army"
Tin leaves on an unnamed grave
                            anonymous
    in fact un amico has written
    "barbed wiz wire tin crosses"
without seeking the cause in money
                without interesting himself in such causes
                Gestalt an interest grief:
Said John Adams "I pity the pore bastids in winter"
as for patterns they see stewed oatmeal in a bowl
                dissociation of ideas seems inhuman
their world a sub-species of porridge bowl
is an imminent conscience to be managed by levers?
    an imminent consciousness working the levers,
    being a spoiled priest from his infancy
    or says Leibnitz and so forth
        God is that one man helps another.

                                            (1970)

DAVID JONES

A, a, a, Domine Deus

I said, Ah! what shall I write?
I enquired up and down.
              (He's tricked me before
with his manifold lurking-places.)
I looked for His symbol at the door.
I have looked for a long while
              at the textures and contours.
I have run a hand over the trivial intersections.
I have journeyed among the dead forms
causation projects from pillar to pylon.
I have tired the eyes of the mind
              regarding the colours and lights.
I have felt for His Wounds
              in nozzles and containers.
I have wondered for the automatic devices.
I have tested the inane patterns
              without prejudice.
I have been on my guard
              not to condemn the unfamiliar.
For it is easy to miss Him
              at the turn of a civilisation.
  I have watched the wheels go round in case I might see the
living creatures like the appearance of lamps, in case I might see
the Living God projected from the Machine. I have said to the
perfected steel, be my sister and for the glassy towers I thought I
felt some beginnings of His creature, but *A, a, a, Domine Deus*,
my hands found the glazed work unrefined and the terrible
crystal a stage-paste... *Eia, Domine Deus*.

                      c. *1938 and 1966.*

                      (1967)

The Sleeping Lord

A Note on "The Sleeping Lord"

A brief note with regard to this fragment called provisionally "The Sleeping Lord" is, for the following reasons, necessary. First, as here printed, various of its passages are subject to revision and there are certain other passages that I had hoped to include, but have excluded, partly on account of length and partly because I have not, for unforseen reasons, been able to get them into the shape I wished in time for publication in this issue of *Agenda* which the editor has most kindly chosen to devote to various aspects of my work.

Secondly, it chances to be a piece that is essentially for the ear rather than the eye. It chances also that owing to its subject matter it contains a number of words, mainly proper and common nouns, in Welsh. This in turn, has made it necessary to try to convey some approximate idea of the sound of those words.

For example, should the reader not know, that the Welsh *au* in, say, *mamau* (mothers) is similar in sound to the terminating syllable in the English words 'lullaby' or 'magpie', or the Latin word *puellae*, then the whole feeling of the sentence in which those words were in juxtaposition would be lost. I have therefore been compelled to append a number of notes attempting to indicate at least something of the sounds of such Welsh terms as I had to use in order to evoke the feel and ethos inherent in the *materia* or subject matter.

Here I must apologize to Welsh readers for these inadequate and elementary attempts. I fully realize that the approximations are extremely arbitrary and in some cases may be wide of the mark, but something of the sort had to be attempted and had to be as brief as possible. I have given the Welsh dipthongs *ae, ai, au, ei* and *eu* as approximating more or less to the English 'ei' in 'height', whereas in fact these dipthongs vary. In a few cases I give the English word 'eye' as corresponding to the Welsh *au*. For one of the two sounds of the Welsh *y* I give 'uh' as in the English 'u' in run, so that *Y Forwyn* (The Virgin) is given as being pronounced uh vór-win.

I have excluded all other notes from this version, except in a few instances.

DAVID JONES
April the 1st, 1967

And is his bed wide
                    is his bed deep
is his bed long
                    where is his bed and
                    where has he lain him
from north of Llanfair-ym-Muallt
                    (a name of double *gladius*-piercings)[1]
south to the carboniferous vaultings of Gŵyr[2]
                    (where in the sea-slope chamber
they shovelled aside the shards & breccia
                    the domestic litter and man-squalor
of gnawed marrowbones and hearth-ash
with utile shovels fashioned of clavicle-bones
                    of warm-felled great fauna.
Donated the life-signa:
                    the crocked viatic meal
                    the flint-worked ivory agalma
the sacral sea-shell trinkets
                    posited with care the vivific amulets
of gleam-white rodded ivory
                    and, with oxide of iron
ochred life-red the cerements
                    of the strong limbs
of the young *nobilis*
                    the first of the sleepers of
Pritenia, *pars dextralis*, O! aeons & aeons
                    before we were insular'd.)
Is the tump by Honddu[3]
                    his lifted bolster?
                    does a gritstone outcrop
incommode him?

---

[1] Llanfair-ym-Muallt: 'Mary's church in Buellt'. The town now called Builth Wells. It was between Llanfair and Llanganten that the Lord Llywelyn, Prince of Wales was killed in 1282. Hence my reference to a *double* piercing in that any place-name with Marian associations necessarily recalls the passage in the gospel of the *gladius* that would pierce the heart of the God-bearer. Pronounce: llan-veir-um-mee-alt.

[2] Gŵyr: The Gower Peninsular; pronounce approximately goo-eer. It was in Gŵyr that human remains, ritually buried, were discovered of a young man of the Palaeolithic period, so many, many millenniums prior to Britain becoming an island.

[3] Honddu: pronounce hón-thee.

does a deep syncline
sag beneath him?
or does his dinted thorax rest
where the contorted heights
themselves rest
on a lateral pressured anticline?
Does his russet-hued mattress
does his rug of shaly grey
ease at all for his royal dorsals
the faulted under-bedding.
Augite-hard and very chill
do scattered *cerrig*[1]
jutt to discomfort him?
Millenniums on millennia since
this cold scoria dyked up molten
when the sedimented, slowly layered strata
(so great the slow heaped labour of their conditor
the patient creature of water) said each to each other:
'There's no resisting here:
the Word if made Fire.'

If his strong spine rest
on the bald heights
where, would you say, does his Foot-holder kneel?
In what deep vale
does this fidell official
ward this lord's Achilles' heel?
Does he lap
the bruised *daudroed*[2] of his lord
and watch lest harm should befall the lord's person (which is all
that is expressly demanded of a *troed*[3]-holder) or over and above
what is of obligation does he do what is his to do with some
measure of the dedication of the daughter of Pebin of the Water-
Meadow, who held in her lap the two feet of the shape-shifting
Rhi[4] of Arfon?[5]
Or, silently, attentively & carefully

[1] *cerrig*: stones; pronounce ker-rig 'er' as in errand.
[2] *daudroed*: two feet; (*dau*, two, + troed, foot). Pronounce approximately die-droid.
[3] *troed*: foot; pronounce troid.
[4] Rhi: King; pronounce rhee, 'r' trilled, 'h' very aspirated.
[5] Arfon: pronounce arr-von.

and with latreutic veneration
as did Mair Modlen[1]
the eternally pierced feet
of the Shepherd of Greekland
the Heofon-Cyning
born of Y Forwyn Fair[2]
lapped in hay on the ox's stall
next the grey ass in the caved *stabulum*
ad praesepem in heye Bedlem
that is bothe bryht and schen.

Does he lean low to his high office
in the leafy hollow
below the bare *rhiw*[3]
where the sparse hill-flora
begins to thicken
by the rushing *nant*[4] where the elders grow
and the talled-stemmed *ffion*[5]
put on the purple
to outbright the green gossamer fronds
of the spume-born maiden's hair.

It were wise to not bruise nor fracture
by whatever inadvertence, these delicate agalma
for of such are the things
made over to her.

Where, too, would you guess
might his Candle-bearer be standing
to hold and ward
against the rising valley-*wynt*[6]
his iron-spiked guttering light
The twisted flax-wick

[1] Mair Modlen: Mary Magdalen. Pronounce approximately meirr (ei as in height) mód-len.
[2] Y Forwyn Fair: The Virgin Mary; mutated forms of *morwyn*, maiden and Mair, Mary; pronounce approximately uh vór-win veir (ei as in height, each 'r' trilled).
[3] *rhiw*: a hill-slope; pronounce, rhee-oo.
[4] *nant*: a small stream.
[5] *ffion*: foxgloves; pronounce fee-on.
[6] *wynt*: mutation of *gwynt*, wind; pronounce wint.

                    (without which calcined death
no uprising, warm, gold-rayed *cannwyll*[1]-life)
                    bends one way
with the wind-bowed elder boughs
and the pliant bending of the wild elm
                    (that serves well the bowyers)
and the resistant limbs
                    of the tough, gnarled *derwen*[2] even
lean all to the swaying briary-tangle
that shelters low
                    in the deeps of the valley-wood
the fragile *blodyn-y-gwynt*[3]

    And the wind-gusts do not slacken
but buffet stronger and more chill
                    as the dusk deepens
over the high *gwaundir*[4]
                    and below in the *glynnoedd*[5]
where the *nentydd*[6] run
                    to conflow with the *afon*[7]
where too is the running of the deer
whose desire is toward these water-brooks.

Over the whole terrain
                    and the denizens of the terrain
the darking pall falls
                    and the chill wind rises higher.

    Is the season sequence out of joint
                    that leafy boughs should tremor so

---

[1] *cannwyll*: from Latin *candela*. Pronounce approximately cánooill; the double 'll' represent the Welsh *ll* for which there is no corresponding sound in English.

[2] *derwen*: an oak tree; pronounce dér-wen, the *er* of the accented syllable is like the 'er' in derelict or errand.

[3] *blodyn-y-gwynt*: flower of the wind or wood-anemone; pronounce blod-din-uh-gwint.

[4] *gwaundir*: moorland; *gwaun*, moor *tir*, land. Pronounce very approximately gwein ('ei' as in height) deerr.

[5] *glynnoed*: plural of *glyn*, glen. Pronounce glún-noithe.

[6] *nentydd*: plural of *nant*, a brook. Pronounce approximately nentith, 'th' as in breathe.

[7] *afon*: river; pronounce áv-von.

for a night-fall gust
                        at this age of the solar year
scarcely descendent as yet
                        from the apex-house
of the shining Twin-Brothers of
                        Helen the Wall?
Be that as it may
                        by whatever freak of nature
or by the widdershin spell
                        of a wand-waver
this night-wind of the temperate Ides of Quintilis
blows half a gale & boreal at that.
                        Indeed, so chill it is
it strikes to the bone, more like the wind
                        of the lengthening light
                        of the strengthening cold
of round or about
                        the Ides of the mensis of Janus
when the wintry Sol has turned his back
                        to the heavenly thack of The Hoedus
and, coursing through the bleaker house of The-Man-that-Pours-
the-Water-Out, careens on his fixed and predetermined cursus,
with the axle-tree of his essedum upward steeved, under the
icicled roof of the februal house of The-Fish-with-the-Glistening-
Tails, when, still on the climb, he has, in part, his cours y-ronne
in the martial house of Aries whose blast is through with a
battering drive the thickest *pexa* of closest weave, and Mavors'
petrabula (artfully virid is their camouflage) are brought to bear
for his barrage of steelcold stones of hail
                        which pelting of this pittiless storme
makes the stripped but green-budding boughs
moan and complain afresh to each other
yn y gaeaf oer.[1]

But whatever may have been the cause of this phenomenon
and altogether irrespective of it and apart too from what is
required and codified in the Notitia of degrees & precedence
touching the precise duties of a lord's candle-bearer and as to
where and when he must stand in the lord's *neuadd*,[2] it is the most

---

[1] yn y gaeaf oer: in the winter cold. Pronounce approximately un uh gúy-av oirr.
[2] neuadd: hall; pronounce approximately nye-ath, 'th' as in breathe.

likely thing in the world that you will, none the less, find him
here, on the open *mynnydd-dir*[2]

for it is his innate habit to be wherever his lord is unless pre-
vented by violence or by one of the lord's chief officers, for he is
listed last on the roster of the named functionaries attendant
upon the lord and is accounted least among them: what is he
compared with the Chief Huntsman let alone the Chief Falconer
or the Bard of the Household? And as for the Justiciar or the Maer
of the Palace,[2] compared with these he is nothing
                              yet is he not the Light-Bearer?
whose but his the inalienable privilege
                       to hold upright
                       before the Bear of the Island
in his timber-pillar'd hall
(which stands within the agger-cinctured *maenol*[3]) the tall, taper-
ing, flax-cored candela of pure wax (the natural produce of the
creatures labouring in the royal hives but made a true artefact by
the best chandlers of the royal *maenol*)
                       that flames upward
in perfection of form
                       like the leaf-shaped war-heads
that gleam from the long-hafted spears
                       of the lord's body-guard
but immeasurably greater
                       is the pulchritude
for the quivering gleam of it
is of living light
                       and light
(so these *clerigwyr*[4] argue)
                       is, in itself, a good
ergo, should this *candela*-bearer
                       presume so far as to argue that
his *cannwyll* does indeed constitute
One of the Three Primary Signa
                       of the Son of Mary

[1] *mynnydd-dir*: mountain-land. Pronounce mún-nith ('th' as in breathe) deerr.
[2] Maer: from Latin *maior*, The Mayor of the Palace. Pronounce very approxi-
mately meir, 'ei' as in height.
[3] *maenol*: the whole area of the lord's *llys* or court, in which the *neuadd* or hall
stands. Pronounce approximately mein ('ei' as height) nol.
[4] *clerigwyr*: clerks, clerics; Pronounce approximately cler-rig-weir.

... *unig-anedig Fab Duw*[1]
...*ante omnia saecula*
lumen de lumine...
by whom all things...
who should blame him?

So whether his lord is in hall or on circuit of the land, he's most
like to be about somewhere, you can count on that.

Whether seated
at his board on the dais wearing such
insignia as is proper for him, his head circled with the pale-bright
talaith[2] of hammered-thin river-gold, his thinning tawny hair of
lost lustre streaked whitish straying his brows' deep-dug care-
furrows
(for *long* has he been the Director of Toil,
the strategos bearing the weight of the defence-struggle on three
fronts and the heavier weight of the treason-tangle of the sub-
reguli of equal privilege, the bane of the island)
when standing near him
is the Priest of the Household
who must chant the *Pater*
and offer the *bendith*[3]
when the knife has been put
into the peppered meat
and drink has been put into the *cornu*
and the Silentiary
has struck the post for the *pared*[4]

---

[1] *unig-anedig Fab Duw*: only-begotten Son of God; pronounce approximately
in-ig an-nédig vahb dee-oo.

[2] *talaith*: diadem, circlet, coronet. Pronounce approximately tál-eith, 'ei' as in
height.

[3] *bendith*: blessing.

[4] *pared* screen or partition, from *parietem*. Pronounce approximately pá-red.

The hall (*neuadd*) of a Welsh chieftain was of wooden construction. Wooden pillars
supported the roof-tree. It was partly divided into an 'upper' and a 'lower' hall by
two half-screens running from the side walls, rather as a church is divided into nave
and chancel (*cancelli*). The fire (which must on no account go out, for it represented
the life of the household) was placed centrally between the two half partitions.
Each of the various officers of the court sat in order of precedence. The Silentiary
(*Gostegwr*) struck with his rod one of the supporting pillars when silence was
required. There is a Welsh proverbial saying about striking the post for the partition
to hear (*Taro'e post i'r pared glywed*) which I presume, but do not know, reflects this
ancient construction of the halls of these rulers as described in the Welsh Laws.

                              to hear
and for all the men
                    under the *gafl*[1]-treed roof-tree
of the *neuadd*, to hear
whether they are seated or standing
                    on either side of the wattle-twined *cancelli*
below or above
                    the centred hearth-stone
(where the life of the household smoulders)
                    to hear
with his face toward the Arglwydd[2] and toward those about him,
after he has said certain versicles, he begins the *bendith* proper,
and with a slight inclination of his body toward the man that
wears the golden fillet, he makes the life sign over all the men in
the smoked-wreathed *neuadd*, saying, in a clear voice:
            Bene ✠ dic, Domine nos
and then, over the food-vessels, and
                    over the distilled, golden *meddlyn*[3]
in the drink vessels
                    over the red-gilt bowl
that holds the blood-red wine
(freighted from Bwrgwyn via Sabrina Aestuarium)
he makes the same signum, saying
                    et haec ✠ tua dona . . .

and when he comes to the words which in the other tongue of
men of the Island signify *trwy Iesu Grist ein Harglwydd*[4] he bows
his head and then, in silence, inly to himself and but for a brief
moment, he makes memento of those who no longer require such
as himself to bless their meat & drink, for elsewhere is their wide
maenol
                    at least, such is his hope.
His silent, brief and momentary recalling is firstly of those
Athletes of God, who in the waste-lands & deep wilds of the
Island and on the spray-swept skerries and desolate *insulae*
where the white-pinioned sea-birds nest, had sought out places

[1] *gafl*: fork. Pronounce approximately gáv-el.
[2] Arglwydd: Lord; pronounce approximately árr-glooith, 'th' as in breathe.
[3] *meddlyn*: mead; pronounce approximately meth ('th' as in breathe) lin.
[4] *trwy Iesu Grist ein Harglwydd*: through Jesus Christ our Lord; pronounce
approximately troo-ee yéss-ee greest ine hárr-glooith, 'th' as in breathe, 'h'
strongly aspirated.

of retreat and had made the White Oblation for the living and the dead in those solitudes, in the habitat of wolves and wild-cat and such like creatures of the Logos (by whom all creatures are that are) and his silent memento is next of those who had made the same *anamnesis* in the cities of the provinces of Britannia which the Survey had aligned according to the quadrilateral plan, *per scamna et strigas* and had determined the run of the *limes transversus* for masons to wall the auspicious area with squared stone, which cities are now either calcined heaps or, if standing intact, are desolate and deserted of people.

Quomodo sedet sola civitas plena populo![1]

How? Why?
It is because of the long, long
and continuing power-struggle
for the fair lands of Britain
and the ebb & flow of the devastation-
waves of the war-bands
for no provinces of the West
were longer contested than these provinces
nor is the end yet
for that tide rises higher
nor can it now be stayed.

And next his recalling is of those who made the same Oblation in the hill-lands and valley-ways, labouring among a mixed folk of low and high estate, some more rapacious, maybe, than the creatures of the wilds, being savaged by much tribulation, uprooted from various provinces, some come by thalassic routes from southern Gaul bringing with them a valuable leaven ...

Or whether they offered the Eternal Victim within the wattled enclosures: *bangorau*,[2] *monasterii, clasordai*[3] where they live in

---

[1] See the First Lesson of the First Nocturn for Matins of Feria V in Coena Domini (Maundy Thursday) which begins *'Incipit Lamentatio Jeremiae Prophetae. Aleph: Quomodo sedet sola civitas plena populo'*.

[2] *bangorau*: plural of *bangor* in the sense of a wattled enclosure of religious. Pronounce approximately ban-gor-rei ('ei' as in height).

[3] *clasordai* (plural of *clasordy*): cloisters or monastic houses; pronounce approximately clas-órr-dei.

common under the common rule of an *abad*[1] who may chance to
be also the Antistita who alone is able to place upon any man the
condition of being an Offerand. But once an *Offeiriad* always an
Offeiriad. Nor does death affect this conditioning; for it is with the
indelible marks of the priesthood of the Son of Mair upon him
that he will, *yn Nydd o Farn*,[2] face the Son of Mair.

Or whether they stood solitary at the *mensa* far from the next
nearest *claswr*[3] in the little white *addoldy*[4] under the green elbow
of the hill, which the chief man of that locality has caused to be
twined of pliant saplings and lime-washed without and within

or whether the merits of the same Victim are pleaded at the
stone in the stone-built *eglwys* (its gapped roofing repaired, more
or less, with thatch, its broken walling patched with unmortared
rubble) that stands by the narrowing and silted estuary where the
great heaped ruins are, that tell of vanished wharves and emporia
and cement bonded brick & dressed-stone store-*cellae* for bonded
goods and where walk the ghosts of customs officials and where
mildewed scraps of sight drafts, shards of tessera-tallies and
fragile as tinder fragmented papyri, that are wraiths of filed bills
of lading, litter here and there the great sandstone blocks of fallen
vaulting . . . where also, if you chance to be as lettered as the Irish
eremite up stream, you can read, freely & lightly scratched in the
plaster of a shattered pilaster, in *mercatores'* Greek, what seems to
mean: Kallistratos loves Julia and so does Henben and so do I
and a bit more
that you can't decipher . . .

or whether the same anamnesis was made in the *capel freninol*,[5]
within the ditched & guarded defences of a *caer* of a lord of the
land
as here & now, in the Bear's chapel.

And next, his rapid memento is of those lords & rulers and

[1] *abad*: abbot, pronounce áb-bad.

[2] *yn Nydd o Farn*: in the Day of Judgement.

[3] *claswr*: man from or in a *clasordy*, a monastic or priest. Pronounce clás-oorr.

[4] *addoldy*: place of worship. Pronounce approximately a-thól-dee, 'a' as in
apple, 'th' as in those.

[5] *capel freninol*: royal chapel. Pronounce cap-el vren-nin-ol.

men of name in the land in times past: *penmilwyr,*[1] *aergwn,*[2] *aergyfeddau,*[3] *cymdeithion yn y ffosydd,*[4] *cadfridogion,*[5] *tribuni militum, pennaethau,*[6] *comitates, rhiau,*[7] *cadflaenoriaid,*[8] *sub-reguli,* pendragons, *protectores, rhaglawiaid,*[9] *strategoi, duces,* saviours & leaders of varying eminence together with *gwyr o galon*[10] of all sorts. Some but recent, others far, far, far back: such as Belinos of whom the Bard of the Household claimed to have some arcane tradition. About which, he, himself, the Priest of the Household, thought of uncertain authenticity; but, to say the truth, he was dubious of much that these poets asserted though they were indeed most skilled artists and remembrancers & conservators of the things of the Island, yet he suspected that they tended to be weavers also of the fabulous and were men over-jealous of their status and secretive touching their *traditio,* but then, after all, their *disciplina* was other than his and this he knew for certain that whatever else they were, they were men who loved the things of the Island, and so did he.

Then there was Cunobelinos the Radiant of whom he fancied he had himself found some mention in a Latin *historia,* but he could no longer at all recollect by what author – perhaps he had merely imagined it, which worried him; but he had in his younger years read in various works the names of which he could barely recall; but there was Eusebius, Orosius, Venantius, Prosper, apart from fragments, at all events, of both Greek and Latin authors of very great fame, *cyn Cred,*[11] and there was Martianus Capella and Faustus called 'of Regensium' because he had

---

[1] *penmilwyr*: commander of soldiers. Pronounce approximately pen-mil-weir.

[2] *aergwn*: warriors, lit. dogs of battle. Pronounce eir-goon.

[3] *aergyfeddau*: battle comrades. Pronounce approximately eir-guv-véth-ei, 'th' as in breathe, 'ei' as in height.

[4] *cymdeithion yn y ffosydd*: companions in the defences or *fossae.* Pronounce very approximately cum-deith-ee-on un uh foss-sith, final 'th' as in breathe.

[5] *cadfridogion*: generals. Pronounce cad-vrid-óg-ee-on.

[6] *pennaethau*: chieftains. Pronounce approximately pen-eíth-ei; 'ei' as in height.

[7] *rhiau*: kings. Pronounce approximately rhée-si 'ei' as in height.

[8] *cadflaenoriaid*: leaders in battle. Pronounce approximately cad-vlein-órr-ee-eid ('ei' as in height).

[9] *rhaglawiaid*: governors of districts. Pronounce approximately rhag-láu-ee-eid. The accented syllable rhymes with 'vow', 'ei' as in height.

[10] *gwyr o galon*: men of valour (lit. men of heart). Pronounce approximately goo-eér o gál-on.

[11] *cyn Cred*: B.C. lit. 'before the Creed'. Pronounce approximately kin kraid.

been consecrated *esgob*[1] to that place, but he was a man of this Island who had written well touching the Victim of the Offering. But now that he was many winters old, the diverse nature of what he had read had become sadly intermeddled and very greatly confused. But anyway his main concern was with Yr Efengyl Lan[2] and he liked to dwell on the thought that the word *efengyl* (owing, he supposed, to the kiss given at that part of the Oblation called the *pax*) could, in the tongue of his country-men, mean a kiss. For what, after all, is the Hagion Evangelion if not the salutation or kiss of the eternally begotten Logos? And how could that salutation have been possible but for the pliancy of Mary & her *fiat mihi*? Which is why Irenaeus had written that this *puella*, Mair Wenfydedig,[3] was 'constituted the cause of our salvation'. Now this Irenaeus, away back, five or more long life-times back, in the days of his great-great-great grandfathers or beyond again, when the Ymherawdr[4] Aurelius, an able enough ruler, but much given to fine thoughts, high-flown principles, moralizings and the like (a type for which he had little use – he much preferred such as the Captain of the Guard) had, either by various *mandata* or by direct Imperial Edict, caused great harm to the *plebs Xti* and had made it perilous for the priesthood of Melchisedec to offer the Oblation for the living & the dead – anyhow, during that time, Irenaeus was an *esgob* in Gallia Lugdunensis, but had come there from the coast of Ionia in Asia (not very far from Galatia where there are men that speak the same tongue as the men of the Island) and this Irenaeus had known the holy man Polycarp who in turn had known Ieuan Cariadusaf[5] to whom had been committed the care & safeguarding of Mair the Mother by the direct mandate of the Incarnate Logos, even when he was reigning from the terrible stauros, his only purple his golden blood-flow

shed PRO VOBIS ET PRO MULTIS

consummating in the unlit noon-dark

on Moel-y-Penglog[6]

the Oblation made at the lighted feast board.

---

[1] *esgob*: *episcopus*. Pronounce éss-gob.

[2] Yr Efengyl Lan: The Holy Gospel. Pronounce approximately ur eh-veng-il lahn.

[3] Mair Wenfydedig: Blessed Mary. Pronounce approximately meirr ('ei' as in height) wen-vud-déd-ig.

[4] Ymherawdr: *Imperator*. Pronounce approximately um-her-row-der.

[5] Ieuan Cariadusaf: John the Most Beloved. Pronounce very approximately yei-an ca-ree-ad-íss-av.

[6] Moel-y-Penglog: 'Skull-Hill'. Pronounce moil uh pen-glog.

Hence what the ecclesia holds touching this *puella*, Mair, is, as stated by Irenaeus, of extra weight, seeing that his *traditio* was received so directly from Polycarp Hên,[1] the Antistita of Smyrna who had known and talked with the beloved Johannes, that the men of the Island call Ieuan or Ioan.[2]

And when he considered the four-fold account in the books of the *quattuor evangelia* he thought what are these if not a kind of Pedair Cainc y Mabinogi[3] *sanctaidd?*[4] in that they proclaim the true mabinogi of the Maban[5] the Pantocrator and of the veritable mother of anxiety, the Rhiannon[6] who is indeed the ever glorious Theotokos yet Queen of Sorrows and *gladius* pierced – what better, he thinks than that this four-fold marvel-tale should be called The Tale of the Kiss of the Son of Mair?

Then there was the Blessed Bran of whom the tale-tellers tell a most wondrous tale and then the names of men more prosaic but more credible to him: Paternus of the Red Pexa, Cunedda Wledig[7] the Conditor and, far more recent and so more green in the memory, the Count Ambrosius Aurelianus that men call Emrys Wledig, associated, by some, with the eastern defences called the Maritime Tract and Aircol Hîr[8] and his line, *protectores* of Demetia in the west…and many, many, many more whose bones lie under the green mounds of the Island; nor in his rapid memento of these many, did he forget the golden torqued *puellae* of gentle nurture, *arglwyddesau*,[9] *matronae* and *breninesau*[10] who, in their life-days, had sustained the men of the Island, but whose bodies lie as hers for whom was digged the square grave on Alaw[11]-bank

---

[1] Polycarp Hên: Old Polycarp. The long Welsh *e* in *bên* is more or less as the 'a' in lane or bane, but is a pure vowel.

[2] Ioan: pronounce very approximately yó-an, as said it's one syllable.

[3] Pedair Cainc y Mabinogi: The Four Branches of the Mabinogi. Pronounce approximately péd-eir-keink uh mab-in-óg-ee.

[4] *sanctaidd* holy, sacred. Pronounce approximately sank-teithe.

[5] Maban: a man-child, but here reflecting Mabon or Maponos the Celtic cult-figure the Son of Modron, the Mother-figure. Pronounce máb-an.

[6] Rhiannon: 'The Great Queen'. Pronounce rhee-án-non.

[7] Cunedda Wledig: pronounce approximately kin-eth-ah ('th' as in breathe) oo-léd-ig.

[8] Aircol Hîr: pronounce approximately íre-col heer. Agricola the Tall.

[9] *arglwyddesau*: the plural of *arglwyddes*, the wife of a lord. Pronounce approximately arr-glooith-és-eye, ('th' as in breathe).

[10] *breninesau*: queens. Pronounce approximately bren-nin-és-eye.

Thus both these words rhyme with *matronae* and *puellae*.

[11] Alaw, rhymes with 'vow', accent on the first syllable.

in Mona Insula, and Creiddylad[1] the daughter of Lear than whom no maiden of the Island or of the isles in the waters that moat the Island could compare in majesty either in her life-time or in the ages before her or in the times yet to be; and Elen[2] the daughter of Coil, lord of Stratha Clauda between the Vallum & the Wall and there was she whose agnomen was Aurfron[3] on account, it would appear, of her numinous & shining virtue, for the epithet 'golden' betokens what is not patient of tarnish...

and there were Slendernecks and Fairnecks and she that was called Bright Day, the daughter of the *gwledig*,[4] Amlawdd (of whom some rumour that he was a *princeps* from over the Sea of Cronos, yn Nenmarc, owing, he supposed, to a complex tangle of like-sounding *nomina*, for according to the genealogies he was a man of this Island and a son of Cunedda Wledig) & there was the lovely Gwenlliant,[5] who though her beauty was indeed great, yet she was named by the men of the Island Y Forwyn Fawrfrydig,[6] because of the shining virtue called *megalopsychia*, the most prized of the virtues, exceeded even her outward splendour of form...

and many, many more whose names are, for whatever reason, on the diptycha of the Island; and vastly many more still, whether men or womenkind, of neither fame nor recorded *nomen*, whether bond or freed or innately free, of far back or of but recent decease, whose burial mounds are known or unknown or for whom no mound was ever raised or any mark set up of even the meanest sort to show the site of their interment; or those whose white bodies were shovelled into earth in haste, without funerary rites of any sort whatever; or those – a very, very great number, whose bodies, whether stripped naked or in full battle-gear were left to be the raven's gain and supper for the hovering kite and for the black-nebbed corbie that waits the *aerfor*[7]-ebb: the deeper the still-

---

[1] Creiddylad: pronounce approximately crei-thúl-ad, 'th' as in breathe.

[2] Elen: pronounce él-en.

[3] Aurfron: Golden Breast. Pronounce approximately eir ('ei' as in height) vron.

[4] *gwledig*: ruler. Pronounce approximately goo-léd-ig.

[5] Gwenlliant: pronounce approximately gwen-llee-ant (stress on the second syllable).

[6] Y Forwyn Fawrfrydig: The Magnanimous Maiden. Pronounce approximately uh vor-win vowr-vrúd-ig.

[7] *aerfor*: tide of battle (*aer*, battle + *mor*, sea). Pronounce approximately eir-vor.

ness of the *aerdawelwch*,[1] the higher heaped the banquet that she loves.

For these and for all the departed of the Island and indeed not only for those of the Island of the Mighty, nor only for those of the Patriarchate of the West, nor yet only for the departed of these provinces together with those of the provinces that are within the jurisdiction of the Patriarch whose seat is Caergystennin[2]
$\qquad$ where Urbs is Polis
far side the narrowing *culfor*[3]
$\qquad$ that links Middle Sea
with Pontus Euxinus
$\qquad$ where the Ymherawdr[4]
$\qquad$ wearing his colobium sindonis
sits in the Sacred Palace
$\qquad$ but for the departed
of the entire universal orbis
from the unknown beginnings
$\qquad$ unguessed millenniums back
until now:
$\qquad$ FOR THESE ALL
he makes his silent, secret
$\qquad$ devout and swift memento.

And discreetly and with scarcely any discernible movement he makes once again the salvific sign, saying less than half-audibly: *Requiem aeternam dona eis, Domine.*

But had he said these words never so low or had the slight movement of his right hand across the folds of his tunica been even less than it was, the Candlebearer would have heard and seen; and though standing a good few paces from him, did hear and see, and, though the office of Cannwyllyd[5] gives him no right whatever to speak in the lord's hall, yet he could not contain himself, and though, the Lord Christ knows, he is not, by any means, a clerk, he sings out in a high, clear and distinct voice, the respond: *ET LUX PERPETUA LUCEAT EIS.*

[1] *aerdawelwch*: silence after a battle (*aer* + *tawelwch*, stillness. Pronounce approximately eir-dou-wél-ooch 'dou' rhymes with 'vow'.

[2] Caergystennin: The fortress (or city) of Constantinus. Pronounce keir ('ei' as in height) gus-tén-nin.

[3] *culfor*: a confined sea-way. Pronounce kíl-vor.

[4] Ymherawdr: *Imperator*. Pronounce approximately um-her-rów-der.

[5] Cannwyllyd: Candle-bearer. Pronounce approximately can-will-led, ('ll' = Welsh *ll*).

So then, whether seated
                    at this board in his hall
or lying on his sleep-board
                    in his lime whited *ystafell*[1]
with his bed-coverlet over him to cover him
                    a work of the Chief Stitching Maid
to Yr Arglwyddes[2] (his, the Bear's wife)
of many vairs of stitched together
                    marten-cat pelts
contrived without visible seam
                    from the top throughout.

                    Or, here, out
on the cold, open *moelion*[3]
                    his only coverlet
his madder-dyed war-*sagum*
                    where he slumbers awhile
from the hunt-toil:
                    carried lights
                    for the lord
in his pillar'd basilica
                    carried lights
                    for the lord
fain to lie down
                    in the hog-wasted *blaendir*[4]
scorch-marks only
                    where were the white dwellings:
stafell[5] of the lord of the Cantref
                    ys tywyll heno
shieling of the *taeog*[6] from the bond-tref

---

[1] ystafell: chamber. Pronounce us-táv-ell. The word here refers to the private apartment of the lord and his wife within the *llys* or court. It derives from late-Latin *stabellum*, a residence, and in the 9th century stanzas about the destruction of Cynddylan's court the word is used of the whole residence: *Stavell Gyndylan* in the original orthography.

[2] Yr Arglwyddes: the wife of the Arglwydd. Pronounce approximately ur ar-glo͞oith-ess, 'th' as in breathe.

[3] *moelion*: plural of *moel*, a bare hill. Pronounce approximately moil-ee-on.

[4] *blaendir*: borderland, but meaning also uplands, high hill-country that is also a place of boundaries. Pronounce approximately blein ('ei' as in height) deerr.

[5] *stafell*: see note above.

[6] *taeog* : a villein or man bound to the land. Pronounce approximately teí-og.

heb dan, heb wely.[1]

And the trees of the *llannerch?*[2]

Why are they fallen?

What of the *llwyn*[3] where the fair *onnen*[4] grew and the silvery queen of the *coedwig*[5] (as tough as she's graced & slender) that whispers her secrets low to the divining hazel, and the resistant oak boughs that antler'd dark above the hornbeam?

Incedunt arbusta per alta
rapacibus caedunt
Percellunt sacras quercus . . .
Fraxinus frangitur . . .[6]

[1] *ys tywyll heno*: is dark tonight. Pronounce us tuh-will ('ll' represents Welsh *ll*) hen-no, *heb dan, heb wely*: without fire, without bed. Pronounce approximately habe dahn, habe wel-ee.

The use here of these two lines requires some explanation seeing that my knowledge of Welsh is so extremely scanty and that I have to rely in the main on translations. The lines quoted form part of one of the earliest fragments of Welsh poetry and seem to me to incant and evoke so much that is central to a great tradition at its strongest and most moving. They are part of a ninth century series of stanzas in which the princess Heledd of Powys laments the death of her brother Cynddylan and the destruction of his court at Pengwern (Shrewsbury) by the Angles. In the older orthography the words of this stanza read

Stavell Gyndylan ys tywyll heno
heb dan, heb wely.

'The "hall" of Cynddylan is dark tonight, without fire without bed.' The words *Stavell Gyndylan* are repeated as the opening words of each of the (sixteen) stanzas so that they burn themselves into the mind, very much as do certain great phrases that echo in a Liturgy, as for example, the words I have ventured to use earlier from the Roman rite of *Tenebrae* 'How does the city sit solitary that was full of people!' Such words, as with these of the princess Heledd have a permanency and evoke a whole situation far beyond their immediate 'meaning' that, in my view, it is our duty to conserve them however little we 'know' the original languages.

[2] *llannerch*: a glade. Pronounce llan-nerch the 'er' as in errand.

[3] *llwyn*: a grove. Pronounce lloo-in.

[4] *onnen*: ash tree. Pronounce ón-nen.

[5] *coedwig*: a wood. Pronounce coid-wig.

[6] *Incedunt arbusta . . .* Perhaps a note is necessary to indicate why I felt impelled to make use of a few words from Ennius, *Annals* Bk. vi, descriptive of the felling by woodmen's axes (*secures*) of the great spreading high trees which he apparently had taken largely from Homer and which Vergil was to use in part from him, and others also, so that the passage has become as it were part of a liturgy whenever the destruction of a woodland is involved. Round about 1936 or 1940 I first heard the Ennius fragment read aloud and the *sound* of the Latin words haunted me and although I could apprehend the meaning only *very* partially and patchily, I *felt* that surely form and content were marvellously wed and a subsequent reading of a translation confirmed my feelings. However, when in 1967

Not by long-hafted whetted steel axe-blades
                    are these fallen
that graced the high slope
                    that green-filigreed
the green hollow
                    but by the riving tusks
of the great hog
                    are they felled.
It is the Boar Trwyth[1]
                    that has pierced through
the stout-fibred living wood
                    that bears the sacral bough of gold.
   It is the hog that has ravaged the fair *onnen* and the hornbeam
and the Queen of the Woods. It is the hog that has tusk-riven the
tendoned roots of the trees of the *llwyn* whereby are the tallest
with the least levelled low and lie up-so-down.
   It is the great *ysgithrau*[2] of the *porcus Troit* that has stove in the
wattled walls of the white dwellings, it is he who has stamped out
the seed of fire, shattered the *pentan*[3]-stone within the dwellings;
strewn the green leaf-bright limbs with the broken white limbs of
the folk of the dwellings, so that the life-sap of the flowers of the
forest mingles the dark life-sap of the fair bodies of the men who
stood in the trackway of the long tusked great hog, *y twrch dirfawr
ysgithrog hir*.[4]

Tawny-black sky-scurries
                    low over

[1] Trwyth: pronounce troíth.

[2] *ysgithrau*: tusks. Pronounce approximately us-gith-rei.

[3] *pentan*: hearth. Pronounce pén-tan.

[4] *y twrch dirfawr ysgithrog hir*: the huge hog, long tusked. Pronounce approxi-
mately uh toorch deerr-vowrr us-gíth-rog heerr.

I wished to evoke some part of this passage it was clearly necessary to again con-
sult a translation, and also a friend with a knowledge of Latin which I have not.
Further I found it necessary to replace *securibus* by *rapacibus* in that my trees were
brought down not 'by axes' but 'by tusks' and similarly *magnas quercus* would not
do because none of the oaks of the Welsh hill-site I had in mind are by any means
'great' or 'mighty', but, on the contrary, strangling and stunted, so I replaced *mag-
nas* by *sacras* seeing that in so far as one is concerned for and stands within the
mythus of this island, the oak, of whatever sort, great or small, has for obvious
reasons, sacral associations.

Ysgyryd[1] hill
and over the level-topped heights
                    of Mynnydd Pen-y-fal[2]
                    cold is wind
                    grey is rain, but
                    BRIGHT IS CANDELA
where this lord is in slumber.

Are his wounded ankles
                    lapped with the ferric waters
that all through the night
                    hear the song
from the night-dark seams
                    where the narrow-skulled *caethion*[3]
labour the changing shifts
                    for the cosmocrats of alien lips
in all the fair lands
                    of the dark measures under
(from about Afon Lwyd
                    in the confines of green Siluria
westward to where the naiad of the *fons*/head
                    pours out the Lesser Gwendraeth[4]
high in the uplands
                    above Ystrad Tywi[5]
and indeed further
                    west & south of Merlin's Caer
even in the lost cantrevs
                    of spell-held Demetia
where was Gorsedd Arberth,[6] where the *palas*[7] was
                    where the prince who hunted
met the Prince of Hunters
                    in his woof of grey
and gleam-pale dogs

[1] Ysgyryd: pronounce us-gúh-rid.
[2] Mynnydd Pen-y-fal: pronounce mun-ith pen-uh-vál; commonly known as 'The Sugar Loaf'. The Welsh name of this mountain means 'the head of the summit'.
[3] *caethion*: slaves. Pronounce approximately keith ('ei' as in height) ee-on.
[4] Gwendraeth: pronounce approximately gwén-dreith ('ei' as in height).
[5] Ystrad Tywi: The Vale of Towy. Pronounce approximately ustrad túh-wee.
[6] Gorsedd Arberth: pronounce approximately gorr-seth ('th' as in breathe) árr-berrth, ('er' as in errand).
[7] *palas*: palace. Pronounce pál-ass.

                              not kennelled on earth-floor
lit the dim chase.)

Is the Usk a drain for his gleaming tears
who weeps for the land
                         who dreams his bitter dream
for the folk of the land
does Tawe[1] clog for his sorrows
do the parallel dark-seam drainers
                         mingle his anguish-stream
with the scored valleys' tilted refuse.
Does his freight of woe
                         flood South by East
on Sirhywi[2] and Ebwy[3]
                         is it southly bourn
on double Rhondda's fall to Taff?[4]

   Do the stripped boughs grapple
above the troubled streams
                         when he dream-fights
his nine-day's fight
                         which he fought alone
with the hog in the Irish wilderness
                         when the eighteen twilights
                         and the ten midnights
and the equal light of the nine mid-mornings
were equally lit
                         with the light of the saviour's fury
and the dark fires of the hog's eye
which encounter availed him nothing.

                         Is his royal anger ferriaged
where black-rimed Rhymni
                         soils her Marcher-banks
                         Do the bells of St. Mellon's
toll his dolour
                         are his sighs canalled
where the mountain-ash

   [1] Tawe: pronounce approximately tau-eh.
   [2] Sirhywi: pronounce approximately seerr-húh-ee.
   [3] Ebwy: pronounce éb-wee.
   [4] Taff: pronounce taf, the 'a' is short.

droops her bright head
for the black pall of Merthyr?

Do Afan[1] and Nedd[2] west it away
does grimed Ogwr[3] toss on a fouled ripple
his broken-heart flow
                    out to widening Hafren[4]
                    and does she, the Confluence Queen
queenly bear on her spume-frilled frock
a maimed king's sleep bane?
                    Do the long white hands
would you think, of the Brides of the Déssi
                    unloose galloons
to let the black tress-stray
                    web the pluvial Westerlies
does the vestal flame in virid-hilled Kildare
                    renew from secret embers
the undying fire
                    that sinks on the Hill Capitoline
   Does the wake-dole mingle the cormorant scream
does man-*sídhe* to fay-queen bemoan
the passage of a king's griefs, westing far
                    out to moon-swayed Oceanus
   Does the blind & unchoosing creature of sea know the marking
and indelible balm from flotsomed sewage and the seaped valley-
waste?
   Does the tide-beasts' maw
                    drain down the princely tears
with the mullocked slag-wash
                    of Special Areas?
Can the tumbling and gregarious porpoises
does the aloof and infrequent seal
                    that suns his puckered back
                    and barks from Pirus' rock
tell the dole-tally of a drowned *taeog* from a
Gwledig's golden collar, refracted in Giltar shoal?

[1] Afan: pronounce áv-van.
[2] Nedd: pronounce very approximately nathe, as in lathe or bathe.
[3] Ogwr: pronounce og-oorr.
[4] Hafren: (Sabrina) pronounce háv-ren.

Or, is the dying gull
                    on her sea-hearse
that drifts the oily bourne
                    to tomb at turn of tide
her own stricken cantor?
Or is it for the royal tokens
                    that with her drift
that the jagg'd and jutting *morben*[1] echoes
and the deep hollows of *yr ogof*[2] echo
and the hollow eddies echo:
                    Dirige, dirige[3]
and out, far, far beyond
on thalassic Brendan's heaving trackway
to unknown *insulae*
                    where they sing
their west In Paradisums[4]
                    and the corposants toss
for the dying flax-flame
                    and West-world glory
in transit is.

But yet he sleeps:
                    when he shifts a little in his fitfull
slumber does a covering stone dislodge
                    and roll to Reynoldstone?
When he fretfully turns
                    crying out in a great voice
                    in his fierce sleep-anger
does the habergeon'd sentinel
                    alert himself sudden
from his middle-watch doze
                    in the crenelled traverse-bay
of the outer bailey wall
                    of the *castell*[5] these Eingl-Ffrancwyr[6]

---

[1] *morben*: headland. Pronounce morr-ben.

[2] *yr ogof*: the cave. Pronounce ur óg-ov.

[3] First Antiphon at Matins for the Dead, *Dirige, Domine, Deus meus, in conspectu tuo viam meam.*

[4] Burial Service, Roman Rite Antiphon. 'In paradisum deducant te Angeli' etc.

[5] *castell*: castle. Pronounce approximately cáss-tell, 'll' represents the Welsh *ll*.

[6] Eingl-Ffrancwyr: Anglo-Frenchmen. Pronounce approximately ain-gl-fránc-weirr.

call in their lingua La Haie Taillée
that the Saeson[1] other ranks
                        call The Hay
(which place is in the tongue of the men of the land,
Y Gelli Gandryll, or, for short, Y Gelli)
Does he cock his weather-ear, enquiringly
lest what's on the west wind
                        from over beyond the rising contours
may signify that in the broken
                        tir y blaenau[2]
these broken dregs of Troea
                        yet again muster?
Does he nudge his drowsing mate?
                        Do the pair of them
say to each other: 'Twere not other
than wind-cry, for sure – yet
                        best to warn the serjeant below.
He'll maybe
                        warn the Captain of the Watch
or some such
                        and he, as like as not
may think best to rouse the Castellan
                        – that'll please him
in his newly glazed, arras-hung chamber
                        with his Dean-coal fire
nicely blazing
snug with his dowsabel
                        in the inner keep
Wont improve his temper, neither, come the morrow
with this borough and hereabouts alerted
                        and all for but a wind-bluster.
Still, you never know, so
                        best stand on Standing Orders
and report to them as has the serjeancy
the ordering and mandate, for
you never know, mate:
                        wind-stir may be, most like to be
as we between us do agree
                        or – stir of gramarye

---

[1] Saeson: Englishmen. Pronounce approximately seis-on.

[2] *tir y blaenau*: land of the border uplands. Pronounce approximately teerr uh blein-ei.

32

or whatsomever of ferly – who should say?
                    or solid substantiality?
you never know *what* may be
                    – not hereabouts.
No wiseman's son *born* do know
                    not in these whoreson March-lands
of this Welshry.

Yet he sleeps on
                    very deep is his slumber:
how long has he been the sleeping lord?
are the clammy ferns
                    his rustling vallance
does the buried rowan
                    ward him from evil, or
does he ward the tanglewood
                    and the denizens of the wood
are the stunted oaks his gnarled guard
                    or are their knarred limbs
strong with his sap?
Do the small black horses
                    grass on the hunch of his shoulders?
are the hills his couch
                    or is he the couchant hills?
Are the slumbering valleys
                    him in slumber
                    are the still undulations
the still limbs of him sleeping?
Is the configuration of the land
                    the furrowed body of the lord
are the scarred ridges
                    his dented greaves
do the trickling gullies
                    yet drain his hog-wounds?
Does the land wait the sleeping lord
                    or is the wasted land
that very lord who sleeps?

November 1966 to March 1967.

33

BASIL BUNTING

On the Fly-leaf of Pound's Cantos

There are the Alps. What is there to say about them?
They don't make sense. Fatal glaciers, crags cranks climb,
jumbled boulder and weed, pasture and boulder, scree,
et l'on entend, maybe, *le refrain joyeux et leger*.
Who knows what the ice will have scraped on the rock
                                        it is smoothing?

There they are; you will have to go a long way round
if you want to avoid them.
It takes some getting used to. There are the Alps,
fools! Sit down and wait for them to crumble!

(1965)

Birthday Greeting

Gone to hunt; and my brothers.
but the hut is clean, said the girl.
I have curds, besides whey.

Pomegranates, traveller;
butter, if you need it,
in a bundle of cress.

Soft, so soft, my bed.
Few come this road.
I am not married;   — yet

today I am fourteen years old.

(1966)

Stones trip Coquet burn;
grass trails, tickles
till her glass thrills.

The breeze she wears
lifts and falls back.
Where beast cool

in midgy shimmer
she dares me chase
under a bridge,

giggles, ceramic
huddle of notes,
darts from gorse

and I follow, fooled.
She must rest, surely;
some steep pool

to plodge or dip
and silent taste
with all my skin.

1970

(1970)

All the cants they peddle
bellow entangled,
teeth for knots and
each other's ankles,
to become stipendiary
in any wallow;
crow or weasel
each to his fellow.

35

Yet even these,
even these might
listen as crags
listen to light
and pause, uncertain
of the next beat,
each dancer alone
with his foolhardy feet.

(1974)

Per Che No Spero

Now we've no hope of going back,
cutter, to that grey quay
where we moored twice and twice unwillingly
cast off our cables to put out at the slack
when the sea's laugh was choked to a mutter
and the leach lifted hesitantly, with a stutter
and sulky clack,

how desolate the swatchways look,
cutter; and the chart's stained,
still, old, wrinkled and uncertain,
seeming to contradict the pilot book.
On naked banks a few birds strut
to watch the ebb sluice through a narrowing gut
loud as a brook.

Soon, while that northwest squall wrings out its cloud,
cutter, we'll heave to
free of the sands and let the half moon do
as it pleases, hanging there in the port shrouds
like a riding light. We have no course to set,
only to drift too long, watch too glumly, and wait,
wait, like the proud.

1977

(1978)

Snow's on the fellside, look! How deep;
our wood's staggering under its weight.
The burns will be tonguetied
while frost lasts.

But we'll thaw out. Logs, logs for the hearth:
and don't spare my good whisky. No water, please.
Forget the weather. Elm and ash
will stop signalling
when this gale drops.
Why reckon? Why forecast? Pocket
whatever today brings,
and don't turn up your nose, it's childish,
at making love and dancing.
When you've my bare scalp, if you must, be glum.

Keep your date in the park while light's whispering.
Hunt her out, well wrapped up, hiding and giggling,
and get her bangle for a keepsake;
she won't make much fuss.

(*says Horace, more or less*)
1977

(1978)

HUGH MacDIARMID

When the Birds Come Back to Rhiannon

Once more a man cried
(Passionately identifying himself
With the whole of Scotland
From top to bottom,
Surveying entire Scotland with his mind's eye
– To hear his phrases was like watching a fog rise;
We saw great tracts of country, roadless, unvisited,
Rare flowers and birds in inaccessible places,
Rocky formations, currents, soils,
Weather conditions, caves, legends, antiquities.
He sang the whole song of Scotland
With a marvellous gift for seizing the moods of Nature,
A profound animistic understanding,
A lyrical genius giving a sense of revelation,
Conjuring up an open country, ploughed all over,
Surging like the sea, its horizons sleeping under a misty haze.
Its landscapes were filled with life
– Alive as those old woodcuts in which we see
Men, animals, and birds all going about their business,
Each completely in character,
As if they had just stepped out of the Ark.
He painted not outside time and space
But rather in a time and space
Enlarged by the force of his emotion
– A comprehensive poetic grasp of appearance)
Quoting from the breastplate of St Patrick:

"I bind to myself today
 The power of Heaven,
 The light of the sun,
 The whiteness of snow,
 The force of fire,
 The flashing of lightning,
 The velocity of wind,
 The depth of the sea,
 The stability of the earth,
 The hardness of rocks."

His indeed was the eloquence
Elusive at shape-shifting as the Mor-rigu,
A power of the word in the blood,
By virtue of which, as Plato says,
He conformed his soul
To the motion of the heavenly bodies.
He had been given to drink of Conndla's Well,
Where grew the hazels of wisdom and inspiration.
(Had his quest been for wisdom only he had
Like Sinann been overcome by its waters
And verily tasted of death!)
Pure of heart and aright with nature
And having read the runes and rubrics of the spirit,
Cliadna Fairhead, of the race of gods,
Had bestowed on him the Cuach of emerald,
Which translates water into luscious wine,
Along with the three duo-coloured birds
Of infinite comfort and beguilement.
He brought the notes from the deeps of time
And the tale from the heart of the man who made it,
Knew the colour of Fingal's hair, and saw
The moonlight on the hoods of the Druids.
He had visited the Golden Tree
Which reaches the clouds for height,
And the words being in his heart for a song
And the beat on his pulse for rhythm,
As Caoilte had it in his foot for running,
He got the notes for the tune
In the music of the branches which,
Says the Filidh with the artful thought,
Guards the eloquence and judgement
Of the children of Gaeldom.

The rede is for the wary.
Druidical tenets demanded and received
Purity of thought and material chastity.
And out of the wonderful artistry
Of the illuminated manuscripts of Celtic art
And the age-laden Sagas
He had seen emerge, and understood,
Anaglyphs of ethnic fusions
– A struggling of the spirit for permanent possession,

And by the antennae of this provective spirit
Vanishing epos reappeared
And for this and many such cognate epos
He had rediscovered the alumni of Dagda;
Amairgen the just; Medb of the Sithe;
Merlin or Merwydn; Oengus Mac ind Oc,
The wisest and most cunning of Tuath de Danann;
Ossian in Tir-nan-Og;
The Fianns in their last convulsions;
And the magic darts of Cuchulain
Defending the royal harp of Tara;
And well he knew the word-magic of the bard, MacCoise,
Who, for the purposes of his art,
Could invoke and receive from Elathan (Skill)
The panegyrics of MacLonam;
The tales of Leech Liathmhuim;
The proverbs of Fitheal;
The eloquence of Fearceartais;
The intellect of the bardess Etain;
The brilliance of Nera,
And the clear truths of Mor-Mumhan.
Having traced and found the footmarks
Of Gael and Cymric from the shadows of the Himalayas,
The mystic regions of Irak,
Across the trail of continents
To the Isle of Saints and to Barra,
He knew from his childhood days
The world must yet seek
Further spiritual creations
From the awakened Celt
Ere the last of the race passed
To join his deathless kin in Tir-nan-Og.
And discovered in himself 'the word of knowledge'
With which Amairgen 'fashioned fire in the head'
And set himself to master 'the marvel of honey verse
With lines of long alliterative words
And sweet compacted syllables, and feet
Increasing upon feet' – and to learn
Enchantments such as Aefi played
On the De Danann children.

And in due time
He raised the wizard horn of the Fingalian heroes
And the voice of bards was tuned in his song.
His was the 'beguiling song of far-off voices',
The spirit-tongued Echo of Prometheus Unbound,
Showing the Coolins of Skye,
The Scurr of Eigg, and the Bens of Jura
As the Crom-Sleuchd of the bard's confessional,
– The beacon-heads from which the shades of the Druids
Transmit the secrets of their Pherylt
To those selected of our race
Who inherit the gift of song.

No longer then need Cathmor transmit
His despairing monody from the Hall of the Winds.
The choristers in the Palace of Enchantment are again astir.
Magnetic clouds raise high the Silver Shield
That it may re-echo the song of joy.
An Deo-Greine, Fionn's banner, cracks crisply all over the world.
The birds have come back to Rhiannon,
The rainbow of promise hangs resplendent over Gaeldom today,
The mysterious prophecies of Merlin
Are being fulfilled in our generation.
Now that the solemn but chivalrous practices
Of the Celtic peoples of history are applied
In the light of modern knowledge
To soften international and individual asperities,
Humanity, with 'a pulse like a cannon',
Will co-ordinate in faith and charity
And swing its aspirations forward
Towards peace and goodwill to men.

(1961)

Bracken Hills in Autumn

These beds of bracken, climax of the summer's growth,
Are elemental as the sky or sea.
In still and sunny weather they give back
The sun's glare with a fixed intensity
        As of steel or glass
        No other foliage has.

There is a menace in their indifference to man
As in tropical abundance. On gloomy days
They redouble the sombre heaviness of the sky
And nurse the thunder. Their dense growth shuts the narrow
                                      ways
        Between the hills and draws
        Closer the wide valleys' jaws.

This flinty verdure's vast effusion is the more
Remarkable for the shortness of its stay.
From November to May a brown stain on the slopes
Downbeaten by frost and rain, then in quick array
        The silvery crooks appear
        And the whole host is here.

Useless they may seem to men, and go unused, but cast
Cartloads of them into a pool where the trout are few
And soon the swarming animalculae upon them
Will proportionately increase the fishes too.
        Miracles are never far away
        Save bringing new thought to play.

In summer islanded in these grey-green seas where the wind
                                  plucks
The pale underside of the fronds on gusty days
As a land breeze stirs the white caps in a roadstead
Glimpses of shy bog-gardens surprise the gaze
        Or rough stuff keeping a ring
        Round a struggling water-spring.

Look closely. Even now bog asphodel spikes, still alight at the
tips,
Sundew lifting white buds like those of the whitlow grass
On walls in spring over its little round leaves
Sparkling with gummy red hairs, and many a soft mass
Of the curious moss that can clean
A wound, or poison a river, are seen.

Ah! Well I know my tumultuous days now at their prime
Will be brief as the bracken too in their stay
Yet in them as the flowers of the hills 'mid the bracken
All I treasure is needs hidden away
And will also be dead
When its rude cover is shed.

(1968)

The Day Before the Twelfth

(Caretaker of Highland Shooting Lodge loquitur)

In come sic a rangel o' gentles
Wi' a lithry o' hanyiel slyps at their tail
That the hoose in a weaven is gaen
Like a Muckle Fair sale.

Ye canna hear day nor door
For their tongues a' hung i' the middle
Like han'-bells: an ilk ane squeakin' an' squealin'
Like a doited fiddle!

rangel o' gentles: lot of gentry folk
lithry o' hanyiel slyps: following of lackeys
hoose in a weaven: house in a hullabaloo
doited: crazy

I wish that the season was owre
Afore it's begun: an' the haill jing-bang
Awa' Sooth again: an' the hurley hoose
Like a deid man's sang,

Like a deid man's sang i' the white birch wud,
A lanely sang in a toom domain,
While the wutherin' heather lies on the warl'
Like an auld bluid-stain!

(1975)

WILLIAM CARLOS WILLIAMS

The Painting

Starting from black or
finishing
with it

her defeat stands
a delicate
lock

of blonde hair dictated
by the
Sorbonne

this was her last
clear
act

a portrait of a
child
to which

she was indifferent
beautifully
drawn

then she married and
moved to
another country

(1960)

Iris

a burst of iris so that
come down for
breakfast

we searched through the
rooms for
that

sweetest odor and at
first could not
find its

source then a blue as
of the sea
struck

startling us from among
those trumpeting
petals

(1963)

from *Asphodel, That Greeny Flower*

CODA

Inseparable from the fire
              its light
                            takes precedence over it.
Then follows
              what we have dreaded –
                            but it can never
overcome what has gone before.
              In the huge gap
                            between the flash

46

and the thunderstroke
                spring has come in
                                or a deep snow fallen.
Call it old age.
                In that stretch
                                we have lived to see
a colt kick up his heels.
                Do not hasten
                                laugh and play
in an eternity
                the heat will not overtake the light.
                                That's sure.
That gelds the bomb,
                permitting
                                that the mind contain it.
This is that interval,
                that sweetest interval,
                                when love will blossom,
come early, come late
                and give itself to the lover.
Only the imagination is real!
                I have declared it
                                time without end.
If a man die
                it is because death
                                has first
possessed his imagination.
                But if he refuse death –
                                no greater evil
can befall him
                unless it be the death of love
                                meet him
in full career.
                Then indeed
                                for him
the light has gone out.
But love and the imagination
                are of a piece,
                                swift as the light
to avoid destruction.
                So we come to watch time's flight
                                as we might watch

summer lightning
        or fireflies, secure,
                by grace of the imagination,
safe in its care.
        For if
                the light itself
has escaped,
        the whole edifice opposed to it
                goes down.
Light, the imagination
        and love,
                in our age,
by natural law,
        which we worship,
                maintain
all of a piece
        their dominance.
So let us love
        confident as is the light
                in its struggle with darkness
that there is as much to say
        and more
                for the one side
and that not the darker
        which John Donne
                for instance
among many men
        presents to us.
                In the controversy
touching the younger
        and the older Tolstoi,
                Villon, St Anthony, Kung,
Rimbaud, Buddha
        and Abraham Lincoln
                the palm goes
always to the light;
        who most shall advance the light –
                call it what you may!
The light
        for all time shall outspeed
                the thunder crack.
Medieval pageantry

is human and we enjoy
                    the rumor of it
as in our world we enjoy
                    the reading of Chaucer,
                              likewise
a priest's raiment
                    (or that of a savage chieftain).
                              It is all
a celebration of the light.
                    All the pomp and ceremony
                              of weddings,
'Sweet Thames, run softly
          till I end
                    my song,' –
are of an equal sort.
For our wedding, too,
                    the light was wakened
                              and shone. The light!
the light stood before us
          waiting!
                    I thought the world
stood still.
          At the altar
                    so intent was I
before my vows,
          so moved by your presence
                    a girl so pale
and ready to faint
          that I pitied
                    and wanted to protect you
As I think of it now,
          after a lifetime,
                    it is as if
a sweet-scented flower
          were poised
                    and for me did open.
Asphodel
          has no odor
                    save to the imagination
but it too
          celebrates the light.
                    It is late

49

but an odor
        as from our wedding
                has revived for me
and begun again to penetrate
        into all crevices
                of my world.

(1963)

WILLIAM CARLOS WILLIAMS

Louis Zukofsky

One lack with imagism, as a definition of effort, is that it is not definite enough. It is true enough, God knows, to the immediate object it represents but what is that related to the poet's personal and emotional and intellectual meanings? No hint is given or only a vague one at the best. Imagism was the takeoff for Zukofsky's poems, I think; at the beginning, he was moved by a number of fairly well known imagistic poets and he was physically part of them but to my mind the amalgam was never successful. There was always a part of this poet which would not blend, something kept him off. I for one was baffled by him. I often did not know what he was driving at.

A disturbing element was his relation to music. It wasn't simple. The contrapuntal music of Bach in particular I knew engaged his attention. It was never a simple song as it was, for instance, in my case. Specifically I am referring to his first long poem 'The' and what ultimately came out of it the culmination of all his efforts, the present poem ('A'). It was sometimes related to another lengthy poem, *The Cantos* of Ezra Pound, but even there the differences are striking, confusing to the reader for the two are far from being the same thing.

It irritated me so that I could not read the works of this poet with anything like complete satisfaction. He was a different bird from me but I was definitely attracted. Something else had been proposed to my mind. I didn't realise the cause of my irritation, how could I? It was an entirely different kind of person who was being presented. The concentration and the breaks in the language didn't add anything to my ease in the interpretation of the meaning. I didn't realise how close my attention to detail had to be to follow the really very simple language. The care, the meticulous care with which the words were put down, chosen after they had been selectively handled, the English of them stressed with a view to their timbre and effectiveness in the particular passage in which they are used ... and, furthermore, in a modern speech which has the interest of the American reader at heart; to be as brief as possible, keeping respect for his times to the forefront of the intelligence, to be never long-winded, witty where wit is called for but brief when the sense permits it.

Add to that the music of the phrase, as with a Campion, to be chosen and protected. It is amazing how clean and effective Zukofsky has kept his composition, I was about to use the word 'sentence' but I thought better of it, for though Z. like many modern poets truncates the sentence for the sake of speed I don't think he does this to the point of unintelligibility. He uses words in more or less sentence formation if not strictly in formal sentence patterns, in a wider relationship to the composition as musical entity.

It is really a very simple language. After all a poem is a matter of words, the meaning of words. The *meaning*. I was seeking, perhaps, a picture (as an imagist poet) to relate my poem to; the intellectual meaning of the word, the pure meaning, was lost, we'll say, on me. Zukofsky when he thought of a rose didn't think of the physical limits of the flower but more of what the rose meant to the mind, to the men who conceived of a rose window in twelfth century France – or at a more remote age, when our language was being formed.

Men were intent on words then – and music; perhaps the monodic theme the words carried, related to the rose which the words spoke of. To speak of a rose shown in a picture by the impressionists would be an irrelevance.

It goes even further back in our memories. The Gregorian chant or its analogue in the world of music the Jewish chant approaches Zukofsky's meaning and the pleasure he means to give us in his poem. No wonder I was baffled. It wouldn't mesh, the sense wouldn't mesh with any interpretation I had ready. Possibly I should have taken the hint from Celia his wife's *Pericles*, an entire Shakespearian play she set to music, phrase by phrase, period by period, which has never been heard but at private performances. To some extent Louis and Celia must be taken as an identity when their lives are weighed. The musician and the poet should be taken as a critical unit in our effort to understand the poet Zukofsky's meaning.

It must not be lost sight of that Zukofsky's first long poem, 'The', was written in 1926 two years fresh after he had been taught his profession of English at Columbia . . . among the others whom he respected. That poem, in part conventional blank verse, had lines which were numbered along the left hand margin like a text to be studied in class. That the young poet had a satiric objective aimed at the whole academic world is not to be denied. It was reprinted in at least one contemporary anthology, an able bit of satire which can still be read with lively interest. But the thing that still arouses my interest is that it is built according to the same model as the later poem, more or less the poem 'A' . . . A whole life has intervened during the composition of these two poems.

In the course of the years, Z. has written many shorter poems, lyrics which have become known especially among writers – for the man has never been widely known. I myself have had my own difficulties with these pieces. Intent on the portrayal of the visual image in a poem my perception has been thrown frequently out of gear. I was looking for the wrong things. The poems whatever else they are, are grammatical units intent on making a meaning *unrelated* to a mere pictorial image.

Furthermore, an obscure music, at least to me obscure, related to the music of John Sebastian Bach, has dominated the poet's mind, beliefs and emotions.

Z. is a Jew who had a devout father not exclusively concerned with the formal minutiae of his religion, a father whom he loved while he found himself unwilling to follow into the details of his ancient religion according, we'll say, to Leviticus. Z. is also a poet, a poet devoted to working out by the intelligence the intricacies of his craft; he is embedded in a matrix of his art and the multiple addictions which govern him, make him, of this time.

I was about to use word 'sentences', as I said, in a description of what this poet does with words but I thought better of it, for Z. uses not overt 'sentences', he uses words like mordents in more or less sentence formation but not strictly in the formal patterns in wider relationship to the composition as a musical entity.

That can be confusing but once accepted releasing the essential nature of the sequences it releases much of the pleasure of the composition. Take the poem on the cover of the book *Some Time*,

> Little wrists
> Is your content
> My sight or hold,
> Or your small air
> That lights and trysts?

That is not an imagistic poem. The author is intent on something else. He represents an image, true enough, but that is not his chief concern, the content, the carefully selected meaning of the poet, what he is burning to say, makes the mere image secondary.

And what is the poet so intent on saying? Something to which his care has always been devoted, the spiritual unity of the world of ideas. The meaning, the *musical* meaning, of the phrase (as with Pound) is paramount – hence their early association as poets. The music of poets varies with the sensitivity of their ears.

CHARLES TOMLINSON

To Louis Zukofsky

The morning
spent in

copying
your poems

from *Anew*,
because that

was more
than any

publisher would
do for one,

was a
delight: I

sat high
over Taos

on a
veranda

Lawrence had
made in

exile here
exile

from those
who knew

how to write
only the way they

had been
taught to:

I put aside
your book

not tired
from copying but

wishing for
the natural complement

to all the
air and openness

such art
implied:

I went
remembering that

solitude
in the world

of letters
which is yours

taking
a mountain trail

and thinking:
is not

poetry
akin to walking

for one
may know

the way that
he is going

(though I did not)
without

his knowing
what he

will see there:
and who

following on
will find

what you
with more than

walker's care
have shown

was there
before his

unaccounting eyes?

Kiowa Ranch.

LOUIS ZUKOFSKY

[By Way of Epigraph:]

The melody! the rest is accessory:

My one voice. My other: is
An objective – rays of the object brought to a focus,
An objective – nature as creator – desire
       for what is objectively perfect
Inextricably of direction of historic and contemporary
                                        particulars.
                              ('A' 6)

For Zadkine

It is a hard thing to say that when I first saw
La Prisonnière I wanted to run
And that I did, only that some birds then sang
In your courtyard, pursuing me
Over stone where you work in stone,
To come upon the prisoner in a field again.
Grass overgrowing ruins of the war
Over which she sprang, her head for other hours,
                        above a wrecked column –
Like none that had ever been –
Nailed together maybe from broken curbs of wells,
                        wood once now stone:
There, she was the Furies sometime called kind
Where the haunted stop on a ray of sun
Tho the bird still dreamed of pursues –
Any bird, that is, over a gravestone
Or a grave lacking one.
In the art of stone it is hard to set one's own
                        seal upon the idea of stone.
And in a world from which most
                        ideas have gone
To take the wreck of its idea

And make it stone
Raised up as a column
In which the prisoner is meant to be,
Over seas and fields and years,
Beside Daphne in the tree
And like a tree
But of stone to be seen in the sun,
Is harder.
There are almost no friends
But a few birds to tell what you have done.

(From *Anew*)

When the crickets
sound like fifty water-taps
forsaken at once

the inclemency
of the inhuman noises
is the earth's

with its roadways
over cabins in the forest

the sheets smell
of sweet milk

all the waters
of the world

we are going
to sleep to sleep

(no. 7. *Anew*)

I walk in the old street
to hear the beloved songs
afresh
this spring night.

Like the leaves – my loves wake –
not to be the same
or look tireless to the stars
and a ripped doorbell.

(no. 16, *Anew*)

'A' 11

for Celia and Paul

River that must turn full after I stop dying
Song, my song, raise grief to music
Light as my loves' thought, the few sick
So sick of wrangling: thus weeping,
Sounds of light, stay in her keeping
And my son's face – this much for honor.

Freed by their praises who make honor dearer
Whose losses show them rich and you no poorer
Take care, song, that what stars' imprint you mirror
Grazes their tears; draw speech from their nature or
Love in you – faced to your outer stars – purer
Gold than tongues make without feeling
Art new, hurt old: revealing
The slackened bow as the stinging
Animal dies, thread gold stringing
The fingerboard pressed in my honor.

Honor, song, sang the blest is delight knowing
We overcome ills by love. Hurt, song, nourish
Eyes' think most of whom you hurt. For the flowing
River's poison where what rod blossoms. Flourish
By love's sweet lights and sing *in them I flourish.*
No, song, not any one power
May recall or forget, our
Love to see your love flows into
Us. If Venus lights, your words spin, to
Live our desires lead us to honor.

Graced, your heart in nothing less than in death, go –
I, dust – raise the great hem of the extended
World that nothing can leave; having had breath go
Face my son, say: 'If your father offended
You with mute wisdom, my words have not ended
His second paradise where
His love was in her eyes where
They turn, quick for you two – sick
Or gone cannot make music
You set less than all. Honor

His voice in me, the river's turn that finds the
Grace in you, four notes first too full for talk, leaf
Lighting stem, stems bound to the branch that binds the
Tree, and then as from the same root we talk, leaf
After leaf of his thought, sounding
His happiness: song sounding
The grace that comes from knowing
Things, her love our own showing
Her love in all her honor.'

From 'A' 12

He who knows nothing
Loves nothing
Who loves nothing
Understands nothing.
Who understands
Loves and sees,
Believes what he knows,
The horse has large eyes
Man's virtue his feeling,
His heart treasures his tongue, certain
That a *yes* means no *no*,
What else is happiness...?

(1964)

PART TWO

A Sheaf of Poems

MICHAEL ALEXANDER

Of Green Fields

for Alexei Tolstoy

Very far from the sea
in a land-locked intemperate country where I have never been
a road leads over my shoulder
down a broad slope as long and slow as a river
to a billowing plain
    where it runs straight for the horizon.

The entire landscape is a field of wheat
thronged golden spears under throbbing heat.
There is no-one on the road.

Somewhere under all this ground
father and mother lie in night
faces spoiled by eternal light.
Shall I see him or her again?
Shall I remember that poem's refrain?

Thomas Hardy

The fire glimmers
on the turned leg of the table you lean on
to peer under eaves
at a sky squeezed beneath the clouds' lid.
The grown-out hedge at the top of the slope
gathers the darkness to the field's shoulder.

Benighted on the sunken track the other side of that bank
you could catch a tree's name from the wind's whisper.

(1965)

Do You Remember That?

The cherry-wood burns on the fire
it is enough
        to illuminate the room
and point the decorations on the Christmas tree.

They kneel on the hearth rug
        either side the chequer-board
and play. The girl is tall and straight
fair hair falling to her shoulders
        candid-eyed.

From where we stand
        by the next year's Christmas tree
and in a different house
        we cannot see the boy's face.

They play, their free hands laced,
quietly, and for a long time.
        Once, he kisses her forehead.
He watches the fire-thrown shadows on her cheek.

All the while
        the sea wind wanders in the orchard

all the while
        the moon spotlit the house

In time the logs burn down.
        She asks him if he would like a drink.
He gets up to make up the fire.

(1975)

WILLIAM BEDFORD

Letter from Cumbria

'We boast our light; but if we look not wisely on
the sun itself, it smites us into darkness.'
Milton

The sky has dropped. I guess you know.
White dust scatters on forest pine.
A brilliant sunlight scalds the snow.

Will there be loud arcades of time,
flowers to erupt their wild grace,
histories for us? You are mine.

I am yours. I know your face,
your hands, our children's blue eyes...
You not here, I whisper into space.

And daffadillies, Coleridge sighs,
growing quickly beside the lake,
leaping from the mirroring skies –

daffadillies melt and shake,
vibrating in the molten air.
Where poets cherished all they make,

these makars witness our despair,
ghosts waiting for the sun to slow.
Alone, I wonder where you are.

The sky has dropped. I guess you know.
White dust scatters on forest pine.
A brilliant sunlight scalds the snow.

(1988)

ANNE BERESFORD

Eurydice in Hades

He once sang to me, saying:
"never go near the Spring by the white cypress
for the water is not for you"

The house is like a cave
vast and cold
he is no longer with me

I must find the lake inside my head
walk by it quietly, listening to the thrush which sings
almost as sweetly as he did

Once, I saw a frog half swallowed by a snake
the frog scrabbled at the bank, desperate,
but it was well and truly caught

Like me, like him and me
caught in coils which we have made
and neither of us gods

To the guardians of my lake
I plead: "I am a child of Earth and Starry Heaven
but my race is of Heaven alone
let me drink from
the cold water of Memory
for I am thirsty and dying"

So, he taught me.

Will he follow me singing, or will I follow him?
the coils unravelled at last by our own making.

(1971)

The Condemned

On the 3rd, 6th, 9th and 40th day after the funeral, old Prussians and Lithuanians prepared a meal to which, standing at the door they invited the soul of the deceased. The meal was eaten in silence and crumbs dropped were left for the lonely souls who had no friends or relations to feed them. After the meal, the priest took a broom and swept the souls out of the house saying: Dear souls, ye have eaten and drunk. Go forth, go forth.

from the *Golden Bough*

Between the mountains
the sun is still glowing.
On the peaks a little snow.
Here on the pastures cows graze
not even their clanking bells
disturb the tranquility
of late summer.

A woman stands at the open door of the house,
she is calling to someone.
Behind her a priest
peers over her shoulder.
They wait quietly.

So it is the fortieth day
and the table set for a feast.
Those plates are not in daily use,
the bread newly baked,
plums, golden, unblemished
picked with such loving care
in the hush of the morning.
I have no appetite.
I enter the house with reluctance.

Their silence is uncanny.
Have they nothing to say
to the lonely souls
who have followed me in?

I, in turn, have nothing to say.
Her face, tanned by the air,
has grown thinner.
Her hands tremble
as she sets the cup on the saucer.
It clatters a fraction.
She needn't fear
I will soon be gone and
have no wish for her to toss
restlessly on the pillows.
Her doom is much like ours –
lonely in the midst of loneliness,
the church bells ringing on Sundays
the long walk down to the village
clutching her rosary.
We understand her. Our silent sympathy
fills the room, with its checked curtains
its geraniums. Everything shining.

She has no appetite.
The slice of cake untouched on her plate.
If only I could tell her
what she is missing –
tell her to look out of her doorway
across the valley and see...
Time is up, we must go forth.
The priest grows old, his bones crack
as he stoops to pick up the broom.

(1975)

The Comforter

This morning, admiring a newly opened rose,
his shadow crept over my shoulder
and the birds uttered warning cries.
A reminder that my country is far away
time to begin the journey home.
I have grown fond of this place

this enclosed garden
with overgrown roses and clustered wistaria,
my many loves,
but he has revealed himself in dreams
his embrace is comforting.

       He has followed me through streets,
       sat near me in the train,
       behind me in my room.
       Always loving.
       Since my birth he has observed my growing,
       looked closely into my living.
       Always impartial.

The rowan berries shine in the setting sun
clouds are gathering across the fields.
Days drop with the leaves
are trodden into the earth – vanish.
When I ask him: 'Now?'
he ruffles my hair with long fingers.
He waits.
High time to start back, a long walk,
and much will have changed.

                              (1975)

August

       Three roads cross
       by the old yew tree
       three moons shine
       on the golden apples
       one grain of wheat
       in the palm of a hand
       one hair threaded
       in a fine needle.

With sweet herbs
and belladonna
I fly to meet you,
your lips stained
by the Lammas wine
and two beating hearts
are knotted in the soft
wax of my arms.

(1975)

Ancestors

Not just the living roam here
the breathless ones gather
peer through the gloom
crowding each other

Curious and sympathetic onlookers
their prayers push away time barriers

On misty mornings
hear them whisper in distant trees
and sigh on the stairs

Their touch is gentle
cold

They are never done with grieving

(1992)

HEATHER BUCK

At the Window

I think of the dead who were buried today
Of those hurried away
Without time for the painful farewells,
And of those who have waited so long,
(Whether waiting for birth or death,
The waiting is long.)

And the strangeness of making a journey
Without the removal van,
And the unfamiliar landscape, where time
Rolls backwards and forwards,
And the mind tossed over earth's shoulder
Clutches the last known thing.

And I look at the steady stare of the sky
And my cat stretched lazily out,
I think of the dead walking naked about,
And how it feels in a mansion of mirrors –
To open a door.

Child's Play

Outside in the thin green aromatic air
Where marble angels and scratched stone declare
The resurrection of the dead,
I heard a dangling helpless sound,
Wind eating the silences, lapping at despair.

In my thoughts perhaps the dead too often grope,
And yet at times, as on a winter's afternoon
When loitering sunlight moves about the room
And softly stirs a crocus into life,
It seems that barriers of space and time
Are wooden blocks that any child can tilt.

(1976)

Psyche

When I rubbed my mind
on the polished rail
of a stale experience
and found only dust,

when I stared at a print
on the wall and found
it had no more to give,

or listened to the murmur
of priests and found
they were building a wall,

I flung my doors
to the alien wind
and let the unexplained scraps
blow undisciplined,
while I walked like Psyche holding
the lamp of interrogation
up to the silences.

Treading the stairs
where the candle-ends
of my search lay
under thickening dust,
I thought they had roped
and bound Eros
locked him away.

74

But I knew in my heart
he was free, I was the one
harbouring tenants
who had somehow
abstracted my key.

One day I'll find him
when the last
of my tenants departs,
leaving me to the dark
of his hands reaching out,
and a voice more urgent
than the whispering chorus
who echo my doubts.

(1988)

STANLEY BURNSHAW

A POEM for Peter Dale – written the night I had taken
my cat of sixteen years to have her put to rest – in gratitude
for all he has done for poetry and poetry translation:

The house hollow. The last of our four-footed children
Dead. Fur, bones, motion, willowy footprints,
Eyes that had looked at mine deeper than all other eyes,
Lost in a palmful of ashes on a cold grass.

No one now to trail my feet or hide under low forsythia,
Watching me while I call. Or late inside the house
Leap to my knees, trace on my quilt a ringful of sleep, wakeful
Eyelids closed, a quiet song in your throat through the night.

I see you move in shadows. The bed trembles.
I hear the song I could not hear, in my empty dark.

(1988)

JOHN CAYLEY

Elsewhere

'Beyond the stars are stars in which there is no combust nor
sinister aspect... neither joined to each other nor separate.'
                                                    – Rumi

Where are they
whom death has not touched?
They are elsewhere.
Other stars beyond the stars.

Before her
image entered his heart, they
were together.
A tree growing on an island.

Their union
knows no limit (be it so) they
know no others.
The turning isle, the song of the wind.

How can we
know what they know: turning away from
others' faces?
The empty lake, the silent waters.

How can they
know what we know: this pain
which has no name?
A light burning in the darkness.

Where are we
who can tell what has ended?
We are elsewhere.
An island under the moon.

To this place
where I am, you are free to come:
be here with me.
A tree growing on an island.

Each of us
knew a separate end. It is hard not
to be alone.
The turning isle, the song of the wind.

How can they
know what we know? They feel
the nameless pain.
A burning light, a silent star.

How can we
know what they know? Naming it:
love at the root.
Branches over the waters of death.

Where is one
shall grow between us all?
Here and elsewhere.
A tree dark branches touch.

(1988)

Against Nature

I have buried it,
safe and high
and far from its kin,

the fleet hare
the remnant
the wit of the moon.

I have bled it
bleed for it
and have buried it with seed.

I

Beneath the surface
of the water-hole
invisible lamprey-mouths
closed on the legs
of a wading dove.
Plump, compact poise
was suddenly awkward.
Head cocked,
feathers awry
unbalanced wings
flapping out of rhythm,
and to no effect.

The unseen horror pulls her down
beneath the water-hole, her drink.

Graceful youth, nourishing beauty,
a lioness, and we two, watched.
None of us could understand.
None of us would rise to stop it.

None of us had known
anything like it before.

Leveret crushed quick by the cold wheel
of the moon: fresh meat for love.

'Why are you sinking, beautiful bird?
Why so suddenly awkward,
so ugly with fear?
Why die, so graceless,
out of your element?'

We growled our discontent.
We yawned.
We slouched away with slack muscles,
longing to maul
or gnaw some half-dead thing.

I tore off another mouthful of the hare.
You looked down at your plate,

at the mass of sinew, bones and rich gravy
which you would leave untouched.

We finished the wine,

witnessed unbelievable escape,
a struggle to the shore
and then...inexplicable hesitation.
Was she waiting for them
to rise from the water,
and cover her with their hard black shells?
Waiting for those mouths of needles
set on blindly searching necks,
to choke themselves on her blood and feathers?

She tore herself away a second time,
emerged and staggered further up the shore,
ravaged and soiled.
They sniffed for her,
craning their blind necks.

Now she has stopped again,
waiting, once more,
for an ending.

But in the end, it seems,
they too had fears:
        of light and air.
Inexplicable
as her hesitation in escape

is their return,
this scuttling back
of bad dreams
to dark waters.

It was quick for the hare.
What about it,
shall we eat?

Remains on the road
but fresh blood, not mistook.
The reek of shit,

its bladder burst,
torn ribs
and severed neck.

Cut, cut,
and disinfect
good meat.

II

I was as she imagined
and she was like you.
She came to tell
of love or lust
– whichever it was –
longing for it,
longing for rest.

I listened to secrets
when she came to meet me.
She cared for you and shared a drink
to romance or to rest?
– What shall we say? –
I'll thirst no longer
and rest in your arms.

I held my silence
and soon she had gone,
leaving you in tears,
– of love or selfish
hatred? Be content.
Don't wish me more,
you give me everything.

III

I keep the child by me
and greet my friend,
poise that simple love
with one more difficult,

against nature.

The stimulation of the hard edge:
we share this bitterness.
But I am softened
by childish, innocent concerns

– remembered love –

and he's too wary to be trying.
My son's relaxed and shares
his joys with my too admirable mate.
Feeling his father's love, he seems

like you, like you.

IV

Still you wished me more of the hare,
urging me to take each bite
I hungered for, not on my plate.
What we wanted was the same,

as we returned from the water-hole,
our drink. Back from Africa, its deserts
and dried meats, its masks and spirits,
its rhythms of light in gold and glass.

Liberated by the rains
we buck like springbok
back in one another's arms.
I look at you and say,

'Sacred, because we come no closer.
You are opaque. I can merely touch you,
merely see your face. Looking into your eyes,
there is only one and then another.
Is it not enough? to be within you,
only in this way.'

Both our blind necks
seek the other out
and snap at feathered breasts
longing to gnaw each other's heart.

And now I
    have caught you,
and cover you with my hard, black shell.
Sink to me, beautiful bird,
drowning in tears.

I will kiss each one away.
Now, as I look at you,
there is no need to say
what you, too sharply, feel.

Jewelled terrapin, supine,
this neck is blind
and my hard tail
pierces your plastron.

In the dance I hold you
down on your carapace.
Your legs wave in the air,
I clutch your face . . .

I have buried you
safe and high
and far from your kin,

bid you remain
to eat the hare and taste
the muscle of the moon.

I have buried you with seed
and bleed for you here,
blood of the hare.

Drop, drop
and grow
the good grain.

V

Against nature

   'we lend it love'

by burying nature
whole in ourselves
we place it over against us.

Embracing now,
we set it over
against itself
and plant the seed
of something
it had never known before

   'with help from elsewhere'

we are, happily,
forced to say.

Give me such words
– my daily
seed of the hare –
and make me say to her

   'another first'

and hear her answer
    'yes'
and hear her, happy, answer
    'yes'
seed of a hare, her answer
    'yes'
against nature,
    answer

'yes, yes, yes, yes, yes, . . .'

              (1988)

HUMPHREY CLUCAS

In Darkness

Since all shall not be well
Under your quiet gaze,
In darkness let me dwell,

Or in some other hell
Play out my tedious days,
Since all shall not be well.

Release me from your spell,
Your burning-glass, your maze;
In darkness let me dwell.

River and tarn and fell,
The hawthorn's earliest haze,
Since all shall not be well,

And the green sea-swell
Have lost their power to amaze;
In darkness let me dwell.

And candle, book and bell
Shall exorcise our ways;
And all shall not be well
In darkness where I dwell.

(1983)

WILLIAM COOKSON

Spell

A Sequence

For P.

Al poco giorno ed el gran cerchio d'ombra

DIS

I dreamt when our love began
we sat on a common, at dusk.

Heather, bronze-gold.

I was beckoned
but wanted to stay.

You looked aside.

'My name is Dis,' he said,
'we'll grow to love each other.'

He led me down many stairs.

Love, lie again in my arms.
Lay the dust of that dream.

FOUR HAIKUS

(i)

Did you take me
        into the gentleness of your hands
just to shatter?

(ii)

Cool air – a leafy dawn.

I need your pale eyes
to lead me back to light.

(iii)

I've been falling
            layer by layer
to the black pit where nothing is.

(iv)

In far regions
            too near and void of light
I fear the universe.

FALL

I tried to share my world with you.

It took fire
            toward light and air.

When you withdrew
            it knotted into grief.

STILLED

The rugged, ancient boughs
of your tulip tree
in the deep garden
where we walked.

No more frantic calls
no more blind visits.

I thought we had changed eyes.

Now I send you love
in token of your gentleness
for a few enchanted weeks:

In the waves
your drifting red-brown hair.
Wild woodlands where we strayed.
Under an oak
that thrust in ecstasy
no words can spell.

Memories etched
on a blank London day.

I have had my earthly joy.

SPELL

A cirrus wing
        webbed in the dawn wind.

Months since you fled
        pale eyes draw me
through heather, bracken
wind-riven woodlands
        desert places
the wilderness is your domain.

            *

Frost-crust fades
        in a later dawn.

Pictures of our brief Summer
        go with me
colour air
soft with an inkling of Spring.

Slow detritus
toward oblivion.

*

Elemental
you cannot break this spell.

DREAM QUEST

Dreaming at dawn
I passed a white ruin
to walk through dusky gold
down a deep lane
knowing neither the place
nor the direction.

*

That dream shadows the day.

Journeying far
I leave flowers
on the threshold
of an empty cottage.

Then see your dull green car.
You're at the cottage window
flowers gone.

*

Slant December gold.

We walk down a deep lane.

*

Grey London.

Your presence
in the holly twigs
you wrenched
to give me.

GIFTS

(*Bonzai, opals*)

I give
        stillness
in this spindly pine.

Stones
        to match colours
in your eyes

A LITTLE LIGHT...

A hillside forest
                moss in tangled light
flickers
        in dark regions of the mind

NIGHT

Stillness of stone pines.

I clamber crumbling crags
searching for your return.

CODA

Occluded banks
                no grass-blade
nor stir of air.

The darkness of time.

What can I give you
but embers from the past?

                    *

In far woods
a room in shade
flood of sunlight outside.

Through ruined oaks
                tangled twigs
search for the golden flower.

Tracts of bright mist.

The tower that shines
                in the sunrise.

*

A solitary bird-cry
                before dawn
renews ancient pain.

(1983-4)

PETER DALE

Last Respects

I know these hands, their feel,
knew the cuts beneath each scar,
wondered when that split nail would heal.

They used to lark
with birds of shadow on the wall
for children scared of the dark.

Fall now –
and all the birds are flown.

Hunched shadows black the wall.

(1964)

Old Poet on a Rainy Day

For David Jones

My old acquaintances and peers
once allied in the lonely art
and rivals in our riper years
gather together now on shelves
after so sure a life apart
and peace becomes their books, themselves.

(1973)

from *Having No Alternative*, a Sequence

THINKING OF WRITING A LETTER

And if I had your address what could I write?
I've seen the shots a cancer patient needs
towards the end. You drift incurably ill,
and your suffering must be worse, the drugs you take.

Suppose I said it's raining here tonight;
shared drinking yarns; sized up rival creeds;
let on I think of easy ways to kill
myself – but pills, not knives, the quarry lake.

They'd need courage.... – Cold comfort that would make
in your despair....So I suppose I'd fill
some sheets with quotes, a rhyme, retort or slight
to draw you on to cap one of my leads.

And you would quote again that Yeats you take
to justify your ways beyond your skill.
Something like: *Whatever flames upon the night*
Man's own resinous heart has fed; it reads.

I see England mapped before me, dark and still,
and for a moment point after point of light
from every room you ever left succeeds
across it. The last melts out like a flake.

For twenty miles around there is no hill.
Time past for beacons that can reach your sight....
The silence of this water; jagged reeds;
shatters of light that lazytong the lake.

Dear Murphy,

(1969)

Old Haunt

Scotch fir, the trunk
staked in the still pools of its boughs
on the old hill.

The needles kill the grass
where we left our shapes
so long ago.

Its criss-crossings
crazed your bare legs.
You tried for a fern pattern.

This stillness was there then;
boughs like green snow overhanging;
and the peace was no trouble to us.

(1972)

Two Sonnets from *One Another*

SHADES

My hand's reach larger than life upon the blind,
the light so limited that the dark leaks in.
You shudder at the shape in mind, you say;
a branch wuthered against the window, bare,
hag-black to stifle you – until my hand
soft as a shadow brushes away your cry.
Dark promises, my love, lie candid there.
I've just the ghost of a touch to sidle down
your spine. Once a shadow, always a ghost.
Remember among windswept oaks or cloistral beech
these hands. They'll haunt your body mostly there.
How they'll remember at arm's reach you comb
    and slowly comb your hair until it gleams
    satisfactorily with my sweat. Sweet dreams.

STORM

Your fear of lightning, my need of the storm.
The great pylons a pale shadow of the cloud
bouldered above us and your slight figure cowed.
Sky cracks like ice and the rain slow and warm.
Your hand in mine. I cannot hold your fear
and you can't draw the need from me, your head
so close I muffle up your other ear.
The two of us, you say, the two of us dead.

The power to drive a city in that flash,
all spent to burn a vacuum in the sky.
I watch it branch and you tense for the crash.
Big drops darken and connect across your dress.
Love, where we hold close we are bone-dry;
you cling, and what comes through is powerless.

(1975)

Memorial (For F.H.)*

I never met you.
        The gut-reaction
to mourn your death is
        driven by anger
that time should wreck not
you as yourself but
as anyone else so
        circled with love,
        gentle with life.

* This poem arose from reading the issue of *New Departures* entitled: 'A Celebration/Of and For Frances Horovitz (1938-83)'

95

Nothing I miss is
    you or yours to
wrench recognition.
        I cannot mourn you.
I'd have to give you
characteristics,
a touch, some charisma
        of others I love to
        feel your destruction.

Eleanor's hands,
        cool even in summer –
the image happens
        with such a sudden
shudder of anguish
and terror I am so
cold that I cannot
        touch myself. My
        hands mourn your death.

(1984)

from *Like a Vow*, A Sequence

UPLAND

1

A dry ditch, with banks of leafmould
    like wet rust, chestnuts overhanging;
a slate sky, contoured with sun-gold

above the horizon where a hamlet
    glistens. There will be rain, rain falling
big and warm and straight as a plummet,

splashing up coronets . . . Forgotten
    the hamlet's name, the last turning,
which next, but southern the location.

But I was on that upland; remember
    a pressure binding and releasing.
My memory haunts it like a spectre.

Perhaps it is the mind of others
    that leaguer there almost a feeling.
You would assume the wild-eyed watchers.

I find you many likely places.
    But if you're there you show no inkling.
You give them all your keenest glances

then off into the woods to savour
    the bluebells' well attested pooling –
ladies'-slippers found one summer.

But what is missing I cannot capture
    in trees, lane, ditch, the cloud purpling.
It is nothing that is in your nature.

But I am nearest it in silence:
    the sound of a bell no longer ringing.
It's almost like an old allegiance,

fealty sworn young to a lost lord.
    You cannot swear faith to my ghost-king.
I cannot breach his word, his gold-hoard . . .

Your bluebells, lass, this is your kingdom.
    In my lord's realm I'm the hireling.
Kneel to the bluebells, the blown blossom.

No once and future king, fore-spoken:
    his line will never see returning.
My oath can never be forsaken.

2

Lord, in the underlight of thunder –
    But if my liege is self-projection,
no ghostly exile of a lost order,

loyalty is no less though kingship
　　　is mine. What worse than king's treason?
I can't break faith by cant or gossip.

I say: no feint of trees and shadow.
　　　Not mine but earthly the dominion;
the bond is real as voice and echo...

No: beeches these; the promised shower
　　　small rain; and the wide sky ocean-
grey, not true to scarp and tenor.

But let it be: a part and parcel,
　　　our common ground of recollection,
the great, downsweeping branches focal.

(Curled husks of nuts like Dutch bonnets,
　　　the short-cut – geese in opposition,
a slate sky harrying high cloudlets...

We used to eat the nuts when children,
　　　nails lifted by the shell's construction...)
Childhood, and the big rain not fallen.

3

Coronets of rain – and the keen-eyed
　　　child recalls their brief existence
sprung from the tarmac of the roadside.

And going up the narrow staircase,
　　　Candleman prancing like a nuisance,
coronets tumbled in a goose-chase

rolling down the gleaming rooftops...
　　　In the stillness of leaves and birds, the silence,
the weathered spirit senses raindrops,

knows the freshness that falls, releasing
　　　the tension, bringing out the fragrance
of the grass, the dry ditch jingling...

Trembler of light on its white column,
    coronets tumbling, dancing attendance,
Candleman, Candleman, once his kingdom.

But to your beeches as I know them,
    my scarp, how shall we plot our credence?
To know another takes a kingdom.

And the big rain is falling, watcher,
    the big drops in their regular cadence,
bigger than any tears, and warmer.

(1988)

Journey

Dearest, I've gone at your pace.
We've lingered on the way;
some route you chose to trace!
It's taken us all day.

Let's have some give and take.
You've named the flowers. Look sharp.
It's not so far to make.
I'm going down that scarp.

That way we're there by dark....
Ah no, don't name the stars!
Sidereal meadow-spark?
Well, not all the stars....

(1993)

DONALD DAVIE

In the Stopping Train

I have got into the slow train
again. I made the mistake
knowing what I was doing,
knowing who had to be punished.

I know who has to be punished:
the man going mad inside me;
whether I am fleeing
from him or towards him.

This journey will punish the bastard:
he'll have his flowering gardens
to stare at through the hot window;
words like 'laurel' won't help.

He abhors his fellows,
especially children; let there
not for pity's sake
be a crying child in the carriage.

So much for pity's sake.
The rest for the sake of justice:
torment him with his hatreds
and love of fictions.

The punishing slow pace
punishes also places along the line
for having, some of them, Norman
or Hanoverian stone-work:

his old familiars, his
exclusive prophylactics.
He'll stare his fill at their
emptiness on this journey.

Jonquil is a sweet word.
Is it a flowering bush?
Let him helplessly wonder
for hours if perhaps he's seen it.

Has it a white and yellow
flower, the jonquil? Has it
a perfume? Oh his art could
always pretend it had.

He never needed to see,
not with his art to help him.
He never needed to use his
nose, except for language.

Torment him with his hatreds,
torment him with his false
loves. Torment him with time
that has disclosed their falsehood.

Time, the exquisite torment!
His future is a slow
and stopping train through places
whose names used to have virtue.

*

A stopping train, I thought,
was a train that was going to stop.
Why board it then, in the first place?

Oh no, they explained, it is stopping
and starting, stopping and starting.

How could it, they reasoned gently,
be always stopping unless
also it was always starting?

I saw the logic of that;
grown-ups were good at explaining.

Going to stop was the same
as stopping to go. What madness!
It made a sort of sense, though.

It's not, I explained, that I mind
getting to the end of the line.
Expresses have to do that.

No, they said. We see...
But do you? I said. It's not
the last stop that is bad...

No, they said, it's the last
start, the little one; yes,
the one that doesn't last.

Well, they said, you'll learn
all about that when you're older.

Of course they learned it first.
Oh naturally, yes.

*

The man in the stopping train
sees them along the highway
with a recklessness like breeding
passing and re-passing:
dormobile, Vauxhall, Volvo.

He is shrieking silently: 'Rabbits!'
He abhors his fellows.
Yet even the meagre arts
of television can
restore them to him sometimes,

when the man in uniform faces
the unrelenting camera
with a bewildered fierceness
beside the burnt-out Simca.

*

What's all this about flowers?
They have an importance he can't
explain, or else their names have.

Spring, he says, 'stirs'. It is what
he has learned to say, he can say
nothing but what he has learned.

And Spring, he knows, means flowers.
Already he observes this.
Some people claim to love them.

Love *them*? Love flowers? Love,
love . . . the word is hopeless:
gratitude, maybe, pity . . .

Pitiful, the flowers.
He turns that around in his head:
what on earth can it mean?

Flowers, it seems, are important.
And he can name them all,
identify hardly any.

*

Judith Wright, Australian

' . . . has become,' I said, 'the voice
of her unhappy nation.'
O wistfully I said it.

Unhappier than it knows,
her nation. And though she will tell it,
it cannot understand:

with its terrible future before it,
glaring at its terrible past;

its disequilibrium, its
cancers in bud and growing;

all its enormous sadness
still taking off, still arcing

over the unhistoried
Pacific, humming to Chile.

Stone heads of Easter Island!
Spoiled archipelagos!

How they have suffered already
on Australia's account

and England's. They will suffer
no more on England's.

Judith Wright, Australian,
'has become,' I said,

'the voice of her unhappy,
still-to-be-guilty nation.'

Wistfully I said it,
there in the stopping train.

*

The things he has been spared . . .
'Gross egotist!' Why don't
his wife, his daughter shrill
that in his face?

Love and pity seem
the likeliest explanations;
another occurs to him –
despair too would be quiet.

*

Time and again he gave battle,
furious, mostly effective;
nobody counts the wear
and tear of rebuttal.

Time and again he rose
to the flagrantly offered occasion;
nobody's hanged for a slow
murder by provocation.

Time and again he applauded
the stand he had taken; how much
it mattered, or to what
assize, is not recorded.

Time and again he hardened
his heart and his perceptions;
nobody knows just how
truths turn into deceptions.

Time and again, oh time and
that stopping train!
Who knows when it comes to a stand
and will not start again?

*

(*Son et Lumière*)

I have travelled with him many times
now. Already we nod,
we are almost on speaking terms.

Once I thought that he sketched
an apologetic gesture
at what we turned away from.

Apologies won't help him:
his spectacles flared like paired
lamps as he turned his head.

I knew they had been ranging,
paired eyes like mine,
igniting and occluding

coppice and crisp chateau,
thatched corner, spray of leaf,
curved street, a swell of furrows,

where still the irrelevant vales
were flowering, and the still
silver rivers slid west.

*

The dance of words
is a circling prison, thought
the passenger staring through
the hot unmoving pane
of boredom. It is not
thank God a dancing pain,
he thought, though it starts to jig
now. (The train is moving.) 'This',
he thought in rising panic
(Sit down! Sit down!)
'this much I can command,
exclude. Dulled words, keep still!
Be the inadequate, cloddish
despair of me!' No good:
they danced, as the smiling land
flared past the pane, the pun's
galvanized *tarantelle*.

*

'A shared humanity...' He
pummels his temples. 'Surely,
surely that means something?'

He knew too few in love,
too few in love.

That sort of foolish beard
masks an uncertain mouth.
And so it proved: he took
some weird girl off to a weird
commune, clutching at youth.

Dear reader, this is not
our chap, but another.
Catch our clean-shaven hero
tied up in such a knot?
A cause of so much bother?

He knew too few in love.

(1973)

PETER DENT

Momentum

The clearing we came to
was a lake, quite small
and dark with lilies, ducks
and, there beyond, a girl
astride a tall white fence.
She sat there moments only
watching ducks in flight
across the lake,
then quietly slipped away . . . .
But we stayed longer,
waiting, watching the lilies
lie still on the dark water.

(1966)

Hesitation

The way you lie in sleep.
Arm flung out, abandoned,
head that almost rolls away.

The cracked floorboard
grates beneath my tread.
No movement, but a smile
hesitates upon your lips.

Behind you a rectangle of night sky
hung with southern stars.
Orion at his best.

(1972)

RONALD DUNCAN

Two Poems from *The Solitudes*

1

Any man might miss
      Your lips or thighs, but I
Miss the slut, the shrew in you;
And hate this quiet peace which lacks your nasty tongue,
Bored with my bed too big without your bum.

Any man might want
      You for your charm, but I
Want the bitch, the nag of you;
And walk this slow evening so dull without your spite,
Sick of my thought, less you're distracting it.

Any man might love
      You for some part, but I
Love you whole, even your heart,
In which I am contained, though I've not entered it,
– Or so you say sometimes, only because you wish to give it me
                                       again.

2

There was no part of you
      my hands did not know.
Now separated,
      let the memory of my hands
Enfold your neck, your breasts, your thighs,
      gently as petals fall
      or the wings of butterflies rise.

Be like a chrysalis contained by my fingers, encased by my touch:
Let the rude world stare at this robe you wear
      Dior could not copy it
      Paquin imitate it;

Go dressed in my hands, my desire the designer
        Clothed in this passion
        You are the height of fashion.

So flaunt the memory of my hands proudly
Till this blind glove with which I now write
Can undress you, and from your nakedness
Receive its flesh, its purpose and its sight,
Embroidering your skin in the fierce tattoo of night.

(1959)

THOM GUNN

Touch

You are already
asleep. I lower
myself in next to
you, my skin slightly
numb with the restraint
of habits, the patina of
self, the black frost
of outsideness, so that even
unclothed it is
a resilient chilly
hardness, superficially
malleable, dead
rubbery texture.

You are a mound
of bedclothes, where the cat
in sleep braces
its paws against your
calf through the blankets,
and kneads each paw in turn.

Meanwhile and slowly
I feel a is it
my own warmth surfacing or
the ferment of your whole
body that in darkness beneath
the cover is stealing
bit by bit to break
down that chill.

You turn and
hold me tightly, do
you know who
I am or am I
your mother or
the nearest human being to
hold on to in a
dreamed pogrom.

What I, now loosened,
sink into is an old
big place, it is
there already, for
you are already
there, and the cat
got there before you, yet
it is hard to locate.
What is more, the place is
not found but seeps
from our touch in
continuous creation, dark
enclosing cocoon round
ourselves alone, dark
wide realm where we
walk with everyone.

(1966)

DONALD HALL

In the Kitchen of the Old House

In the kitchen of the old house, late,
I was making some coffee
    and I day-dreamed sleepily of old friends.
Then the dream turned. I waited.
    I walked alone all day in the town
where I was born. It was cold,
    a Saturday in January
when nothing happens. The streets
    changed as the sky grew dark around me.
The lamps in the small houses
    had tassels on them, and the black cars
at the curb were old and square.
    A ragman passed with his horse, their breaths
blooming like white peonies,
    when I turned into a darker street
and I recognized the house
    from snapshots. I felt as separate
as if the city and the house
    were closed inside a globe which I shook
to make it snow. No sooner
    did I think of snow, but snow started
to fill the heavy darkness
    around me. It reflected the glare
of the streetlight as it fell
    melting on the warmth of the sidewalk
and frozen on frozen grass.
    Then I heard out of the dark the sound
of steps on the bare cement
    in a familiar rhythm. Under
the streetlight, bent to the snow,
    hatless, younger than I, so young that
I was not born, my father
    walked home to his bride and his supper.
A shout gathered inside me
    like a cold wind, to break the rhythm,
to keep him from entering
    that heavy door – but I stood under

a tree, closed in by the snow,
   and did not shout, to tell what happened
in twenty years, in winter,
   when his early death grew inside him
like snow piling on the grass.
   He opened the door and met the young
woman who waited for him.

(1963)

MICHAEL HAMBURGER

Travelling I

Mountains, lakes. I have been here before
And on other mountains, wooded
Or rocky, smelling of thyme.
Lakes from whose beds they pulled
The giant catfish, for food,
Larger, deeper lakes that washed up
Dead carp and mussel shells, pearly or pink.
Forests where, after rain,
Salamanders lay, looped the dark moss with gold.
High up, in a glade,
Bells clanged, the cowherd boy
Was carving a pipe.

And I moved on, to learn
One of the million histories,
One weather, one dialect
Of herbs, one habitat
After migration, displacement,
With greedy lore to pounce
On a place and possess it,
With the mind's weapons, words,
While between land and water
Yellow vultures, mewing,
Looped empty air
Once filled with the hundred names
Of the nameless, or swooped
To the rocks, for carrion.

Enough now, of grabbing, holding,
The wars fought for peace,
Great loads of equipment lugged
To the borders of bogland, dumped,
So that empty-handed, empty-minded,
A few stragglers could stagger home.

And my baggage – those tags, the stickers
That brag of a Grand Hotel
Requisitioned for troops, then demolished,
Of a tropical island converted
Into a golf course;
The specimens, photographs, notes –
The heavier it grew, the less it was needed,
The longer it strayed, misdirected,
The less it was missed.

Mountains. A lake.
One of a famous number.
I see these birds, they dip over wavelets,
Looping, martins or swallows,
Their flight is enough.
The lake is enough,
To be here, forgetful,
In a boat, on water.
The famous dead have been here.
They saw and named what I see,
They went and forgot.

I climb a mountainside, soggy,
Then springy with heather.
The clouds are low,
The shaggy sheep have a name,
Old, less old than the breed
Less old than the rock
And I smell hot thyme
That grows in another country,
Through gaps in the Roman wall
A cold wind carries it here,

Through gaps in the mind,
Its fortifications, names:
Name that a Roman gave
To a camp on the moor
Where a sheep's jawbone lies
And buzzards, mewing, loop
Air between woods and water

Long empty of his gods;
Name of the yellow poppy
Drooping, after rain,
Or the flash, golden,
From wings in flight –
Greenfinch or yellowhammer –

Of this mountain, this lake. I move on.

(1969)

A Walk in the Cotswolds

with Frances Horovitz

Moon-pale even there, in the valley
She'd learnt by heart, showing me marjoram
Wild and abundant as common grasses,
So lightly she stepped, I thought
She'd never need more of earth
Than the pull of it, against
An urge less to rise than to hover.

But "flowers became stone",
Her lunar nature weighted
With love, for a man, a child
And a place that would hold them, hold her,

Till she hovered again, heavier,
Pulled this way and that, wrenched;
And for healing must hurtle down.

(1989)

IAN HAMILTON

Birthday Poem

Tight in your hands
Your Empire Exhibition shaving mug.
You keep it now
As a spittoon, its bloated doves
Its 1938
Stained by the droppings of your blood.

Tonight
Half-suffocated, cancerous,
Deceived,
You bite against its gilded china mouth
And wait for an attack.

(1964)

At Evening

Arriving early, I catch sight of you
Across the lawn. You're hovering:
A silver teaspoon in one hand
(The garden table almost set)
And in the other, a blue vase.
For the few seconds I stand watching you
It seems half-certain you'll choose wrong
– Well, not exactly, wrong, but dottily,
Off-key. You know,
That dreaminess in you we used to smile about
(My pet, my little lavender, my sprite),
It's getting worse.
I'd talk to you about it if I could.

Again

That dream again: You stop me at the door
And take my arm, but grievingly.
Behind you, in the parlour, I can see
The bow of a deep sofa, blanketed in grey,
And next to it, as if at harbourside,
A darker grey, rough-sculpted group of three.
Three profiles sombrely inclined,
Long overcoats unbuttoned, hats in hand:
Night-mariners, with eyes of stone,
And yet the eyes seem stricken.
Is it that they too can hardly bear
What's happened? What *has* happened? Who?

Soliloquy

'We die together though we live apart'
You say, not looking up at me,
Not looking up.
                    'I mean to say.
Even were we actually to die in unison,
Evaporating in each other's arms,
We'd still have ended up – well, wouldn't we? –
Dying for a taste, our first and last,
Of unaloneness:
                    we'd have dreamed,
Dreamed up a day utterly unclouded
By the dread that not quite yet but soon,
Although, please God, not very soon,
We will indeed be whispering
Wretchedly, in unison, your breath on mine:
I might as well be dead,
Or we might. Do you follow? Are you
With me? Do you see?'

The Garden

This garden's leaning in on us, green-shadowed,
Shadowed green, as if to say: Be still, don't agitate
For what's been overgrown –
Some cobbled little serpent of a path,
Perhaps, an arbour, a dry pond
That you'd have plans for if this place belonged to you.
The vegetation's rank, I'll grant you that,
The weeds well out of order, shoulder-high
And too complacently deranged. The trees
Ought not to scrape your face, your hands, your hair
Nor so haphazardly swarm upwards to impede
The sunlit air you say you need to breathe
In summertime. It shouldn't be so dark
So early.
　　　　　All the same, if I were you,
I'd let it be. Lay down your scythe. Don't fidget
For old clearances or new. For one more day
Let's listen to our shadows and be glad
That this much light has managed to get through.

(1993)

120

SEAMUS HEANEY

from *Station Island*

Note: Station Island, on Lough Derg in Co. Donegal, is the site
of a penitential pilgrimage where the exercises include praying
while making the rounds of various stone circles 'beds'.

Black water. White waves. Furrows snowcapped.
A magpie flew from the basilica
and staggered in the granite airy space
I was staring into, on my knees
at the hard mouth of St Brigid's bed.
I came to and there at the bed's stone hub
was my archaeologist, very like himself,
with his scribe's face smiling its straight-lipped smile,
starting at the sight of me with the same old
pretence of amazement, so that the wing
of woodkerne's hair fanned down across his brow.
And then as if a shower were blackening
already blackened stubble, the dark weather
of his unspoken pain came over him.
A pilgrim bent and whispering on his rounds
inside the bed passed between us slowly.

"Those dreamy stars that pulsed across the screen
beside you in the ward – your heartbeats, Tom, I mean –
scared me the way they stripped things naked.
My banter failed too early in that visit.
And I could not take my eyes off the machine.
I had to head back straight away to Dublin,
guilty and empty, feeling I had said nothing
and that, as usual, I had somehow broken
covenants, and failed an obligation.
I half knew we would never meet again...
Did our long gaze and last handshake contain
nothing to appease that recognition?"

"Nothing at all. But familiar stone
had me half-numbed to face the thing alone.
I loved my still-faced archaeology.

The small crab-apple physiognomies
on high crosses, carved heads in abbeys . . .
Why else dig in for years in that hard place
in a muck of bigotry under the walls
picking through shards and Williamite cannon-balls?
But all that we just turned to banter too.
I felt that I should have seen far more of you
and maybe would have – but dead at thirty-two!
Ah poet, lucky poet, tell me why
what seemed deserved and promised passed me by?"

I could not speak. I saw a hoard of black
basalt axeheads, smooth as a beetle's back,
a cairn of stone force that might detonate,
the eggs of danger. And then I saw a face
he had once given me, a plaster cast
of an abbess, done by the Gowran master,
mild-mouthed and cowled, a character of grace.
"Your gift will be a candle in our house."
But he had gone when I looked to meet his eyes
and hunkering instead there in his place
was a bleeding, pale-faced boy, plastered in mud.
"The red-hot pokers blazed a lovely red
in Jerpoint the Sunday I was murdered,"
he said quietly. "Now do you remember?
You were there with poets when you got the word
and stayed there with them, while your own flesh and blood
was carted to Bellaghy from the Fews.
They showed more agitation at the news
than you did."

                    "But they were getting crisis
first-hand, Colum, they had happened in on
live sectarian assassination.
I was dumb, encountering what was destined."
And so I pleaded with my second cousin.
"I kept seeing a grey stretch of Lough Beg
and the strand empty at daybreak.
I felt like the bottom of a dried-up lake."

"You saw that, and you wrote that – not the fact.
You confused evasion and artistic tact.
The Protestant who shot me through the head
I accuse directly, but indirectly, you
who now atone perhaps upon this bed
for the way you whitewashed ugliness and drew
the lovely blinds of the *Purgatorio*
and saccharined my death with morning dew."

Then I seemed to waken out of sleep
among more pilgrims whom I did not know
drifting to the hostel for the night.

(1984)

DAVID HEIDENSTAM

"The land stands silent..."

The land stands silent in the sun:
Solid; green; encompassed; known;
Till a crow's caw sounds, like a great door opening,
And makes of the dark wood an inhabited thing.

(1988)

A.L. HENDRIKS

The Tree-Lady

She talked to trees
As she did to dogs   cats   children
Her voice gentle soft low   crooning
You are beautiful   I love you
Kissing them   caressing them.

She mounted trees
As she did her ponies
Using no block
Stirrup or leg-up
Nimbling like an acrobat
Or cat.

She rode the trees
Sitting them   she used to say
Bare-branch
Rode them in every weather
Especially rain and high wind
Stringy thighs   wrinkled veined hands   gripping
The leaves a green mane flowing
Her own grey streaming behind
She singing un chanson sans paroles.

Never did she fall;

When we found her she was self-composed lying supine
Amid leaves that had.

Unbruised   unbroken   unpoisoned

Fingers of both hands clasped about a stem of blossom
Lips lately parted in a smile of wonder and delight
Eyes   wide   staring
Not at the beyond sky
But into those green havens she had loved

Under which now her neat bones lie.

(1988)

125

GEOFFREY HILL

Soliloquies

1 THE STONE MAN, 1878

for Charles Causley

Recall, now, the omens of childhood:
The nettle-clump and rank elder tree;
The stones waiting in the mason's yard:

Half-recognised kingdom of the dead:
A deeper landscape lit by distant
Flashings from their journey. At nightfall

My father scuffed clay into the house.
He set his boots on the bleak iron
Of the hearth; ate, drank, unbuckled, slept.

I leaned to the lamp; the pallid moths
Clipped its glass, made an autumnal sound.
Words clawed my mind as though they had smelt

Revelation's flesh . . . So, with an ease
That is dreadful, I summon all back.
The sun bellows over its parched swarms.

2 OLD POET WITH DISTANT ADMIRERS

What I lost was not a part of this.
The dark-blistered foxgloves, wet berries
Glinting from shadow, small ferns and stones,

Seem fragments, in the observing mind,
Of its ritual power. Old age
Singles them out as though by first-light,

As though a still-life, preserving some
Portion of the soul's feast, went with me
Everywhere, to be hung in strange rooms,

Loneliness being what it is. If
I knew the exact coin for tribute,
Defeat might be bought, processional

Silence gesture its tokens of earth
At my mouth: as in the great death-songs
Of Propertius (although he died young).

(1965)

From the *Songbook* of Sebastian Arrurruz

1

Ten years without you. For so it happens.
Days make their steady progress, a routine
That is merciful and attracts nobody.

Already, like a disciplined scholar,
I piece fragments together, past conjecture
Establishing true sequences of pain;

For so it is proper to find value
In a bleak skill, as in the thing restored:
The long-lost words of choice and valediction.

2   COPLAS

(i)

"One cannot lose what one has not possessed".
So much for that abrasive gem.
I can lose what I want. I want you.

(ii)

Oh my dear one, I shall grieve for you
For the rest of my life with slightly
Varying cadence, oh my dear one.

(iii)

Half-mocking the half-truth, I note
"The wild brevity of sensual love".
I am shaken, even by that.

(iv)

It is to him I write, it is to her
I speak in contained silence. Will they be touched
By the unfamiliar passion between them?

3

What other men do with other women
Is for me neither orgy nor sacrament
Nor a language of foreign candour

But is mere occasion or chance distance
Out of which you might move and speak my name
As I speak yours, bargaining with sleep's

Miscellaneous gods for as much
As I can have: an alien landscape,
The dream where you are always to be found.

4

A workable fancy: old petulant
Sorrow comes back to us, metamorphosed
And semi-precious. Fortuitous amber.
As though this recompensed our deprivation.
See how each fragment kindles as we turn it,
At the end, into the light of appraisal.

(1966)

AN UNCOLLECTED ARRURRUZ COPLA

('Aqui esta encerrada el alma de...')

The fox goes hungry to earth. At dawn
The owl, surfeited with fur and bone,
Sleeps. I rise from your dream, you from mine.

(1972)

Lachrimae

or
Seven tears figured in seven passionate Pavans

Passions I allow, and loves I approve, only
I would wish that men would alter their
object and better their intent.

ST ROBERT SOUTHWELL, *Mary Magdalen's*
Funeral Tears, 1591.

1   LACHRIMAE VERAE

Crucified Lord, you swim upon your cross
and never move. Sometimes in dreams of hell
the body moves but moves to no avail
and is at one with that eternal loss.

You are the castaway of drowned remorse,
you are the world's atonement on the hill.
This is your body twisted by our skill
into a patience proper for redress.

I cannot turn aside from what I do;
you cannot turn away from what I am.
You do not dwell in me nor I in you

however much I pander to your name
or answer to your lords of revenue,
surrendering the joys that they condemn.

Splendour of life so splendidly contained,
brilliance made bearable. It is the east
light's embodiment, fit to be caressed,
the god Amor with his eyes of diamond,

celestial worldliness on which has dawned
intelligence of angels, Midas' feast,
the stony hunger of the dispossessed
locked into Eden by their own demand.

Self-love, the slavish master of this trade,
conquistador of fashion and remark,
models new heavens in his masquerade,

its images intense with starry work,
until he tires and all that he has made
vanishes in the chaos of the dark.

3   MARTYRIUM

The Jesus-faced man walking crowned with flies
who swats the roadside grass or glances up
at the streaked gibbet with its birds that swoop,
who scans his breviary while the sweat dries,

fades, now, among the fading tapestries,
brooches of crimson tears where no eyes weep,
a mouth unstitched into a rimless cup,
torn clouds the cauldrons of the martyrs' cries.

Clamorous love, its faint and baffled shout,
its grief that would betray him to our fear,
he suffers for our sake, or does not hear

above the hiss of shadows on the wheat.
Viaticum transfigures earth's desire
in rising vernicles of summer air.

Crucified Lord, however much I burn
to be enamoured of your paradise,
knowing what ceases and what will not cease,
frightened of hell, not knowing where to turn,

I fall between harsh grace and hurtful scorn.
You are the crucified who crucifies,
self-withdrawn even from your own device,
your trim-plugged body, wreath of rakish thorn.

What grips me then, or what does my soul grasp?
If I grasp nothing what is there to break?
You are beyond me, innermost true light,

uttermost exile for no exile's sake,
king of our earth not caring to unclasp
its void embrace, the semblance of your quiet.

Loves I allow and passions I approve:
Ash-Wednesday feasts, ascetic opulence,
the wincing lute, so real in its pretence,
itself a passion amorous of love.

Self-wounding martyrdom, what joys you have,
true-torn among this fictive consonance,
music's creation of the moveless dance,
the decreation to which all must move.

Self-seeking hunter of forms, there is no end
to such pursuits. None can revoke your cry.
Your silence is an ecstasy of sound

and your nocturnals blaze upon the day.
I founder in desire for things unfound.
I stay amid the things that will not stay.

Crucified Lord, so naked to the world,
you live unseen within that nakedness,
consigned by proxy to the judas-kiss
of our devotion, bowed beneath the gold,

with re-enactments, penances foretold:
scentings of love across a wilderness
of retrospection, wild and objectless
longings incarnate in the carnal child.

Beautiful for themselves the icons fade;
the lions and the hermits disappear.
Triumphalism feasts on empty dread,

fulfilling triumphs of the festal year.
We find you wounded by the token spear.
Dominion is swallowed with your blood.

7 LACHRIMAE AMANTIS

What is there in my heart that you should sue
so fiercely for its love? What kind of care
brings you as though a stranger to my door
through the long night and in the icy dew

seeking the heart that will not harbour you,
that keeps itself religiously secure?
At this dark solstice filled with frost and fire
your passion's ancient wounds must bleed anew.

So many nights the angel of my house
has fed such urgent comfort through a dream,
whispered 'your lord is coming, he is close'

that I have drowsed half-faithful for a time
bathed in pure tones of promise and remorse:
'tomorrow I shall wake to welcome him.'

(1975)

Terribilis est locus iste

Gauguin and the Pont-Aven School

Briefly they are amazed. The marigold-fields
mell and shudder and the travellers,
in sudden exile burdened with remote
hieratic gestures, journey to no end

beyond the vivid severance of each day,
strangeness at doors, a different solitude
between the mirror and the window, marked
visible absences, colours of the mind,

marginal angels lightning-sketched in red
chalk on the month's accounts or marigolds
in paint runnily embossed, or the renounced
self-portrait with a seraph and a storm.

(1975)

Five Sonnets from
An Apology for the Revival of
Christian Architecture in England

"...*the spiritual, Platonic old England*..." STC, Anima Poetae

1   QUAINT MAZES

And, after all, it is to them we return.
Their triumph is to rise and be our hosts:
lords of unquiet or of quiet sojourn,
those muddy-hued and midge-tormented ghosts.

On blustery lilac-bush and terrace-urn
bedaubed with bloom Linnaean pentecosts
put their pronged light; the chilly fountains burn.
Religion of the heart, with trysts and quests

and pangs of consolation, its hawk's hood
twitched off for sweet carnality, again
rejoices in old hymns of servitude,

haunting the sacred well, the hidden shrine.
It is the ravage of the heron wood;
it is the rood blazing upon the green.

Pitched high above the shallows of the sea
lone bells in gritty belfries do not ring
but coil a far and inward echoing
out of the air that thrums. Enduringly,

fuchsia-hedges fend between cliff and sky;
brown stumps of headstones tamp into the ling
the ruined and the ruinously strong.
Platonic England grasps its tenantry

where wild-eyed poppies raddle tawny farms
and wild swans root in lily-clouded lakes.
Vulnerable to each other the twin forms

of sleep and waking touch the man who wakes
to sudden light, who thinks that this becalms
even the phantoms of untold mistakes.

Autumn resumes the land, ruffles the woods
with smoky wings, entangles them. Trees shine
out from their leaves, rocks mildew to moss-green;
the avenues are spread with brittle floods.

Platonic England, house of solitudes,
rests in its laurels and its injured stone,
replete with complex fortunes that are gone,
beset by dynasties of moods and clouds.

It stands, as though at ease with its own world,
the mannerly extortions, languid praise,
all that devotion long since bought and sold,

the rooms of cedar and soft-thudding baize,
tremulous boudoirs where the crystals kissed
in cabinets of amethyst and frost.

The pigeon purrs in the wood; the wood has gone;
dark leaves that flick to silver in the gust,
and the marsh-orchids and the heron's nest,
goldgrimy shafts and pillars of the sun.

Weightless magnificence upholds the past.
Cement recesses smell of fur and bone
and berries wrinkle in the badger-run
and wiry heath-fern scatters its fresh rust.

'O clap your hands' so that the dove takes flight,
bursts through the leaves with an untidy sound,
plunges its wings into the green twilight

above this long-sought and forsaken ground,
the half-built ruins of the new estate,
warheads of mushrooms round the filter-pond.

So to celebrate that kingdom: it grows
greener in winter, essence of the year;
the apple-branches musty with green fur.
In the viridian darkness of its yews

it is an enclave of perpetual vows
broken in time. Its truth shows disrepair,
disfigured shrines, their stones of gossamer,
Old Moore's astrology, all hallows,

the squire's effigy bewigged with frost,
and hobnails cracking puddles before dawn.
In grange and cottage girls rise from their beds

by candlelight and mend their ruined braids.
Touched by the cry of the iconoclast,
how the rose-window blossoms with the sun!

(1977)

Ritornelli

For Hugh Wood on his 60th Birthday

(i)

Angel of Tones
                flame of accord
exacting mercies
                   answerable
to rage as solace

I will have you sing

(ii)

For so the judgement
passes
            it is not
otherwise
               hereafter
you will see them resolved
in tears
           they shall bear
your crowns of redress

(iii)

Lost to no thought
of triumph he returns
upon himself goes down
among water and ash
and wailing sounds confused
with sounds of joy

143

Sobieski's Shield

(1)

The blackberry, white
field-rose, all others
of that family:

steadfast is the word

and the star-gazing planet out of which
lamentation is spun.

(2)

Overnight   as the year
             purple   garish-brown
aster   chrysanthemum
         signally restored
to a subsistence of slant light
as one would venture
                   Justice Equity
or Sobieski's Shield even
                        the names
and what they have about them dark to dark.

(1992)

Of Coming-into-being and Passing-away

to Aileen Ireland

Rosa sericea: its red
spurs
      blooded with amber
each lit and holy grain
the sun
      makes much of
as of all our shadows –

prodigal ever returning
darkness that in such circuits
reflects diuturnity
         to itself
and to our selves
         yields nothing
finally –

      but by occasion
visions of truth or dreams
as they arise –
         to terms of grace
where grace has surprised us –
the unsustaining
         wondrously sustained

(1993)

Psalms of Assize

I. Hinc vagantur in tenebris misere,
quia non credunt veritati ipsi...
Querunt lumen confisi ipsis et non
                    inveniunt.

Why should I strike you with my name
why trade impress of proud wounds
come now belated
                        patrons of wrath
anxieties are not rectitudes
holiness itself falls
to unholy rejoicing
to resurrect the dead
myth
        of our salvation
blasphemies no less
mercies
            let us pray
Gabriel descend
as a mood almost
                        a monody
of chloroform
or florists roses
consensual angel spinning his words
                        thread
he descends
                and light
sensitive darkness
                        follows him down

II. *Non potest quisquam utrisque*
servire, simulque ascendere et de-
scendere; aut ascendas aut descend-
as oportet . . .

Ascend through declension
the mass the matter
the gross refinement
   gravitas
everlasting obsession
vanity by grace
the starred
        misattributed
works of survival
attributes even now
hallowing consequence
chants of the trace elements
the Elohim
       unearthly music
given to the world
message what message
         doubtless
the Lord knows
when he will find us
      if ever
we shall see him
with the elect
      justified
   to his right hand

III. *Hac sola ratione semper eris liber: si volueris quaecuumque fiunt ita fieri, et omnia in bonam partem verte.*

Seeing how they stand
with what odds
                    by what rule
of accidence resolved
the irresolute
                    the feats
of hapless jubilo
                    the gifts
set down to derision
rejoice in them
as things that are mourned
loving kindness
                    and mercy
righteousness
patient abiding
and whatever good
is held
        untenable
the entire complex dance
of simple atonement
as in a far fetched
                    comedy
making of sleep and time
timeless healers

Note: the epigraphs are taken from Sears Jayne, *John Colet and Marsilio Ficino*, (Oxford, 1963), pp. 119-20.

Sorrel

Very common and widely distributed . . . It is called Sorrow . . . in some parts of Worcestershire.

Memory worsening – let it go as rain
streams on half-visible clatter of the wind
                    lapsing and rising,
that clouds the pond's green mistletoe of spawn,
seeps among nettlebeds and rust-brown sorrel,
perpetual ivy burrowed by weak light,
makes carved shapes crumble: the ill-weathering stone
salvation's troth-plight, plumed, of the elect.

(1993)

ROLAND JOHN

Memory

The quietude
when there
is time
to remember
and recall
your name
these quick
moments
like presence
preserve
your myth,
there was
no lilt
in your
voice
your body
had its
complement
of flaws.

(1975)

PETER LEVI

Didactic Poem

For Iain Watson

Lingering time itself records itself, –
think time is over, say good-bye to it;
bird after bird expires into belief,
the sun among the stationary trees
touches the blue to level green and white:
there are no riddles in remarks like these.

Some of the young are poets I suppose
picking about in one another's lines
cobwebbing their own eyesight in shadows:
austere nature has ways to execute
the lively figures of her rough designs,
time is their voice and nature strikes them mute.

Time moves among the frosty rushes where
the daylight dies out with a rasping sound, –
these are the shortest days of the whole year,
trailing from fog to fog through seas of dew;
the ruffled birds desert the startled ground,
streams run in chains of ice, and weeds grow few.

Think time is over, say good-bye to it,
taking new words to make a new season;
draw bleak horizons working by lamp-light,
and let your eyes rest with a new surprise
on men and steel and jobs they use it on
and on the wild birds settling in their eyes.

(1963)

For Denis Bethell

(d. Feb. 15, 1981)

(i)

Two swallows in the shed, the snow falling,
then the long days, the mysterious late year,
then low, low down over the withering hayfield
the young swallows swooping out of the air.

Memory is the ringing of the iron hooves of horses,
the turf thundering silent long ago,
the rampart of the downs stretching away in sunlight,
death was a distant willow shadow.

Angels with a few leaves hand in hand with the Muses
honour those long grasses and starlit bones
where an old saint's beard trails down out of heaven
and touches the black water into swans.

(ii)

The shiver of the storm-light on the trees,
the coloured flowering of the dark trees,
and gleam of the cold grass under the trees,
speak of our greenish brown and swallow-skimmed
river of water in the sea of grass.
The dark wood-flowers ripened in the shade.
How cow-parsley smells heavy in the shade,
how light it is, grown up above the grass,
when three parts of the world are green and white.
In summer the dog panted in the shade.
Now the night-birds are quiet in the field
and the slow breath of the expiring fields
hangs on the night-air more roughly than mist.
The mountain drapes his ribs in dewy black
and stony smells like an unlevel field.
Dawn breaks as delicate as a dog-rose,
it drenches every field and mountainside.
All over. That is all over now.
The world was dying in his eyes dying,

summer and winter took ten years dying.
The yellow streaks were in the leaden sky,
he was not in the field, he was white bones
when three parts of this world were green and bright.

(iii)

Walking at night retold the Odyssey
on gravel roads under the boughs of elms,
beyond the village houses chewed away
by water-streams and the rainfall of time.
The white deer in the forest of darkness,
and the white cattle on the lost island,
and the sad charcoal-coated deer pursued
through the dim wood between glimmering trees.
The yelling of a thousand birds at dawn.
The gentle treading of the feet of death.
A faint smell of an orange stuck with cloves.
We drank port and ate bacon sandwiches,
light found us washing in the empty Thames.
How long ago that is, how cold it is,
the air blowing today from that dark year.
Conversation I can no longer bear,
as innocent and formal as Shakespeare.
The Odyssey meandered on all night.

(iv)

The hill so clear and the field evergreen;
along the margins of the summer road
poppy here, cranesbill there, that whistling like
the thistle-bearded fathers of our lives,
words nesting on roadsides like thistle-down.
There is a peace that sits on snowy hills
a counterblast that cools the wit of man,
and something breathing on this summer road,
without a name, that had the tread of peace.
They, in their conversation mystical,
made time go backward, talking away time,
into a silver-fruited, bearded age,

while clear water ran onward in the brook
and the old fisherman bent to the brook:
and secret poachers in the darkest pools
fished scaly salmon by starlight alone.
These are the fathers of the British church,
black and grey are the colours of their words.
George Herbert's green breath was a dying breath,
green and white flowers sprout out of his death.
I praise my God, my God is all to me.
The never-ending non-sequiturs of the sea,
greener and whiter than George Herbert's grave,
salt-green, salt-white, console only the brave.
The seashore is where my life has ended.
The silver fruits have crumbled in my hand
Denis, and the white beards are blowing wild,
the Spirit has rested in the wild stones,
he sings terribly loudly in your bones.
When we were young we saw two lovers lie
embracing in a sunlit snowy field,
we thought them like two figures in John Donne.
We had not understood what human weight
John Donne dragged after him as poetry.
Whose heaven is the heaven of sermons,
sunday by sunday, snowfall by snowfall?
There are no lovers lying in that snow.
Our ghost of love has melted in that snow,
our ghost and our unstudied quietness.

(v)

Looms through the flashing mist the British isle.
The mist is sunstruck, the low cliff milkwhite,
and the green turning and returning sea
will loll and gasp away midsummer night.
May to December so easily runs,
and the machine of stars to ruin,
tugging the scholar from his bookish dark
and the cold mermaid under the salt sea.
The oracle silent a hundred years
in voices of the island watersprings,
our horse scars in the grass, two or three lines;

swallow and swift breed in the sunny sheds,
earth under beams is white with swallow-dung
and the deep walnut and the shooting plane
have their pleasure in sunlight and fine air.
Sun glitters on the plain glass of the church:
stone in flower by pure mathematics
which is the observation of nature.
Autumn in our lifetime and the leaves fall,
the forest chapel is a pile of stones,
the leaves have dropped around your hermitage.
Neither the robin redbreast nor the wren
is busy now under the churchyard wall.
Who had the heart for building in our times?
Words for the true and good, words for the brave,
your building-stone paper under the lamp,
by the edge of the never silent sea.
The British islands swam like summer birds
in plumes of foam and slated plains of sea,
and they were generous in elements
and sang the music of their native stars
which they had learnt at their awakening.
Sleep Denis, the island is asleep
and in your heart the circle of our year
has ended in sleep and the fall of leaves.
The ocean rocks in its vast bed, the earth
is slowly heaving its green dragon scales
and it is time your world and mine should sleep.
And Izaak Walton's Lives sleep in their book,
a world that never lived until it died,
one that was pleasant on an old man's tongue
in holy conversations and good thoughts
and lingering irony like crab-apples.
I mean those scholars Walton thought should be
likes Dukes in Shakespeare under the green bough.
Trees that were growing then are withered now.
Only the sky at night is star-freckled
and the deep grass freckled with coloured weeds
draws the one sheet over all our white bones.

Denis, I have been thinking of a world
that will go on forever, never dies.
Grey and blue shadows and a waterfall,
between the thin trees in the winter sun:
treasures of autumn blacken underfoot,
winter will come then with amazing light.
It is the stream of water fresh on stone
and the thin forest in the early sun,
where the scholar of water and of stone
stood all night through in the devouring moon,
then like an owl mused as the world grew bright
pure yellow eyed in the blue winter light.
It is the spirit of our dying time
moving through shadows like an autumn stream.

(1982)

EDDIE LINDEN

The Miner

For my Father

Your face has never moved,
it still contains the marks of toil,
deep in blue.
These slag heaps now in green
have flowers instead of dust
and many men are buried here
whose shadows linger on.

(1984)

EDWARD LOWBURY

Learning to Walk Again

What never seems to figure in
Nostalgic playbacks of childhood –
Learning to walk! That shaky start
In the forecourt led us to the Garden,
The Paradise of make-believe
Where trees walked and tigers let
Themselves be stroked and called names,
And the Bird of Paradise
Preached love all day, – a place
Filled with a light like Benedictine;
There, at the Garden's end, we stumbled
On a gate marked ENTRANCE –
Walked through into the world we know,
Filled with the light of common day.

Today, once again,
I'm in the forecourt, learning
To walk, because a clot
Has blocked some footpath in my head,
Has knocked me sideways – turning
The walls to roundabouts
That won't support me when I lean.
I coax my wayward feet
To obey urgent instructions:
Mother Earth leaves more to chance
Than did the one to whom I clung
When I was here before.
From the forecourt my feet find
Their way to the Garden; it is filled
With the light of common day;
Trees know their place, and tigers
Look dangerous behind bars.
Again I stumble on a gate;
This one is labelled EXIT;
'There's a light like Benedictine
Beyond it', they tell me;
I won't try the handle.

PATRICIA McCARTHY

Circe

Where I led you: along tested tracks
whose bracken, smelling of commons
and high places, still topped your head
as if a boy's, hiding my reputation.

Evacuated from other lives, you collected
pellets of sheep that charged at us –
unafraid of anomalies. You didn't guess
it was mine: the slippery witchgrass,

nor that nosed-up mounds held truffles
for the metamorphoses of men into swine.
Or you might have refused to head for
the pond where barbed wire, cloven pines

and brambles springing up drew blood
and our images thickened with lilies –
stilled too soon to shimmer into geneses.
For genesis it was with water in the breeze,

irises and foxgloves like chieftains
in the clearings. I didn't mean you to lose
your way among horseflies that blitzed
the primeval light we could not defuse.

Part-redeemed from the myth and glad
as you of the seas of wheat we walked upon
like gods, I welcomed the oaks offering
vaults for the exigencies of a passion

poor in words. For, love, apart from
a stump twisting in the turning earth
into a bowel, I have no heart to break
but yours. So don't ask yet its worth.

Simply tell and retell your dream
whose wild garlic seeded itself in me
and, lost as you in bowers no longer styes,
I at last surrendered the name Circe.

(1983)

Last Rites

(to my mother)

Year round you spring clean,
sorting belongings into presents and jumble,
keeping only the bare essentials.

The odd hint is dropped: about the value
of the chandelier or the lump sum
saved for the burial when it comes.

We would encourage a simple change
in house, but never this ultimate move.
Like parents, we firmly disapprove.

Age would have eased you into acceptance
if you had had age; not the spirit to forgo
the will in your drawer for the shy trousseau

of the unstoppable girl still in your voice.
Though you'll travel light, we should give to you
more precious moments rather than taboos

for the trunk that you have kept in store;
pack it with the flowers that you have grown.
But we do not. Petrified of the unknown –

we, too, are trying to sort things out
to remember you by. Meringues on doilies
and newspaper crosswords become tiny legacies

which we can claim our own. Unashamedly
we use you, getting octagonals of patchwork
sewn into a quilt – too late berserk

for your bits when even full daylight
puts a strain on the eyes. How consoling it is
that you can yet play a game of tennis

and, supply contorting, garden for hours,
ruthless to what spreads, uncontrolled.
Risking a stroke, you seem almost too bold.

We know you'd deal with your imminent gap
by letting nature abhor it in your favourite chair,
then start again making the wilderness bare.

Just recently we urged you to commit your life
to an exercise book. Now – we stare
at the virgin pages – unable to prepare.

Nor can you alert us, however you try –
suggesting the crutch and consolation
of images bogus to you in religion.

We should reassure with the many who have gone;
invite you to plant a tree of heaven
by our doors, leave bread to leaven

as you labour eternally in us: daughters
of your stature. At your going, a quake
will rip up our foundations where we shake.

(1985)

Visiting the Horses at Midnight, Midwinter

My feet cross both Poles. A fox barks, rivalling me
for this territory. The bale, trailing twine, bends
my back. The hot kettle cracks a ringmaster's whip
across the thick mirror of ice on the watering-can.

The horses jump, ears pricked for danger, relaxing
at my wellknown voice. Their exhalations send
clouds up to the clear sky to dispel the zeros.
The small bay mare has pulled hay over her bedding

for extra warmth, nature insisting how best to fend
for herself despite a domestication which makes her
dependent on me in extremes. She breathes with me, long
and slow, listening to the frost stiffen blades, twigs,

even the shiplap sides of the stable. The gelding
licks my benumbed hands, his hot tongue coddling
my blood, proving ours a mutual dependency.
I persist with my rituals, straightening their rugs,

filling water buckets. Both move to their doors
as an owl's hoot skims the surface of the adjacent field,
confirming it a rink. I resume my rituals
while the stillness resumes its creaks. We are all alert.

Gone, though, are the mindless terrorists that squirm
from hedges in gales. Instead, sentries stand to ward off
the hour of merciless killings: of fur and feather.
I intrude in this non-human time. And yet my skin,

useless in such rigours, needs a proximity
to tension and rootings. The little bay mare nudges
my side knowingly. A sudden shaft of moonlight
claims her as a moon horse, blanched by myth,

I do not want her taken away. As I scoop up droppings,
I kneel to each horse in turn, any blame incurred
for their taming cancelled by my homage. I shuffle
around, their slave, denying myself for them willingly.

Thankfully, their crunching on the slices of hay
that I shake out is a lullaby, easing me back
into the security that they are mine and I am theirs.
Slinking back up the garden path, I can see in the dark.

In the hoary morning that has not thawed, I turn them out.
The milky mists, now, are rustlers out to dissolve
their outlines but my golden and mahogany horses
know their strength. In a Houdini act, they get out

of their domestication as if out of a rug, rolling over
and over to leave it, done up, on the rock-hard ground.
Performing a ballet to their own inner music of freedom,
they gallop off, racehorses of the sun, side by side,

trained already to pull the chariot of Apollo. Up the hill
they pound rhythmically, chasing away the mists,
casting their iron shoes. I see them as streaks in the sky,
not mine again til they wait at the gate in the evening.

(1993)

JEAN MacVEAN

Return

For Kathleen Raine

In an abyss
outside love

I who have run
so far from myself

meet myself
returning

. . .

at the heart
the fire
dangerous
volcano

but also
the purification
gold of the alchemists

burning
to an integer

. . .

was it for this
the agony

the loss
the departure

of dangerous loves
this ending
of begging for love

go forward
weak heart

. . .

I have trodden water
too long
in shallow seas

yet heard the message
of the green islands

seen the hewn caves
of saints
in the holy one

above the ambiguous water
the raging of wind
and the highpitched melancholy
of seals

grey ancestors

beyond all stupidity
folly
cruelty
the green of solitary islands
a song we thought lost
sea birds wheeling

small animals
peer from grass
shy recognition
of timid creatures
a point of healing
hard earned
paradoxical tenderness of sun

. . . . . .

sky life
soft creatures

the small ones
how afraid of us

the others
how majestic
in heights
we cannot know
in freedom
we cannot reach

stunted flight
of machines

Icarus
falling

sunchariots
wrecked by tumultuous horses

and beyond

the ultramarine skies
the natural elegance
of wings
and their signs to us
a few feathers

falling

. . . . . .

Only here
in this sky
outside humanity
lies
the bright lake
of death

the swan singing

. . . . . .

166

elected silence
Hopkins wrote

and silence
is indeed elected

king and emperor
of truth

the quiet pilgrim
beyond
the desecrated
lands of fury

. . . . . .

peace over the heights

deep in the earth
deep burning fire

then the sun and sea
marriage

centre

and the child
new risen

sea christened

sun engendered

return journey

(1989)

EVE MACHIN

Sea Phantom

An ebb-tide in full season
will spell hieroglyphs on the bitter sand
and in the story's telling
I will return
to murmurs of kindred
and the earth's sleep.

On your Journey towards the Dead

Dip your hand
in the lake's dark water
feel the ripple
from the far-off shore:

Believe it
as you believe in starlight
which annihilates a million years.

(1993)

SYLVIA MANN

For Three Lords

I have seen the lords rise
from their graves
like black stones
and the funeral bathed in dew.

(1975)

VIRGINIA MASKELL

Heat touching heat

Heat touching heat –
I should have died last year
And cut the webs that wove me
And the innocence that drove me
                first to you.

Cold growing cold –
I should be living now,
Spinning webs to bind me
In a life that blinds me
           to all but you.

Still growing still –
I should be born soon now,
Knowing that the web of pain
Was the reason that you came
            first to me.

(1959)

The Sunday Hours

The day beats in limbo,
Too slow my hand lies across the page,
And your burnt form hides
Its grave talent in the sand.

The afternoon breaks promise.
Too slow my limbs stretch blind,
And your dark words teach
Other lips to love.

(1962)

170

ALAN MASSEY

Three Extracts from *Leechcraft*

Michael Robartes remembers forgotten beauty
and, when his arms wrap her round, he presses
in his arms the loveliness which has long faded
from the world. Not this. Not at all. I desire to
press in my arms the loveliness which has not
yet come into the world.

– James Joyce,
A Portrait of the Artist as a Young Man.

I   UNDER-CHILDREN

Bred in captivity, briefly alive. Tinder
For the glow of culture and empire. Corporeal
Movables. Species of
Vegetable matter: that they should flower
Was judged against the interest
Of their owners. Accordingly the frost
Of terror fell, actual here, potential hereafter.
When terror failed – pack-raped
In mind and body, butchered, trampled
On the named street, at the named field,
In the named wood. How many unnamed shrines
For each one named?
                                    If memory grew. If,
To remind us, dependable silvery taps
Each morning ran hot and cold
Blood.
                  Under-children of shrines, of named
Shrines! Where cavalry sealed them, eyes hoofed
Into sudden mire. Where (holding their
Breath, afraid to breathe) they
Breathed. Where they cowered in a ditch-end
Under the precise fire-power of
The obedient.
                        No more birthdays, best friends, jokes,
Nicknames.
                        Such things no longer happen – in England?

Precariously true, and the Board's attempts
To turn back the clock shall
Fail. The clock ticks on and it is theirs.

And England is not Earth.

The guilty? Abstractions – *capitalist economics,*
State Christianity? Not abstractions. Men and women.
Who conjures the frost that kills the flower?
Whether they will it or not, the rich.
Whether they will it or not, the priestly.
More, the glazer of eyes, diplomatic
Cougher, keeper of a clean nose.
Most, the under-man and the under-woman
Who smother emotion, keep out of trouble,
Say nothing, smile: their children are murdered by
Persons known. They are taken from the living
To encourage conformity among the survivors.
They shall be raised unceasingly from the dead
For much the same reason. 'Those
Who do not remember the past
Are condemned to relive it.' Neither abstractions
Nor statistics, these under-children
Briefly lived and left those who loved them
Grief. See them too (invoked
Or not invoked) grimacing in misery,
Tear-streaked, silent.
                                        These being present,
Get thee, muse, to a glass museum. No sop
To their myths, the peripatetic with motorist's cramp,
The clerk of the Athens Tourist Board.

IV   THE PASTORAL SYMPHONY

To shrug off the weight.
To be, for a season, Nature's clerk.
To stroll off somewhere in shirt-sleeves.

To celebrate skies
Amassing their heraldry, white

And blue, blue and accumulative white
Absorbing the loud birds, while broad July
Unleashes cool green tongues on the air –
Perfoliate, palmate, serrate and sinuate,
Green on green on green, flowing
With fine interstitial blue. Fastidious magpies
Strut and chuckle in lavish fields.

To douse the mind. To observe. To log
The season's minutiae, held in a soft regression
To dreaming Albion.

To celebrate birds.
                              Yellow ducklings
Fitfully darting along the stream as though jolted
By sudden shocks.
                              On a scorched afternoon, in her shady bed
The thrush turning over.
                              Swifts in furious play
High over tranquil streets of limestone
In a grey-blue, luminous-opal
Evening sky.
                      Swallows entering and
Re-entering, entering and re-
Entering Wick Rissington's church, where
Gustav Holst played the organ.
                              Ineffable
Sang-froid of seagulls, plummeting towards
The sea-crash, sheer
From the megalith's weak brink-stone!

The sublime can kill. I fear ocean and rock-face,
Am most myself on
Downland, say the bright Ridge Way:
Wild rose and cornflower, poppy, the cleanly
Wind; skylark and chalkhill blue. This habitat
Lulls, serene.

To sustain the idyll, arching
Racemes of days. The hot weeks grow
Of goldfinch, azure dragonfly. I contemplate
On tall and sweetly-tasting meadows

The lyrical opening and shutting of
Tortoiseshell wings. What I hear is whirr and tick
And buzz and cheep and chirrup. Balm of sunlight
Sets off the richness of beech; the Lombardy
Poplars are green quill pens, or
Greenly shimmering
Exclamation marks. Spiccato ripple of
Water-spider stirs the pool...
                                    Shrink and fade, you
Questions.

              Galactic light
Dances in still and widening rings.

Autumn. Fruits
Minutely swell in yellowing woods. Drunkenly
I breathe the fermented smell of
Berry, nut and falling leaf.
                              Autumn. Fall.
Herbst. Clang of Mahlerian
Cow-bells. Day-sleep and night-sleep pace
With gentle feet my long dream. Drowsy
Horns among leaf-stir call and counter-
Call...

Height of the blue bell-clang morning,
Pure. Not imaginable now
The torrent stream in rainfall, ferocious-shattering.

White of the quarter-moon yawning,
Pallid melon-slice in the brow
Of explicit blue, expressionlessly flattering.

Flight of the wild jay adorning
Cobweb woods, fern to fir-tree bough,
Jay-quack and jay-honk spread on chaffinches' chattering.

Fight of the squirrels: mock fawning,
Then brilliant double-tracks endow
With dignity even the mad hare's mad-hattering.

174

Light of the multiple awning,
Shelter bland cep-clusters allow
Cartwheeling leaves a soft sudden wind is scattering.

Night of the winter's forewarning
Sweetly falls, slowly, falls with how
Simple a cumulus-calm, as if not mattering . . .

Treacherous melody!
Nature's delicate aria, sweet,
Sweeter, sours
To siren song. My love is spilt on the cumulus cloud,
The black-and-bright cattle: what use to them
Is my love?
                My love, retracted,
Parches, and parches worse
For a summer's immersion (O incestuous sheets!)
In crooning Nature. Freedom has drifted me
To the packed snows.
                This is the hour
Of cock-crow in eternal dazzling morning,
A time for truth, the difficult *Summa Humana;*
Too much for one man. Our only song
Is human song now, made to answer
A crying. The human body, the human mind,
Human labour – here is the true source, fountain-
Spray, the freshet
Generously cool, nidus of gaiety.

V   WORLD-SONG

Later they blinded me, but in the beginning I saw
With perfect vision. I saw
Laboured-for lineaments of peace.
                        The immense garden
Islanded me among almond boughs, peppery lupins,
Canterbury bells: creation
Of a tree-tall human at work in simple majesty.
The sunned earth,
Damp-dark and pale, was freshly raked

Into trim civility. Slowly Dad bent, scourge of greenfly;
Then reared off upward, sunburnt,
Smiling. At the kitchen window Mum elevated the bowl
Of excellent raw cake-mix.
                                        At Primary School
The boys and girls went out. With shock
We learned that we (age: five) had
Fallen: we must love the defined God above all
And subtract correctly. Slowly, slyly we grew adept
At pretending that we had understood.
At Grammar School there was certain talk
Of 'Western Civilization'; it was Europe they meant –
Belching, blood-soaked Europe! (Since,
I have made my own list of
Great Europeans.
                                Martyrs, recluses, maddened exiles.)

Drowning, drowning I choked   *death*   I spat out
A mouth, a mouthful of black mud, rats' dung,
Venom. 'Into the world
To seek his fortune.' Into the
Commonplace commercial sewer, the deep end: baptism
Sent me retching ashore, shaking my
Scales. Had I been warned? Humans
Approached. In secret fear I
Backed away: who were they? Surely not
The Eternal Feminine – 'You coming home for a good time,
Dear?' God moved vaguely, bird-song from
Nowhere.
                    A cold draught of music
Seized me, a music made of discords
Perpetually unresolved. That it was made so
Pleased me: an acrid symbol. *This*
Was better. I got the taste of it. I got drunk on it.
I fell asleep for twenty years.

Dream sucked me in
As an oil-slick sucks in a sea-bird.
Smoothly the dreams came round in a circle,
Dreaming me. I mimed and puppeted, saint, devil,
Prophet, buffoon; I shone like a crazy sun
Lurching from pole to pole in my sleep,

Distracting the helpless satellites. That
Nothing, nothing was forbidden *to me*
Was as clear as the highest shout
Of trumpets cast in silver. I would sliver
The barriers of Time and Space; overcome Death;
Sing out innocent joy in the twelve note system.
Incredible communions occurred. Co-equal
Fears, *I am defiled; I shall be defiled*
Writhed. Insane, I walked
In greater dread of insanity than of
Death or life. Blankly I rejoiced,
Dizzy over fragments, suffering at times
The splitting light: 'Why this is hell!'

I stirred, half-awake. I awoke. I am awake.
All my projected shadows live and move
In the urban street, and I name them with my own name
Now and for ever. I wake to my own voice muttering *I am you*
With little joy. But see, two women trudge
From door to door: cheerful, grim-jawed,
Vividly they endure. A postman, bent on local such-ness,
Sings out a plangent aria into the
Murk. The school is an opened box, strews children
Comically running. The boisterous girls
Have not read Hugh MacDiarmid; derisory curls
Hang on their unawakened lips and cloud their eyes;
But their faces are lilac-fresh from
Living.
          Suddenly-green adoration wells.
                                                  This
Materia prima is raw as ever – therefore ripe
For the alchemy of due concern. Mountainous credo,
Crush the unreal; make me recite
The heart's facts – a memory of Russell's
Noble ancient head (his eyes a mythic bird's),
The *Hammerklavier* Sonata, Voltaire's artillery
Blasting *l'infâme*, Shostakovich's dulcet harp
Dismissed by the taps of *tamburo militare*;
Or merely show me that fledgling housewife
Walking her gravely neuter children! A red bus
Roars by, massively swift. The boy,
Delighted, flinches; the girl

Grimaces, pointing to a bland incontinent
Puppy. Unceasingly the dead and the living
Reach for us, touch, beseech
The to-be-reconciled: they conquer
Death-in-life as a flight of emerald birds
From the world-tree rooted in drizzling gutters
Of blossom, excrement, fall-out,
Trodden toccatas of beech-mast.

Sunlight on frosty acres, thinly tree'd.

Eyesight improving. But to re-forge
The oneness of self, that crystal
Splintered by the Witch of the West, Aliena –
Serious work; like art, proportioned
Fruition.
            To make one seminal poem, to be
Poet-as-catalyst, once! To permeate each line with truth
As the single, simple ground bass permeates
A Purcell chaconne. At least
To go no more a-whoring with Formalisma
(Aliena's twin), whose triple orifice has sucked me in
For the last time with bravura, nostalgia,
'Objectivity'... To make a poem as vivid
As landscape is to a map; as locking limbs
To mind-itch; as the real to the abstract –
Deft and cool, phrase after phrase in ever-fresh
Perceptions; not common coinage – newly minted
Doubloons; not diluted – neat. Look in
From eternity, Ezra Pound, at my ideogram
Of the poet's poem:

                    Jewel-setting
                    Woven tapestry
                    Painter's brush-strokes
                    Orchestral score
                    Spider's web
                    House of limestone

To marry truth to the ancient ravishment.
To see a full-grown epic spring from my three-word
Ars Poetica: Notice; note; notate.

                                        A crystal poetry
To match the re-forged crystal of
Personality: 'a definitely-shaped psychic abundance,
Capable of resistance and endowed with energy.'
For Earth's late coming-of-age, a poetry
To lay at the feet of God and Man.

Inevitable, given his background, Wordsworth's
Retreat, apostasy. Byron's and Shelley's too,
Had they lived? For privileged young *literati*
Will coquet with the Left, till breeding tells:
Hardening arteries drag them to the Centre,
Then to the Right.
                           But nobody now shall frost
The flowering of my class. The children's choir
Starts helplessly weak, polytonal, polyrhythmic;
With time and work what song we shall hear,
What world-song! Let us teach them the music of
Consciousness. And, between rehearsals,
Let us teach them to laugh (and let us laugh)
At leech-ideology in all its modes,
Bishop-mode, banker-mode, judge-mode,
Lawyer-mode, duke-mode, monarch-mode. To be
The proud proletarian! From such consciousness
Shall spring the more than Mozartian
World-song. Meanwhile, limping behind, my words
Of fellowship for those I shall never meet,
Working men and women of Lima and Lucknow,
Children of Ako, Omsk, Aberdare. Where is England?
In heart and brain-cell, bloodstream and soul
Of the working class who remember,
Awake to history, aware of shrines.
England, in this, is Earth.

Man-nature is fellowship! Swindlers, liars,
Clammy apostles of leech-freedom,
Man is not competitive. Shall we write it
In crimson letters as high as the walls
Of the ruined Stock Exchange? Man hungers for
Brotherhood, co-operation in works of sanity,
Passionate husbandry of Woman and Earth.
Woman-nature is love. How much does a baby

Pay its mother for her breast? How much
Does she ask? What fashions Man and Woman
Is rapture of love and
Lust, their hungry and beautiful tiger
Not to be tamed this side of eternity. Give him
His head, a protected species
Free within spacious bounds! And let there be
Adoration; let there be life-curiosity
Quiet as a child's. From the body's consciousness too
Unheard-of world-song.

'A kid I have fallen into milk'

My numina physical, my arcana the nest-caves
Thirsted for, remembered
With wild, unshakeable love. O Margaret, Jenny,
Strolling in bright July, your eyes
Are water-bearers for the parched sick
Who lost our nature. I worship
You who will grow and mother and suckle,
Human!
            Skylark ascending, flown
From the pain-wheel, strews the dazzling beads
Of his one song. Each curious dawn evokes
His one song. And we shall be like birds,
Our song direct and lovely as lark-song,
After the moment of choice
When past and future interlock like lovers. We
Shall see the leech-blown bubble 'freedom'
Burst.
            To praise, undermine, with stronger words. To rouse
The cheated child of the continents. I choose
A part of the field – no Eden yet: thrawart,
Rank, smelling of blood – under pulsating larks. Earth
Is one, universe one: this fragment
Of dewy clay fell from the crust of Arcturus.
England, 8.34 a.m., at a chance conjunction
Of grass, horse-chestnut trees and morning sunlight
I am witness, guest, warrior, brother.

(1974)

W.S. MILNE

Hesperus
(Christmas, 1992)

     Venus   Mercurie
whitiver ye are
     evening-star
luik doun
     and peetie man
this Christmas-tide
     (bairns, their mas,
     their das
        deid, or dying)
luik doun
     and peetie man
Andromache
     for her husband
Hecabe
     for her son
Priam
     for his son
and owre them aa
     Cassandra's cries
for Hector
     bi Achilles' sword, deid
     Venus   Mercurie
whitiver ye are
     morning-star
luik doun
     and turn
to the end o War

(1993)

In Memoriam Hugh MacDiarmid

The rowan-tree's fu laden,
the berries glitter bluid-reed.
The snaw'll sain be bidin,
but your sangs still chitter,
though I ken ye're deed.

(1981)

GEORGE OPPEN

Psalm

Veritas sequitur . . .

In the small beauty of the forest
The wild deer bedding down –
That they are there!

        Their eyes
Effortless, the soft lips
Nuzzle and the alien small teeth
Tear at the grass

        The roots of it
Dangle from their mouths
Scattering earth in the strange woods.
They who are there.

        Their paths
Nibbled thru the fields, the leaves shade them
Hang in the distances
Of sun

        The small nouns
Crying faith
In this in which the wild deer
Startle, and stare out.

(1966)

PENELOPE PALMER

To My Grandmother

A young girl now,
Face soft-smooth and flushed
With first life-light of death,
Eyes of lavender cleansed
Of experience, though gentle, stab
Mine with their purity.
So light, moving to dust
In your stillness, my dearest,
I did not know dying could come so light
To this dark room, could come
Warm gleaming in your hair, and take
Softly the cold that ticked through hours
As you slept, and I thought of you
Old and alive in chair, warming me then
Cross-legged on the floor, with your laugh
And lavender scent. Now that you wake
To night for the last time, physically moving
From age to birth, you say: 'Goodbye my darling,'
I whisper goodbye, wanting words...
These words to reach you afterwards.

(1963)

The Chapel

A small, barred room at Herculaneum,
Rented towards the end, it's thought,
To small-time merchants or to craftsmen.

I don't know whether they escaped
In 79; the lava flowing...
Most people surely fled; were safe:
Herculaneum does not smell of death,
And the trees blossom.

A block of whitish stone juts from the wall,
A slender cross is deeply chanelled in it,
The effect's curious: a shadow cross
Gravely moving between stone and spirit,
And I can't make out
Whether it's damaged at the top,
Or indicates a tired head.

A Roman altar stands in front of it,
Squat, solid,
It's like a little stove,
The door swung partly open
As though someone looked to see
Whether the bread was risen.

The earliest Christian chapel found
In the Roman Empire:
I'm glad they keep the small door locked
– Not just from us – but from
All heavy splendour.

It haunts me still,
An atmosphere detached, companiable
Of signs and shadows barred against
So much of our concern, and readiness.
He showed men how to live with grace
And goodness, in this nether world.
The chapel breathes, and waits.

Green Beads

The darkening night
Has washed her features bare,
Her beads lie on the floor

Like the flinging off of a person,
Green gleaming beads, which alone seem whole;
He flung them there.

The colder breeze
Comes through the windows, generously open,
Suddenly, the night's too huge,

And full of remote, portentous sounds,
More than her body, white on the bed
Can conquer.

She might be anyone; he can't remember
How she looks when she smiles
Or how her voice sounds.

She seems asleep,
She might be dead – her skin's cold,
No, of course she breathes,

Whoever she is.
How stupid the truth is –
That he's known her a year.

Her beads tell on the floor
Of oncoming space, of naked pain;
They mock green gleaming days, green nights that were.

(1968)

The Cornflowers

Blue radiance; stained glass – say in the chapel;
My single image of what endures:
I don't know why you chose the cornflowers.

Later you said you weren't quite sure
That they were really blue at all.
I said: well, I know they are.

That night, by artificial light
The flowers were purple. They looked dead;
An ancient, though a royal shroud.

The next day (vindicated) you left.
The cornflowers, world upon deep blue world
Held my certain need to love.

After a week, a few blooms faded;
Lavender, grey; – a bit like people,
You, scattered by uncertainty.

I threw some out,
Recalling the moments you might have grasped
But let drift into the past;

Perhaps you wanted it that way,
The flowers were dead by artificial light,
And now they teach me with their life.

But wan as clouds and deep as paradise
They move in the flux and make my images;
And everything and nothing lasts.

(1977)

RACHEL PELHAM BURN

Fragment from Sleep

Brightness of phosphorescence in sea,
          clinging to figures
struggling through coloured water
          moving in oil.
The boy, the man in his archaic helmet.

No doubt some ancient seafarers
straining in shining darkness
out to sea –

Figures long since forgotten
          in the chaos of time.

(1982)

KATHLEEN RAINE

Fire

On my hearth a clear flame flickers:
What more secure, familiar, than this
Room built of ever-speeding light?
So swift its motion it seems to stay
Constant, yet nothing still but this steady seeming,
And I, habituate to what appears
Present before these eyes,
This known, unknown familiar place

Beautiful, flickering, translucent flame,
Blue, and yellow, and bright, and glowing embers
From earth's deep-buried forests return to me here
Sun's heat and light: love and wisdom
Of what foreknowing holds in one
Moment those green fronds drinking the sun
And an old woman by her autumn fire?

Fire, wild and free, across millennia
You come to me
From carboniferous forests where none ever walked:
What knowledge of beginnings and endings
Carries this room and all it holds
After my ending, before my beginning
This moment of the ever-changing never-changing?

You will take this body and scatter its ashes, fire,
Your flickering flames, like Loge's music
At the world's end, blaze
Into such a star as those who send their rays
To comfort us with infinite forgiveness
Of your undoing into unending beginning:
What world's consuming
Sends out that constant light?

Fire, subtle undoer, loosener of bonds,
Free, you are the freer
Of all that is destructible, perishable, but we
By flame cannot be burned, nor can you consume away
The intangible thought I offer you in praise
As you roar in glory through houses and worlds and universes
Turning our dust to stars.

II

Not tonight,
I am too tired, I say, to write
Burning words of angels, I,
Poor instrument
Fall towards ashes of fire burned out,
Let me forget
The ever-present beauty, the high thought
I cannot contemplate. It is too late,
I say, it is night,
I would rest, would dream, pass through the gate
Into that other space
Where there are such mountains, such swift rivers,
Such clear waters, given
To the sleeper. Not, I say
Now, unsleeping daimon, do not try
To lift my heart, to raise
My thoughts, my sight
To the glory of that place
Where you are and I am not.
I fall to dust, to ashes of that fire
That kindled me, desire
With heart's small residual glow
Spacious dream. I am old,
I say, spare me now
Beauty and delight.

My body speaks such words
Seeking its term in dust –
I have forgotten how it was,
How it is when day's first light touches the eyes
When the morning sun rises on this world
With all the power and glory of a dream.

Charity

Caritas – love, as some translators give,
Or charity. There was a meaning once
For something the world needed, then as now,
To turn the sword of violence,
The eviscerator, the hangman, the crucifier,
The indifferent. Now we have a word,
But what it named is lost, somewhere among the dead –
Greater than Plato's Good True or Beautiful, or Faith
    or Hope, they said,
Not sexual desire or romantic love, that grandiose dream.
Kindness comes near, and we'd be glad of that.
Some scrutinize the Buddha's tranquil face
Whose secret the stars share,
But only the poor human heart can hold us dear.

(1988)

THEODORE ROETHKE

The Rose

I

There are those to whom place is unimportant,
But this place, where sea and fresh water meet,
Is important –
Where the hawks sway out into the wind,
Without a single wingbeat,
And the eagles sail low over the fir trees,
And the gulls cry against the crows
In the curved harbors,
And the tide rises up against the grass
Nibbled by sheep and rabbits.

A time for watching the tide,
For the heron's hieratic fishing,
For the sleepy cries of the towhee,
The morning birds gone, the twittering finches,
But still the flash of the kingfisher, the wingbeat of the scoter,
The sun a ball of fire coming down over the water,
The last geese crossing against the reflected afterlight,
The moon retreating into a vague cloud-shape
To the cries of the owl, the eerie whooper.
The old log subsides with the lessening waves,
And there is silence.

I sway outside myself
Into the darkening currents,
Into the small spillage of driftwood,
The waters swirling past the tiny headlands.
Was it here I wore a crown of birds for a moment
While on a far point of the rocks
The light heightened,
And below, in a mist out of nowhere,
The first rain gathered?

As when a ship sails with a light wind –
The waves less than the ripples made by rising fish,
The lacelike wrinkles of the wake widening, thinning out,
Sliding away from the traveller's eye,
The prow pitching easily up and down,
The whole ship rolling slightly sideways,
The stern high, dipping like a child's boat in a pond –
Our motion continues.

But this rose, this rose in the sea-wind,
Stays,
Stays in its true place,
Flowering out of the dark,
Widening at high noon, face upward,
A single wild rose, struggling out of the white embrace of the
                                        morning glory,
Out of the briary hedge, the tangle of matted underbrush,
Beyond the clover, the ragged hay,
Beyond the sea pine, the oak, the wind-tipped madrona,
Moving with the waves, the undulating driftwood,
Where the slow creek winds down to the black sand of the shore
With its thick grassy scum and crabs scuttling back into their
                                        glistening craters.

And I think of roses, roses,
White and red, in the wide six-hundred-foot greenhouses,
And my father standing astride the cement benches,
Lifting me high over the four-foot stems, the Mrs. Russells, and
                                        his own elaborate hybrids,
And how those flowerheads seemed to flow toward me, to beckon
                                        me, only a child, out of myself.

What need for heaven, then,
With that man, and those roses?

What do they tell us, sound and silence?
I think of American sounds in this silence:
On the banks of the Tombstone, the wind-harps having their say,
The thrush singing alone, that easy bird,
The killdeer whistling away from me,
The mimetic chortling of the catbird
Down in the corner of the garden, among the raggedy lilacs,
The bobolink skirring from a broken fencepost,
The bluebird, lover of holes in old wood, lilting its light song,
And that thin cry, like a needle piercing the ear, the insistent
cicada,
And the ticking of snow around oil drums in the Dakotas,
The thin whine of telephone wires in the wind of a Michigan
winter,
The shriek of nails as old shingles are ripped from the top of a
roof,
The bulldozer backing away, the hiss of the sandblaster,
And the deep chorus of horns coming up from the streets in
early morning.
I return to the twittering of swallows above water,
And that sound, that single sound,
When the mind remembers all,
And gently the light enters the sleeping soul,
A sound so thin it could not woo a bird.

Beautiful my desire, and the place of my desire.

I think of the rock singing, and light making its own silence,
At the edge of a ripening meadow, in early summer,
The moon lolling in the close elm, a shimmer of silver,
Or that lonely time before the breaking of morning
When the slow freight winds along the edge of the ravaged
hillside
And the wind tries the shape of a tree,
While the moon lingers,
And a drop of rain water hangs at the tip of a leaf
Shifting in the wakening sunlight
Like the eye of a new-caught fish.

IV

I live with the rocks, their weeds,
Their filmy fringes of green, their harsh
Edges, their holes
Cut by the sea-slime, far from the crash
Of the long swell,
The oily, tar-laden walls
Of the toppling waves,
Where the salmon ease their way into the kelp beds,
And the sea rearranges itself among the small islands.

Near this rose, in this grove of sun-parched, wind-warped
                                    madronas,
Among the half-dead trees, I came upon the true ease of myself,
As if another man appeared out of the depths of my being,
And I stood outside myself,
Beyond becoming and perishing,
A something wholly other,
As if I swayed out on the wildest wave alive,
And yet was still.
And I rejoiced in being what I was:
In the lilac change, the white reptilian calm,
In the bird beyond the bough, the single one
With all the air to greet him as he flies,
The dophin rising from the darkening waves;

And in this rose, this rose in the sea-wind,
Rooted in stone, keeping the whole of light,
Gathering to itself sound and silence –
Mine and the sea-wind's.

(1964)

PETER RUSSELL

Russell's Rest

For Tom Scott

For I not whider I shall, ne hou longe her duelle

Half way up the hill,
And half way down the dale,
Is the ruined one-time mill
Where the waters never fail.

The mill-wheel, yes, has disappeared,
A flower grows from the ground;
The rusty gears no longer heard,
But in the silence – dying sound –

Lament triumphant – on and on –
Descants above the other birds.
It is, it is, the dying swan –
Apollo's voice, that needs no words

To say how bleak the landscape is
Without the laurel's crown,
And how these modern melodies
Sadden the modern town.

(1993)

N.K. SANDARS

S.F.

Let there be no more talk of the god who exploded
the universe, nor the drab alternative:
creation round the clock. Let the words be
to my humanity, the moon be a station
on my journey,
let my eyes be familiar with Mars
and my ears read messages from Betelgeuse.

The language of Mars is very nearly intelligible,
I am touched by the beauty of Betelgeuse,
my own beauty is buried two feet down in earth,
a pair of crutches lie beside me that once
were stilts on which I walked.

I have tried to read the cryptogram
of the senses, jargonning through the cells
and down the capilliary passages,
but the signals were unfamiliar,
infrequent and faint.

I waited at the station but nobody came,
I heard on the public address-system
programmes without words, music without tones,
mathematics so pure they could never propagate.

The air is thin on the way to Betelgeuse,
I pass the precipices of nearer stars;
I turn to admire earth's narrow nimbus
of bright atmosphere, the five-barred gate
into the irides. The small moon
is green like grass, and now I cannot turn,
they do not speak to my humanity.

Words shake from me like drops of water,
like static electricity they do no harm,
there is no going back to what is buried
two feet down on earth.

Do not talk to me of moons today or Mars
tomorrow, do not talk of Betelgeuse.
Let the words be to my humanity.

The animal inside is doomed,
flesh-marks of fossil fibre, or like the dinosaur
a footprint in Arizona.
It is not yet too late, I still can understand,
after a fashion, the talk of small birds,
the small-talk of the senses, the few words;
when a life is hurt
I feel it through the endings of my nerves.
Blood is allied to blood
and words to words, only the physics of futility
threaten my no-philosophy.

When they have cut the cord
and made me free from the invasive tyranny
of someone else's heart and blood –
But no,
I do not think that it will ever happen,
the science-fiction nightmare already is as obsolete
as the god who exploded the universe,
or the god who planted a garden,
or creation round the clock.

(1971)

TOM SCOTT

Cursus Mundi

(for R.L. Matheson)

one man	For yae chiel up
	There's ten are doun,
	And for yae brim cup
empty	There's ten that's toom;
	As a miller's wheel
	In a mill-race birled
	Turns aye abreel,
	Sae rowes this world.
	Whaur ane hes ten
	There's ten got ane
	And a hunder men
	That hevnae got nane;
hoop	Like a bairn's gird
	Doun the Cougate dirled,
	Wild owre the yird
smacks	Skelps on this world.
	Thon landrowth man
	Frae greed o gear
	Gars his brither gan
	In want and fear,
mud	For a spadefu o glaur
shrunken	His saul is nirled:
	For better and waur
	Sae rowes this world.
	The rivers and lochs
	Are claimed by Greed
property	As his proper auchts
	Frae the fowk in need;
wave	Ay, the welteran swaw,
	Tho snarled and gurled,
	He claims an' aa,
	And the lave o this world.

Greed maks the law
That creates the crime,
And guid fowk aa
Are daean time;
As a fistfu o sand
In the wind's teeth hurled,
On the punishan hand
Blaws back this world.

Genius and sant
Rage out in pain,
And reformers rant,
But aa in vain;
old woman As a carlin's shawl
Is plained and purled,
Sae o dirt and saul
Plats up this world.

idiot A cuif's preferred
Tae a man o sperit,
And the faithless herd
Til ane o merit;
Like a prize bull
dressed Aa dautit and curled,
The vainest fuil
Wins this world.

Wha shouts maist loud
Is heard the maist,
And wha maks maist gowd
Is deemit the best;
Like an auld duin bell
awry, broken gate At a jee yett tirled,
Maugre hevin and hell
Jows on this world.

state of confusion As a deer in a baize
Owre a muir is whirled
On tapper taes,
Sae flees this world.

200

And Daeth in the end
Indifferently will
Gravewart send
Baith guid and ill;
Like a deid lament
On the great pipe skirled,
lost   Sic distinction shent,
Sae keens this world.

(1993)

The Annunciation

alone   Ye'll lig your waddin-nicht yourlane
astride   Your legs aspar ti nocht but air,
And it will get in ye a son
Yet never pairt your maiden-hair.

protect, save   Ye'll hain yersel baith nicht and morn
And letna your guidman stier ye, will ye,
Afore the ferlie bairn is born
And broached your virgin nipples til ye.

care   Tak tent nou, I maun gang my road:
Ilka word I've said is true.
And aa I've ever envied God
Is bairnin o a lass like you.

(1966)

201

from *The Ship*

III

Whaur will it end afore it ends us aa?
Wi juist as muckle pride, irreverence
And want o sense and harmonie wi God,
Thon ancient 'fear of the Lord' that means 'respect
For aa the operations o the Real
Throu aa his kosmic, infinite machine',
We follaed up the Ship wi ae gret war,
Learnt nae lesson, sae anither follaed that.
We stand the day like a scorpion ringed wi fire
Ready to sting oor racial self ti daeth
Raither nor brek throu the bourgeis creed
Clearly condemned by wyce men as by God
As totally unreal and moribund.
Ither ships we're biggan ti the stars
Ettlan to mak a mercat o the kosmos
Ruled by the profiteer and usurer.
FREEDOM they shout, but SLAVERIE they mean,
No juist for the mony exploitit fowk
But even for the damned exploitan few.
CHRIST, they shout and are lucky their Yeshua
Isna bye wi scourge in hand to answer.
They talk aboot their 'way of life' and aa
Historie echoes DAETH, Daeth, daeth.
They rant o values wha nae value ken
That cash registers arena fit to meisure.
They talk o morals and gae on as afore
Corruptan generations and their ain bleck sauls.
Pouer concentrates in fewer hands,
Fascism lost the war and won the peace.
The liberal lie rules the deludit 'west'
And hands us owre ti fascist generals.
We pollute the seas, the rivers, lochs, the air
Oor bairns breathe wi mony kinds o foulness,
Material and spreital, the fumes and fall-out
Frae car and lorry, experimental bomb
Surpasst by the shit that drips inti ilka hame
Thru television and twanglin radio;
Double-talk and falsehood rule the land

And Truth is shut in hospital and prison.
God and Nature gie each creature born
The sun and moon for free, the noble Earth,
Yet men are everywhere the slaves o Money,
Their slave, lang become their tyrant,
Thou nou it's nocht but figures o credit in books.
On ilka haund the evidence comes in
Minute by minute demands a change o hert,
An end o Profit and Usurie a system sane,
Resilient ti human needs and natural law.
Hou lang afore the lesson will be learnt?
Hou lang, o lord, will we consent to dree
As slaves o 'freedom' in sic miserie?

Lament for Eurydice

Your absence is more pain than I can bear
    Eurydice,
disembowelling   The loss a kind of gralloching of soul.
What is this world to me and you not there?

The burden laid on me was less than fair,
Not to see your eyes a cruel toll,
    Eurydice.
Your absence is more pain than I can bear.

Descent into hell again I'd gladly dare
    Eurydice,
For while you're in it I've no better goal.
What is this world to me and you not there?

What can I know of paradise but where
You are, be it heaven or hell, or the Arctic pole,
    Eurydice,
Your absence is more pain than I can bear.

Are you and I not one, and no mere pair
    Eurydice,
Either apart but one half of the whole?
What is this world to me and you not there?

If you cannot be here, better I share
Your fate, so each with other may condole,
    Eurydice.
Your absence is more pain than I can bear.
What is this world to me and you not there?

Let Go Who Will

In this time I would ask three things,
    As the solitudes round me close:
Spare but the sensitive nerve that sings,
    The stormcock and the rose.

For none I can lose are really lost
    Traitor no friend could be:
Bury the dead and forget the cost
    Love only who stand with me.

Let all those go that want to go,
    Let only the leal remain:
The half-and-half would melt like snow
    Or as ice dissolves in the rain.

(1993)

C.H. SISSON

Numbers

1

Now you have left that face I am perplexed
To find no-one where I have loved best.
That is why, in the High Street, I stare
Wondering whether there is anyone anywhere.

2

Nothing that is remembered is true.
– And what precisely does that make of you?

3

Please now leave indignation alone.
It is enough if you are a stone.
There are the mountains, the waving trees, and you
Flat on the open ground from which they grew.

4

If there were time it would be time to go
– It is the lack of it makes me rage so.
Yet you may say, laughter would do as well
Since for the eternal all things are possible.

5

I said this man would fall and he fell.
With power dreams become terrible.
The power is nothing and the dream is all.

6

Let me escape the burning wheel of time.
There is no other purpose in rhyme
– As if a man could be identified
At least by his folly after he has died.

7

You come from sleep like a body from the womb
A moist wisp, to straggle into bloom.
There is an instant of delicacy, then
You strumpet unnoticed through a world of men.

8

Lechery in age is not kind.
It is the last exercise of the mind.

9

Do not burn, my heart
– That would be to exaggerate your part.
It would not do for you to reduce to tears
One who has carried you for fifty years.

10

If there were not air what would there be?
The voice passed my ear musically
Yet somehow I managed to be aware
Of what she was talking about – the air.
There were spirits in it, not least her own.
They are a substance immediately known
So there was no trouble about using the body
And that, for the moment, satisfied me completely.

11

Clifford says the mind is destroyed by work
And I agree my mind is destroyed by work.

12

Age, you have reached others before me.
They do not again expect to see me.
As they say good-bye they do not even have tears
Lest they seem to acknowledge their fears.

13

They do not know whether they are going to rest
Or a long recession from what they have loved best.
The truth in those old eyes and in my own
Is all that was said in that conversation.

14

He says good-bye from his wooden chair.
We go out and he is left there.
But which of us sees most vividly in the street
The boys and girls passing on featherweight feet?

15

I saw five hares playing in the snow.
That was only a winter ago
Yet they dance in my eyes and are as wild
As if I were old and had seen them as a child.

(1963)

In Flood

A word for everybody, myself nobody,
Hardly a ripple over the wide mere:
There is the winter sunshine over the water,
The spirits everywhere, myself here.

Do you know it? It is Arthur's territory
– Agravaine, Mordred, Guenivere and Igraine –
Do you hear them? Or see them in the distant sparkle?
Likely not, but they are there all the same.

And I who am here, actually and statistically,
Have a wide absence as I look at the sea,
– Waters which 'wap and wan', Malory said –
And the battle-pile of those he accounted dead.

Yet his word breathes still upon the ripple
Which is innumerable but, more like a leaf
Curled in autumn and blown through the winter,
I on this hill-side take my last of life:

Only glad that when I go to join them
I shall be speechless, no-one will ask my name,
Yet among the named dead I shall be gathered,
Speaking to no man, not spoken of, but in place.

(1979)

On Living Rather Long

What wind blows now? For all is still,
Yet somewhere, certainly, a breeze
Assaults the summit of some hill
And carries foliage from the trees
While I, whom nothing now can please
Accept my stationary position
And cannot change my own condition.

Youth is a time when an event
Is bound to happen or impend
Without our knowing what is meant,
And ignorance is then our friend,
Giving us hope that, in the end,
Either we move on to despair
Or learn to relish the hot air.

And middle age is for design:
We think we know what we are doing
And where it's best to draw the line,
Content that we are not renewing
The follies of our youth, pursuing
The good we know until we find
That it was only in the mind.

We stand impeccably aloof
At last, and see the empty plate:
The eating was the only proof
The pudding could excogitate
– And that will always be too late
For hungry men, and when they're full
They find the appetite grows dull.

So listen for the wind, without
Asking what quarter of the sky
It comes from, what it is about,
Or either how it blows, or why.
It blows. However hard you try
You cannot mitigate its force,
Still less deflect its final course.

(1992)

W.D. SNODGRASS

Owls

for Camille

Wait; the great horned owls
Calling from the wood's edge; listen.
There: the dark male, low
And booming, tremoring the whole valley.
There: the female, resolving, answering
High and clear, restoring silence.
The chilly woods draw in
Their breath, slow, waiting, and now both
Sound out together, close to harmony.

These are the year's worst nights.
Ice glazed on the top boughs.
Old snow deep on the ground.
Snow in the red-tailed hawks'
Nests they take for their own.
Nothing crosses the crusted ground.
No squirrels, no rabbits, the mice gone.
No crow has young yet they can steal.
These nights the iron air clangs
Like the gates of a cell block, blank
And black as the inside of your chest.

Now, the great owls take
The air, the male's calls take
Depth on and resonance, they take
A rough nest, take their mate
And, opening out long wings, take
Flight, unguided and apart, to caliper
The blind synapse their voices cross
Over the dead white fields,
The dead black woods, where they take
Soundings on nothing fast, take
Soundings on each other, each alone.

(1973)

R.S. THOMAS

Two Versions of a Theme

I

You couldn't, I thought, ask for
A seedier crowd than these Welsh
People, men and women, in their
Cheap shoes and expensive
Hats, blowing their noses, shuffling
Their cold feet, listening between lulls
In the gossip to the minister
Praying, while the stiff corpse lay
In its coffin beyond the reach of
Such cant. I would have turned
Furiously from those lurid
Noses and blear eyes to my
Car, but that a low sound
Arrested me, a hymn tang-
Led in that misshapen
But human wood, that directly
Freed itself and became art,
Palpable beauty hovering over the
Bent heads, waiting to be
Owned by them, had they looked up.

II

So, having said it, what have you said?
Made intelligible noises;
Beaten about a small bush
With the bird flown.

You went to a funeral, the same old thing,
And were disgusted:
Bleary eyes, and bald heads, and the prayers
A collection of cant.

You were turning away – they began singing,
Effortless beauty,
Spiring as most art has spired
From soiled fountains.

You forgot the crowd, the flowerless manhood
In its rank garden;
Seeing only the way the hymn
Endeared itself

To more distant mourners, the Welsh hills.
For a long moment
The music became the poem, that became you.
It is quenched now.

(1965)

CHARLES TOMLINSON

Winter Journey

I

When you wrote to tell me of your arrival,
    It was midnight, you said, and knew
In wishing me *Goodnight* that I
    Would have been long abed. And that was true.
I was dreaming your way for you, my dear,
    Freed of the mist that followed the snow here,
And yet it followed you (within my dream, at least)
    Nor could I close my dreaming eye
To the thought of further snow
    Widening the landscape as it sought
The planes and ledges of your moorland drive.
    I saw a scene climb up around you
That whiteness had marked out and multiplied
    With a thousand touches beyond the green
And calculable expectations summer in such a place
    Might breed in one. My eye took in
Close-to, among the vastnesses you passed unharmed,
    The shapes the frozen haze hung on the furze
Like scattered necklaces the frost had caught
    Half-unthreaded in their fall. It must have been
The firm prints of your midnight pen
    Over my fantasia of snow, told you were safe,
Turning the threats from near and far
    To images of beauty we might share
As we shared my dream that now
    Flowed to the guiding motion of your hand,
As though through the silence of propitious dark
    It had reached out to touch me across sleeping England.

Alone in the house, I thought back to our flood
    That left not an inch of it unbaptised
With muddy flux. Fed by the snow-melt,
    The stream goes lapping past its stone flank now,
And the sound beneath all these appearances
    Is of water, close to the source and gathering speed,
Netting the air in notes, letting space show through
    As sound-motes cluster and then clear
Down all its course, renewing and re-rhymed
    Further-off from the ear: I listen
And hear out what they have to say
    Of consequence and distance. That night
The wave rose, broke, reminded us
    We cannot choose the shape of things
And must, at the last, lose in this play
    Of passing lights, of fear and trust:
Waiting, as I wait now, I wish you could hear
    The truce that distills note-perfect out of dusk.

III

I must tell you of the moon tonight
    How sharp it shone. You have been gone three days.
Cold burnt back the mist. The planetarium
    Set out in clarity the lesson of the sky –
Half lost to me: I thought how few
    Names of the revolving multitude I knew
As they stood forth to be recognised. I saw
    The plough and bear – were those the Pleiades?
A little certainty and much surmise, what is the worth
    Of such half-recognitions? They must be
For all their revelation of one's ignorance
    Worth something – let me say this at least:
Though bidden by darkness to the feast of light,
    I came as one prepared, and what I could not name
Opening out the immensity flame by flame
    Found me a celebrant in the mass of night,

Where all that one could know or signify
    Seemed poor beside the reaches of those fires,
The moon's high altar glittering up from earth,
    Burning and burgeoning against your return.

IV

I lay the table where, tonight, we eat.
    The sun as it comes indoors out of space
Has left a rainbow irising each glass –
    A refraction, caught then multiplied
From the crystal tied within our window,
    Threaded up to transmit the play
And variety day deals us. By night
    The facets take our flames into their jewel
That, constant in itself, burns fuelled by change
    And now that the twilight has begun
Lets through one slivered shaft of reddening sun.
    I uncork the wine. I pile the hearth
With the green quick-burning wood that feeds
    Our winter fires, and kindle it
To quicken your return when dwindling day
    Must yield to the lights that beam you in
And the circle hurry to complete itself where you began,
    The smell of the distance entering with the air,
Your cold cheek warming to the firelight here.

(1985)

PETER WHIGHAM

The Orchard Is Not Cut Down

The orchard is gone. A space, con-
      ventionally like Paaschendaele,
      linearly framed by black rail-
ings, rises to a wide field on
which, inert, the milk-brown cows sun
      themselves and where the busy mail-
      van and the bus brightly curtail,
on the road sudden as a gun,
the field, – the vanish'd grove.

                  No dream
      of priest or king can empower mind
      to seize the blossom on the wind;
only, in passing, I have seen

      swan leaning on confused swan
      fall inwards like a folding fan.

                    (1959)

JULIE WHITBY

After 'The Road in Louveciennes'

by Camille Pissarro

Do you remember that road in Louveciennes?
The trees taut with their secrets,
and the road tight with snow?

We were close but not touching, as though
what we had was enough, we already knew
all that we needed to know.

How far from reality the road in Louveciennes!
You, a cypress in your dark green dress,
and I, in what my grandfather might have worn,
quaintly mysterious.

How sure the future seemed on our road in Louveciennes:
a sweet cold apple for us to eat.
Those trees, too, would tell us their secrets,

the snow bless us with blossom –
we were close but not touching,
ignorant of love's need, of the drab tread of years.

Do you remember, oh my love, the road in Louveciennes?
Before it grows dark we must find it somehow,
and clasp each other close, since
only we can weep real, unpainted tears.

(1983)

CAROLINE WRIGHT

Leaves

Autumn. Leaves along the bank.
Painted boats.
People fought here.
Took their horses to drink
washed their wounds
died here.

His armour shook the sun.
The plumes in his helmet
took their colours from the land.
He liked the way the leather strained
liked to flex his muscle
so the leather stretched

he *liked* that.

They'd been riding since first light
had seen the mist freeze the land and lift,
watched a mountain ridge unfold
beneath its quilt.
You could hide an army in that mist,
but now it's lifting; sun breaks through.

He didn't know where they were going.
Somewhere up north...
Only he knew that he
was quite a wonder to behold.
Plumes bobbing on the water.

When he lay dying he noticed
the whiteness of his hand
against the grass
the river's quiet slip
the leather on his arm

leaves near his face
brown and red.

(1980)

218

Time and Place

Face.
Whose face?

She looks through the black trees
into the clearing.
Milky green dew-spray hovers.
The gate.

Head back
eyes sealed
mouth? open?
closed.
Whose face?

'I shall stand by the gate
and wait for you.'

Head back
eyes sealed
mouth? closed.
Hair like –
Traffic in the distance.

'I hope it doesn't rain.'
Bird catches the air.
'Don't rain.'

Traffic; another world,
time's over with here.
Head back, eyes, mouth
hair like a falling scale,
nose tilted.
Traffic in the distance.

'I shall meet you here.
I'll tell you how I hurt my ankle
crossing the stream. How I saw
a tramp in the woods. Ask you
what took you so long.'

The hands that touch the face
compress the features
smooth the cheeks
clean the nose
make the face a little . . . real.
Traffic unnoticed;
another world.

'I wear the ring you gave me
it's too big.
I'll hope for other gifts.
I'm standing by the gate.
The quiet hums. When you arrive
you'll silence it.'

The hands push back the hair,
placate the unresisting image
of dead things.
Traffic –

Another world.
Her hands go through her hair.
'I'll ask you if you saw the old tramp.'
She throws her head back.
'Ask what took you
so long.'

Dead of Night

Bat flight through darkness.
Pinpricks of blood
the stars appear;
wounds across the night.

Martha turns the lie upon herself
and sleeps among the shadow shapes, alone;
an innocent warrior romantic to the core.
'Make me a mobile home beside your door,
and pull at my torn heart within the dark,
write long epistles of invented love
and make them live, even in the dead of night.'

Bat flight through darkness
and the pinpricks might just be
salvation's wounds.
She puts her mouth on his
and takes a chess piece from the table.
'Everything you own is fine,' she says,
allowing it to fall from her loose grasp.

'Martha, you have looks,' her mother'd said,
'never let bad taste destroy your face.'
But Martha couldn't grasp the words
nor yet a bird in flight through swollen air.
She never looked beyond the thing itself.

'Martha, you have...' looks into the small
dark-curtained room. She feels like Alice.
'It's so small!' Her hands before her mouth
like a wide eyed Dodgson child.
The Caterpillar leans back on the cushions,
she touches his green eyes to make them close.
'I love your colour, butterfly,' she says.
His wings enfold the dark.

Martha turns to lie quite by herself
and all night long she wonders if the bat
that flies the night was not the butterfly
or the butterfly the bat.

221

'It's hard to tell the difference in the dark.'
But she knows anyway what losers people are.
She lights a cigarette and takes the glow
to be the one star left alight.

'Martha, you have looks,' her mother'd said.
Martha looks and sees the pinpricks
dry up and expire.
'The wounds are closing and the dawn will come.'
But Martha faces solitude all day
and all day listens
for the creatures that might take her
through the night.

(1981)

PART THREE

Translations

PETER WHIGHAM

Five Translations from Sappho

LOVE

The wind threshes the mountains oaks.
Eros is frenzied in the soul of Sappho.

Irresistible & bitter
the mastery that sweetly melts my limbs.

ORCHARD

Cool water among apple boughs..
sleep falling from quicksilver leaves

THE MOON

The stars
            that circle
her bright face
                        cloak theirs
when the night-queen
                              sheds
her silver..
            light..
at the full

LONELINESS

Midnight,
             and the small hours
creep on,
             the Pleiads
& the moon
                   have set.
I lie alone.

OBLIVION

Sans record
             sans regret
you'll lie
             who have no memory
of Pierian Roses:
             unknown
among the unknown dead
             your ghost
must go
             in the House of Dis.

                                              (1966)

226

PETER JAY

Three Translations from Ibycus

LOVE

In spring Cydonian quinces, watered by running
streams in the holy virgins unapproachable
garden, and grapes that swell
clustered in vine-shoots' tendrilled shade,
ripen.

       But at no time of year
is love now restful within me –
Cypris has shot it
             burning
like a Siberian wind charged
with lightning – reckless, dark
it has stormed me,
          grips, shakes
and beats in my heart.

CAPTIVE

Again Eros flashes his glance towards me
(tenderly) from those dark eyelids;
his multiple spells will cast me into
Cypris's fathomless nets...
               And
I swear his approach makes me shudder – like
a champion horse in old age
yoked once more to the chariot, wearily
plodding toward the start.

227

COMET

Blazing
        through the vast night
like streaky-tailed
            dog-stars

(1966)

HORACE

Eheu fugaces, Postume, Postume

A Version by Basil Bunting

You cant grip years, Postume,
that ripple away nor hold back
wrinkles and, soon now, age,
nor can you tame death,

not if you paid three hundred
bulls every day that goes by
to Pluto, who has no tears,
who has dyked up

giants where we'll go aboard,
we who feed on the soil,
to cross, kings some, some
penniless plowmen.

For nothing we keep out of war
or from screaming spindrift
or wrap ourselves against autumn,
for nothing, seeing

we must stare at that dark, slow
drift and watch the damned
toil while all they build
tumbles back on them.

We must let earth go and home,
wives too, and your trim trees,
yours for a moment, save one
sprig of black cypress.

Better men will empty
bottles we locked away,
wine puddle our table,
fit wine for a pope.

(1970)

229

PETER WHIGHAM

from *The Poems of Catullus*

31

Apple of islands, Sirmio, & bright peninsulas, set
in our soft-flowing lakes or in the folds of ocean,
with what delight delivered, safe & sound,
                                        from Thynia
from Bithynia
            you flash incredibly upon the darling eye.
What happier thought
            than to dissolve
the mind of cares
            the limbs from sojourning,
and to accept the down of one's own bed
under one's own roof
            – held so long at heart . . .

and that one moment paying for all the rest.

So, Sirmio, with a woman's loveliness, gladly
echoing Garda's rippling lake-laughter,
and, laughing there, Catullus' house
                        catching the brilliant echoes!

(1960)

230

ARTHUR COOPER

Three Poems translated from the Chinese

WANG WEI (8th century):

On empty slopes
we see nobody,
Yet we can hear
men's echoed phrases:

Retreating light
enters the deep woods
And shines again
on the green mosses.

P'EI TI (his friend) replies:

As the day fades
see the cold mountain,
Suppose us those
travellers alone:

We'd never know
the deep wood's business
But for traces
of a stag or doe.

(1974)

FLOWER OR NOT FLOWER?

(Song Lyric, traditionally ascribed to Po Chü-i, 772-846)

Flower or not flower, mist or not mist, was here –
At midnight, came – with day, no longer there!
Came, as a dream of spring, a time;
Went, like a cloud at dawn, no where.

(1978)

MICHAEL ALEXANDER

The Ruin

from the Old English

Well-wrought this wall: Wierds broke it.
The stronghold burst....

Snapped rooftrees, towers fallen,
the work of the Giants, the stonesmiths,
mouldereth.
                    Rime scoureth gatetowers
                    rime on mortar.

Shattered the showershields, roofs ruined,
age under-ate them.
                    And the wielders and wrights?
Earthgrip holds them – gone, long gone,
fast in gravesgrasp while fifty fathers
and sons have passed.
                    Wall stood,
grey lichen, red stone, kings fell often,
stood under storms, high arch crashed –
stands yet the wallstone, hacked by weapons,
by files grim-ground...
...shone the old skilled work
...sank to loam-crust.

Mood quickened mind, and a man of wit,
cunning in rings, bound bravely the wallbase
with iron, a wonder.

Bright were the buildings, halls where springs ran,
high, horngabled, much throng-noise;
these many mead-halls men filled
with loud cheerfulness: Wierd changed that.

Came days of pestilence, on all sides men fell dead,
death fetched off the flower of the people;
where they stood to fight, waste places
and on the acropolis, ruins.
                              Hosts who would build again
shrank to the earth. Therefore are these courts dreary
and that red arch twisteth tiles,
wryeth from roof-ridge, reacheth groundwards....
Broken blocks....

                    There once many a man
mood-glad, gold-bright, of gleams garnished,
flushed with wine-pride, flashing war-gear,
gazed on wrought gemstones, on gold, on silver,
on wealth held and hoarded, on light-filled amber,
on this bright burg of broad dominion.

Stood stone houses; wide streams welled
hot from source, and a wall all caught
in its bright bosom, that the baths were
hot at hall's hearth; that was fitting...
....

Thence hot streams, loosed, ran over hoar stone
unto the ring-tank....
        ...It is a kingly thing
        ...city....

                                              (1962)

ALAN MASSEY

From the Provençal of Arnaut Daniel

XVII: ER VEI VERMEILLS, VERTZ, BLAUS, BLANCS,
GRUOCS...

Cerise, snow-white, green, azure, gold
The meadow, orchard, river-bank;
Song-birds whistle and interweave,
Early and late, sharp, sweet, forlorn;
And I would make an April tree of song,
Its clustered blossom shaken by such singing
Birds; a miracle of scented light.

When to her light my thoughts unfold
As young leaves to the sun, I thank
Amor for ecstasies that grieve
And sing to heaven! Each new-born
Desire takes to its flames: those who belong
To Love, Love moves to mirror Him, unstringing
Selves: humility is all our might.

Willingness to be bought and sold,
To sweat as kitchener or swank
In livery, and never leave
Her seigneurie: mark of the sworn
Man! The hoped-for self concedes, along
With reputation, power and the ringing
Coin of those who nod that black is white.

And Love's outfacings are as bold
As theirs: we lie outright, look blank,
Deceive the fools who would deceive
Amor. Bernard of Ventadorn,
Maker of ecstasies, your skylark-song
Catches the very tremor-shaken winging
Of all love-shaken humans in their plight.

Exiled to Alexandria, cold
Rain-lit London or the flank
Of Rus, this virtue would reprieve:
I'd see her in my heart. Untorn
By time or place or counsel right or wrong
From their one theme, these melodies and springing
Syllables are turned for her delight.

And all the court's diversions rolled
Out into play, austere or rank,
Sicken: I should prefer to cleave
The snail-clock in my rage and scorn!
O sun, unshifting weight, your light's too strong;
Grow faint for great Amor, who rises, bringing
Fragrant song to loose the dazzling night.

Go, song, to her to whom I shall belong
For ever. Say Arnaut despairs of singing
Sweetly enough of her, his heaven-light.

(1983)

DANTE

Sestina

Translated by Peter Dale[1]

To day drawn in, great ring of shadow,[2]
alas, I come, to whitened hills
where colour vanishes from grass
and yet desire stays evergreen
so rooted is it in the stone
that speaks and feels just like a woman.

And frozen hard is this young woman
as snow that lingers in the shadow;
she stirs no more than hardest stone
in the soft season that warms the hills
and mellows them from white to green
and spreads their slopes with flowers and grass.

She wears a coronet of grass
and out of mind goes every woman;
the curling yellow and the green
blending so well that in their shadow
dwells love that in between small hills
has locked me more than mortar, stone.

Her beauty has more power than stone
nor can her blows be healed by grass;
so I have fled through plains and hills
attempting to evade a woman,
but in her light can spread no shadow
from mountain, wall, or boughs of green.

---

[1] Long ago I made it a rule never to translate from languages I could
not read. My irritation with all the versions of this sestina that I have so
far read is my sole excuse for now breaking that rule. If I have added to
the irritations of life, I plead excuse for my crime of passion.
[2] *Al poco giorno ed el gran cerchio d'ombra*, quoted by Pound in Cantos V
and CXVI. *Ed.*

I saw her once all clothed in green
that might have moved the hardest stone
with love that I feel for her shadow;
so I've desired her in the grass –
as much in love as any woman –
surrounded by the greatest hills.

Yet rivers shall return to hills
before fire catches wood so green,
because of me, in that young woman
and yet I'd even sleep on stone
for all my days and eat the grass
to see where once her dress cast shadow.

Wherever hills cast darkest shadow,
in her rich green, then, this young woman
hides it like stone beneath the grass.

(1979)

W.D. SNODGRASS

with Simone Draghici & Ioan Popa

Miorita

from the Romanian

Near a low foothill
At Heaven's doorsill,
Where the trail's descending
To the plain and ending,
Here three shepherds keep
Their three flocks of sheep,
One, Moldavian,
One, Hungarian,
And one, Vrancean.
Now, the Vrancean
And Hungarian
In their thoughts, conniving,
Have laid plans, contriving
At the close of day
To ambush and slay
The Moldavian;
He, the wealthier one,
Had more flocks to keep,
Handsome, long-horned sheep,
Horses, trained and sound,
And the fiercest hounds.
One small ewe-lamb, though,
Dappled grey as tow,
While three full days passed
Bleated loud and fast,
Would not touch the grass.
'Ewe-lamb, dapple-grey,
Muzzled black and grey,
While three full days passed
You bleat loud and fast;
Don't you like this grass?
Are you too sick to eat,
Little lamb so sweet?'
'Oh my master dear,

Drive the flock out near
That field, dark to view,
Where the grass grows new,
Where there's shade for you.
Master, master dear,
Call a large hound near,
A fierce one and fearless,
Strong, loyal and peerless.
The Hungarian
And the Vrancean
When the daylight's through
Mean to murder you.'
'Lamb, my little ewe,
If this omen's true,
If I'm doomed to death
On this tract of heath,
Tell the Vrancean
And Hungarian
To let my bones lie
Somewhere here close by,
By the sheepfold here
So my flocks are near,
Back of my hut's grounds
So I'll hear my hounds
Tell them what I say:
There, beside me lay
One small pipe of beech
With its soft, sweet speech,
One small pipe of bone
With its loving tone,
One of elderwood,
Fiery-tongued and good.
Then the winds that blow
Would play on them so
All my listening sheep
Would draw near and weep
Tears, no blood so deep.
How I met my death,
Tell them not a breath;
Say I could not tarry,
I have gone to marry
A princess – my bride

Is the whole world's pride.
At my wedding, tell
How a bright star fell,
Sun and moon came down
To hold my bridal crown,
Firs and maple trees
Were my guests; my priests
Were the mountains high;
Fiddlers, birds that fly,
All birds of the sky;
Torchlights, stars on high.
But if you see there,
Should you meet somewhere,
My old mother, little,
With her white wool girdle,
Eyes with their tears flowing,
Over the plains going,
Asking one and all,
Saying to them all,
"Who has ever known,
Who has seen my own
Shepherd fine to see,
Slim as a willow tree,
With his dear face, bright
As the milk-foam, white,
His small moustache, right
As the young wheats ear,
With his hair so dear,
Like plumes of the crow,
Little eyes that glow
Like the ripe, black sloe?"
Ewe-lamb, small and pretty,
For her sake have pity,
Let it just be said
I have gone to wed
A princess most noble
There on Heaven's doorsill.
To that mother, old,
Let it not be told
That a star fell, bright,
For my bridal night;
Firs and maple trees

Were my guests; my priests
Were the mountains high;
Fiddlers, birds that fly,
All birds of the sky;
Torchlights, stars on high.'

    – from Vasile Alecsandri,
       Poesii populare ale Românilor.

(1974)

FRANÇOIS VILLON

Ballat o the Hingit

Translated by Tom Scott

                Brither-men that eftir us live on,
                Harden no yir herts agin us few
stare   But petie the puir chiels ye gove upon,
forgive And God's mair like yir ain faults ti forhou.
                Five or sax o's strung up here ye view,
corpses Our tramorts, doutless pettit whiles wi stew,
rather sour Theirsels are suppit, tho gey wersh the brew.
                When that our banes ti dust and ashes faa,
endure Dinnae lauch at the sinners dree sic rue
                But pray the Lord has mercie on us aa.

                And gin we caa ye brethren, dinnae scorn
                The humble claim, even tho it's true
                It's juist we swing: ye ken weill nae man born
                No aa the time is blest wi mense enou.
                Sae for our cause, guid-hertit brethren, sue
                Wi the Virgin's Son they hingit on Calvary's bou,
descend That grace devall afore our judgment's due
snatch   And kep us up in time frae hell's gret maw.
complain Sen we are deid, ye neednae gird at's nou
                But pray the Lord has mercie on us aa.

                We hae been washed and purifee'd by rain.
                The sun has tanned our hides a leathery hue.
                Craws and pyes hae pykit out our een
                And barbered ilka stibble chin and brou.
                Nae peace we ken the twenty-fowr hours through
                For back and furth, whiles braid-on, whiles askew,
                Wi ilka wind that blaws we twist and slue,
pitted   Mair stoggit nor straeberries, and juist as raw.
Mingle See ti it you never mell wi sicna crew
                And pray the Lord shaws mercie ti us aa.

Prince Yeshu, wha haud aa mankind in feu,
Watch Satan duisnae rive us serfs frae you:
Wi him we's bide nae langer nor we awe.
Guid fellae-men, dinnae ye mock us nou
But pray the Lord shaws mercie ti us aa.

(1993)

Ballat o the Leddies o Langsyne

Translated by Tom Scott

Tell me whaur, in whit countrie
Bides Flora nou, yon Roman belle?
Whaur Thais, Alcibiades be,
close   Thon sibbit cousins. Can ye tell
Whaur cletteran echo draws pell-mell
Abuin some burn owrehung wi bine
Her beautie's mair nor human spell –
Ay, whaur's the snaws o langsyne?

Whaur's Heloise, yon wyce abbess
For wham Pete Abelard manless fell,
Yet lovin aye, at Sanct Denys
Wrocht out his days in cloistrit cell?
And say whaur yon queen is as well
That ordrit Buridan ae dine
sacked cast   Be seckt and cuist in the Seine to cool –
Ay, whaur's the snaws o langsyne?

Queen Blanche, as pure's the flour-de-lys,
Whase voice nae siren's could excel,
Bertha Braidfuit, Beatrice, Alys,
Ermbourg that hent the maine hersel?
Guid Joan of Arc, the lass they tell
distant   The English brunt at Rouen hyne –
Whaur are they, Ledy, I appeal?
Ay, whaur's the snaws o langsyne?

244

Prince, this week I cannae tell,
Nor this year, whaur they aa nou shine.
enquire Speir, ye's but hear the owrecome swell –
Ay, whaur's the snaws o langsyne?

(1993)

Ballade

Translated by Peter Dale

Now tell me where has Flora gone,
the lovely Roman, her country's where?
Archipiades, Thais that shone,
her cousin once removed? And there
was Echo once, a trace on air,
by ponds and commons she would show
a beauty more than humans bear:
where is the drift of last year's snow?

Where Heloise, whose wisdom shone,
whose love helped Abelard to bear
the gelding he had undergone
when sworn to vows a monk must swear?
And where now is that Queen so fair
who ordered them to sack and throw
Buridan in the Seine down there?
Where is the drift of last year's snow?

Where's Blanche the Queen, white as a swan,
her siren's voice upon the air?
Big-footed Bertha, Beatrice gone;
Alice, and Arembourg once heir
to Maine. Good Joan in Rouen square
burnt by the English. There they go,
but where, O Virgin, tell me where,
where is the drift of last year's snow?

245

Prince, do not ask in a fortnight where,
nor yet again in a year or so.
This is the burden of the air:
where is the drift of last year's snow?

(1971)

FRIEDRICH HÖLDERLIN

But when the heavenly . . .

Translated by Michael Hamburger

But when the heavenly
Have built, it is quiet
On earth, and well-fashioned stand
The mountains they have struck. Their brows
Are marked. For they were hit,
When the straight daughter untenderly
Held back the Thunderer,
By the god's tremulous ray
And rebellion quenched from above
Exhales a good fragrance.
Where within, assuaged, here
And there,   is the fire.
For joy the Thunderer
Pours out and almost would have
Forgotten heaven at that time,
Enraged, if the wise had not
Warned him.
But now it blossoms
In a place of dearth.
And wonderfully great
Desires to stand.
Alpine ranges hang   sea
Warm   deep   but the breezes cool
Islands and peninsulas,
Grottoes   to pray,

A gleaming shield
And quick, like roses,

                         or else
A different manner creates,
But there sprouts
            very lushly an envious
Weed that dazzles, faster it shoots
Up, the awkward, for the creative

Is joking, but they
Do not understand. Too wrathfully
It grips and grows. And like a conflagration
That devours houses, it flares
Up, heedless, and does not spare
Space and a steaming cloud,
Widely in ferment, covers
　　　　　　the helpless wilderness.
So it would seem divine. But
Dreadfully inhospitable through
The garden confusion winds,
The eyeless, when with clean hands
Scarcely a man can find
The way out. He goes, on a mission,
And, like an animal, searches
For what is needed. True, with his arms,
Full of foreknowledge, one may attain
The goal. For where
The heavenly need a fence or a sign
To mark their
Way, or a bath,
There is a stirring like fire
In the hearts of those men.

Yet others the Father
Keeps at his side.
For above the alps,
Because by the eagle
They must be guided, lest with their own minds
In fury they interpret,
The poets, they dwell above
The bird's flight, around the throne
Of the god of joy
And cover the abyss
For him, they who like yellow fire, when time is in spate,
Are above the brows of those men,
The prophetic, would begrudge
It them, because they love
Fear, shades of hell,

But they were driven away,
Opening up a pure

Fate, from
The holy tables of earth,
By Hercules the cleanser
Who, candid always, remains, even now,
With the ruler, and, breath-bearing, still
The Dioscuri descend and rise
On inaccessible steps, when from the heavenly fortress
The mountains draw far away
By night, and away
The times
Of Pythagoras

In remembrance, though, lives Philoctetes,

Those help the Father.
For they like to rest. But when
They are roused by mischievous
Happenings on earth and the heavenly
Are robbed
           their senses, burning then
They come,

The breathless –

For the pondering god
Hates
Untimely growth

(1989)

Translator's Note

One of the fragmentary drafts in the so-called Homburg Folio, loose sheets folded over that served Hölderlin for new work and reworkings of earlier texts over a long period extending well beyond what was taken to be the onset of his 'madness'. D.E. Sattler, the editor of the current Frankfurt Edition of Hölderlin's works and of the facsimile edition of the Homburg Folio has shown that the work in this manuscript dates from October or November 1802 to its confiscation as late as May or June 1807, when the carpenter Ernst Zimmer, to whom Hölderlin had been entrusted after his discharge from the Tübingen mental clinic, took it away from the poet and handed it over to his family. (This may well have been the true watershed between the work of Hölderlin and that of the entirely different poet he became in his Tübingen tower in later years.)

The fragment is part of Hölderlin's most ambitious project, a series of 'hymns' or cantos that were to have ranged over the cosmology, myths and history of ancient and modern civilization, from the revolt of the Titans to the discovery of America and Hölderlin's own era.

Columbus was the subject of one of them. Luther and Shakespeare were among the titles jotted down for poems never written or lost. The change in Hölderlin's person and the collapse of his poetic ambition made it impossible for him to execute the project. So we are left with fragments and drafts, most of them in a state that almost forbids interpretation, makes all datings of the contents of the Folio highly conjectural, and invalidates the conjectural dates of all previous editors, who had assumed that Hölderlin became incapable of such work after his return from Bordeaux in July 1802.

GEORG TRAKL

De Profundis

Translated by Michael Hamburger

There is a stubble field on which a black rain falls.
There is a tree which, brown, stands lonely here.
There is a hissing wind which haunts deserted huts –
How sad this evening.

Past the village pond
The gentle orphan still gathers scanty ears of corn.
Golden and round her eyes are grazing in the dusk
And her lap awaits the heavenly bridegroom.

Returning home
Shepherds found the sweet body
Decayed in the bramble bush.

A shade I am remote from sombre hamlets.
The silence of God
I drank from the woodland well.

On my forehead cold metal forms.
Spiders look for my heart.
There is a light that fails in my mouth.

At night I found myself upon a heath,
Thick with garbage and the dust of stars.
In the hazel copse
Crystal angels have sounded once more.

(1968)

PETER RUSSELL

Three Versions of Osip Mandelstam

When the urban moon comes out on the squares
And slowly the teeming city shines with its light,
And night comes down, full of despair and darkness
And the melodious wax yields to harsh time:

Then also the cuckoo cries from his stony height,
And the pale reaper-girl comes down to the stifling world,
Silently turns the huge spokes of the shadows,
And flings herself down on the ground with the yellow straw . . .

(1920)

(1959)

LENINGRAD 1930

I have come back to my city, familiar to the point of tears,
To the blood in my veins, to my childhood's swollen tonsils.
You have come back here – so swallow up quickly
The cod-liver oil of the Leningrad river-lamps:

Quickly make up your mind to the short December day
When the air is a mess of egg-yolk and evil tar.
Petersburg! I do not wish to die yet –
All my telephone numbers are with you.

Petersburg! I still have addresses
By which I shall find the voices of the dead.
I live on a back staircase – wrenched out with the flesh
The noise of a bell strikes in my temple,

And all night long I wait for welcome guests
Stirring at the fetters of door-chains.

(1960)

TRISTIA

I have learned the whole art of leave-taking
In bare-headed night-lamentations.
The oxen chew: anticipation lingers –
And I honour the ceremony of that cock-crying night
When raising their burden of sorrow for a departing traveller
Eyes that were red with weeping gazed into the distance
And the wailing of women mingled with the song of the muses.

In that word "leave-taking" who can tell
What kind of separation is in store for us,
What it is the crying of cocks promises
When fire burns on the acropolis:
And in the first red dawn of some new life
When lazily the ox is chewing in the shade,
Why does the cock, the new life's own town-crier
On the city wall beat madly with his wings?

I love the way the thread is spun –
The shuttle runs to and fro, the spindle hums –
Look now – already like swansdown
Barefooted Delia flies to meet you!
O the meagre pattern of our life –
Even our happiest words are threadbare!
Everything has been of old and will be again:
For us, only the moment of recognition is sweet.

So let it be: the little gleaming figure
Lies on the spotless earthen dish.
Like the stretched-out skin of a squirrel
Stooping over the wax the young girl gazes.
It is not for us to guess about Grecian Erebus:
What's bronze for man for woman is only wax.
Our destiny befalls us only in battles –
They see the future as they die.

                              1918

                                        (1959)

Cover drawing by Jean Cocteau for 1960-61 issue of *Agenda*.

JEAN COCTEAU

Leoun

Translated by Alan Neame

I

Leoun I dreamed on the night of the 28th.
Padding with lioness paws across the night
She walked, Leoun, between the burnt-out fires.
Greek actors walk in clogs with comparable poise.

II

Leoun went forward until bedworthy dawn.
Skilfully walking on the night went Leoun.
Leoun walked on the night itself, I mean.

III

The dream hung in my head and Leoun in my dream.
Hearse and mutes were hard put to keep up with her
The roundabout twisted its corded copper
The robot scanned her shepherded footfall
All seemed to turn yet nothing moved at all
For, expert in the properties of mirrors, Leoun
Climbed backwards up the ladder the rain let down.

IV

She straddled the bodies of showmen asleep.
Halted. Counted her enemies. Thought deep.
Under her cloak hid the Head of Holophernes
(You see, this head was the lamp for her journeys
Deaf blind frightful with its brilliant beam)
And resumed the course designed by my dream.

V

That's how she walked, relentless Leoun,
For Leoun walking was chameleon,
Taking form and colour from everywhere she trod
Moving with the grace of a thief on the job.

VI

She walked on the fringe of the Dew's eye-lash.
Her undertaking was unspeakably rash
For at the jetty-corner and from cardinal points
The soldiery of morning patrolled the battlements.

VII

Monuments on the ages drifting
Sported their light rig of scaffolding.
History was marking houses with an X.
The queen was at the chymist buying a portpest.
Lurid in mauve patches between the bridges flowed
The virgin-seeming waters, often enough widowed,
And Leoun Leoun at the foot of the quay wall
Went on her way with disguised footfall.

VIII

Where the streetlamps were out painted women were towed
By stark naked cyclists to the pretty crossroad
While heedless of its human cattle the city held
Its great palm open under a sky ciphered with gold.

IX

Avoiding camper sleeper and false swan
Leoun followed the lines traced on that palm.

X

The cyclists went walking down by the water
Girls in one hand and bike in the other.
A whiz of dragonflies and insect flutterings
Paced these angels who had no wings
Who put a like warmth and equal zest
Into guiding the handlebars and squeezing a waist.
Just so at the fair you find the wretched shack
Alongside signs of chance and of the Zodiac.

XI

So walked Leoun so did the lioness walk
Under an inkblue sky spattered with milk.
Lovers suckled on these garret-skies
Laughed at night's gates and monitoring eyes.
They twined together under the eaves.
Their crushed pollen takes the bloom off the seasons.
Everywhere tramps above the city riddles
The frantic gallop of motionless couples.
But Leoun attuned to a rhythm other than man's
Knows nothing of this love armed with two pairs of hands.

XII

In the shadow theatre on its fly-over bridges
Light slit the throats of the cocks and pigeons.
The Antigonè was showing. Leoun on her road
Saw actors draped in mantillas of blood.
The bloody shadow twined round the incest tree
Trickling from each twig of heroic poetry
And Leoun saw (or could she?) far below her the light
From projectors crossing swords with the swords in the fight.

XIII

Could she pierce up beyond the heaven of patriots
To the wingèd triumph of its anagogues?
Thousands of angel dancers, wings golden and lush,
Swelled the opera with marble and plush.
Leoun's veils were the sails of a schooner.

XIV

Herodias Elsa Thais Iseult Elvira
Clinging to the shipwreck of a solo-number
Trailed their seaweed hair through the armorial lumber.

XV

But for those Leoun was already out of sight.
Blindly she wandered down the endless street
Leading to your doorstep – greenroom to hellfire.

XVI

She had to pick her way past the bramble of barbed wire.

XVII

What are those bakers asleep in their dough?
For flinging these bodies off the hasty naked soul
Had uprooted them and tossed them anyhow.
These sleepers had passed out, neck arched in a bow.
Only the wristwatch survived on the lifeless arm
The future ticked to waste in each open palm
And each man wore in victory or defeat
A viper coiled where his heart should beat.
But Leoun stepped clear of their disordered feet
Scattered arms hands limp over the ciphered lot
Mouths where silence framed itself to a shout.

XVIII

What sort of loaf is this of blood and mud and moon
Baked by these bakers in the dough-trough lolling?
Who is to eat this bitter macaroon
And who will buy this bread of my friends' body?

XIX

Leoun untouched by such ignoble grace
With feet unsullied trampled the rank grass.
(Her feet were marble and entirely cleared
Our human spillikins lying inert.)
She could not see the crimson berries rotting
On the quickset hedge or the blue rags dropping
Nor how the rose triumphant on the sleeping earth
Sucked its scarlet at the springs of death.

XX

High over the houses dances the sleepwalker.
Below like a tightrope-walker the baker
Down the airshaft flours his bare torso.
Shall we recapitulate what Leoun cannot know? –
Above we have a sleepwalker inspecting her theatre.
Below on night-shift down the ventilator
Brewing their batch, nude Pierrots and plaster Apollos.
Pointless. Walking is all her work. Nothing else follows.

XXI

Bedroom wallpaper and sewing-machines shock
When the thunderbolt has ripped open the block.
The flats part their flesh to the soul at their core.
The people are gone. They don't count anymore.
Warm heads fall beneath the shaken tree,
Golden greengage the colour they bleed,
And Leoun like a peahen teasing the cock
Rolls them over with the hem of her frock.

XXII

That was Leoun's manner, arrogant lady,
Death walks like her, so does Antigonè
Flouting the law in insolent disdain.
So pass the Coronation, kingly train,
Children college-bound in crocodile,
Deer on the forest moss. Leoun the same.
And the young murderer down dead man's mile
From the condemned cell to the guillotine,
The Great Bear likewise, move and the wood-louse,
Water as it boils and quicksilver.
(Only my waking could disrupt her course.)
I must sleep on and to the uttermost help her.

XXIII

O March, why would you have me brave your Ides?
Your horn had warned me that your Doom abides.
Forty was catastrophic, thirty-nine too sweet.
Why must the Virgin sit beneath an egg?
This mystery-mongering painter is too smart!
Why do you never speak, you works of art?
Cry out, defend yourselves, mock death, be rude!
Need a masterpiece nag to qualify as good?

XXIV

Brittany is an urn of opalescent clay.
Black the hill and black the slanting tree
Black Tristram's lying sail and black the fiend.

XXV

The knight lies waiting on his granite bed.
Brittany directs her wide unfocussed gaze
On bishops at their scourging by the waves.
She listens to the flight of a thousand shrieking birds
Battering the rainbows to foggy shreds.

XXVI

Leoun made her way through the curded opal
Of hard Brittany where all is mild and pastel.

XXVII

Run wreckers, make the windows rattle
Scarify men with the stormy petrel
Tie torches to the horns of the cattle
Add chapters to the Dark Prowesse.

XXVIII

Thatch arches window glances here and, yes,
Here be dead-eye oysters and sweet cider-press –
Brittany where Scotland finds herself grown fairer
Like a woman lighting on a distant mirror.

XXIX

Heedless of the mists' refracting glass
Leoun moves through the milk opal and floss.
(The misty lens marks detail:
Milk oak and stormy petrel
Moon and moonbeams turned to fairies
Wrecks uprearing beastly trophies)
Leoun's map is plotted in her hand.

XXX

If not in hers then in another's planned.
Perhaps my hand relaxed in sleep
Plots the bearings on her map.
All else irks her and means change of set.

XXXI

Tristram may linger for the horn's lament
Leoun despises him and laughs at his distress.
She and the Zeitgeist walk abreast.
I dream her and I contain the dream.
Yet I still cannot tell Leoun's final aim.
Flat on my bed how could I follow her?
No. I can only snuff her out altogether.

XXXII

Snuff her out? Can a Leoun really die?
What does her name mean? What does the sleeper do?
He lies. Offers himself for a dream-stage.
Now the dream fills me as water fills a sponge.

XXXIII

Perhaps, striding over the shock when I wake up,
Leoun will step into another's sleep,
Going from sleep to sleep without remission
Towards the one to whom she owes submission.
Which is he?

XXXIV

The sleeper gives nothing of his own.
My dream makes a mere passage for Leoun,
Knowing my impotence my sole reward.
I have no means to trap her off her guard.
Who can tell whence Leoun or whither away?

XXXV

So plied Gradiva through the streets of Pompeii
With a grace somewhat reminiscent of Leoun
So on the water pranced the Colleoun
So the Commendatorè kicked the ground agape
So trod the Venus d'Ille with brazen step
So flew Icarus plumed with artifice.

XXXVI

Now Tristram dwelt at the Inn of Sacrifice.
Wounded waiting perched on a cardboard box
In an open-air theatre on the Breton rocks.

XXXVII

Why waste weeping on one Iseult aghast?
If Leoun tarried she would herself be lost.
Perish Tristram perish Iseult whose hair shines so bright.
I sleep that Leoun may glide on through the night.

XXXVIII

I sleep and I know and I know that I dream
I alone can decide when the dream is complete
And when Leoun shall leave me once and for all.

XXXIX

Were Leoun to return after an interval
To tread again the dream that fills me now
Qualmless I should wake up quick. But, no,
She only walks us each one night in time.
Today from all eternity was mine
For me to play the link in Leoun's chain
Not knowing where or when she walks again.
If only I knew that sleeper designate
To whom Leoun elects to turn her feet
And he could tell the sequel to the story!
Or sleep maybe will flaw his memory
Perhaps he will say: I never dream, not I!
Or I may hear one day – should she comply –
Some sleeper quite unknown
Waking from you uttering your name – *Léone!*
Telling of other paths your feet pursue.

XL

What shall I do, Great God, if I lose track of you?

XLI

Ink upon paper spells infatuation.
There are no verses of the pen's creation.
A monochrome ribbon a melody of grief
Cut the heraldic crochet of the fated life.
I only see the back of the piece I embroider.
Look, against the sunset Leoun looks shorter.
I finger a shadow – Leoun is the gnomon.

XLII

Up, reluctant sleeper! up sleeper, up and on!
Quick march! Keep up! Leoun won't stand waiting.
Don't snap the thread she sets her heart on plaiting.
And honour what you do not understand!

XLIII

Lie on your bed do not stir hand or foot
Run without motion and motionless fly
Sleeper cribbed by a cheap society
For Leoun has chosen the gulf of your being
To play out her drama and set her scene in.

XLIV

You can run without stirring a limb
You can follow Leoun on your back in your room
You can bathe in speed while you relax
Lock the pedals let go the brakes
And let the front wheel of your cycle
Wind the fine-threaded stare of prowheads on its spindle.
False night false sun false wind – world of seeming.
Be warned. Dreamers may lose themselves in dreaming.

XLV

Don't let her go. Keep your eyes skinned. Only see
How Minerva's shadow is shaped like a key
Revealing her far clearer to the mind of man
Than the temple reared on the flat of her hand.

263

XLVI

Run sleeper fettered in deep sea tresses
Your mouth is open and your leg aggressive
And your closed eye bent on the riddle of the blood
Seeks a world more potent recreate and good.

XLVII

That is where hope must be fastened to win her.
She is a fountain. A column. And in her
Nothing inheres of the nature in us.
She walks without moving, lifting her knees.
And has she any knees?

XLVIII

       At last I am in step.
From plinth to point the obelisk slept.
For obelisks sleep on their feet at night.
The silence brimmed with babbling gold light.

XLIX

Fantomas the King of 1911
Keeps a king captive under the bronze siren
There where Memnon's organ rolls its muted tone
There from her palace where the long-armed moon
Moves her stone chessmen down the ivory
There where the future creeping like an ivy
Up Egypt hides herself in gilded words
Her eyes night-waking and adored her birds.

L

Kiosk and grill and grove lawn armoury
Ghosts of young men of occult stabulary
Saddling horses of wrath unknown to the sun –
There History and dream melt in continuum.

LI

Pole-less Leoun balanced along the cord
For the showmen were camping Place de la Concorde.
By the light of their fires I could see from above
The shadows of the caravans and horses move.
We could pick out the noise of distant brawls
The fountain-bowl clanging to the iron pails
And the tap . . . tap . . . tap of a boy with a peg-leg.

LII

Here fall the moonlight and the crownèd head
Here beat the hearts of tambours of Santerre
The showman sleeping on the ground are here
(They sleep three-quarter-face or in profile)
Here walks Leoun *all skilful on the wire.*

LIII

Here Leoun goes walking, I follow where she walks.
Here green soldiers sleep in their sentry-box
Here France at half-mast hears the caravan
Dreaming aloud of Egypt and Leviathan.

LIV

Here on a hazardous path Leoun
Flew o'er the checkerboard of night and moon.
She walked, Leoun, with wingèd step
Above the showmen black and striped.
The square had furled its wings to sleep.
Leoun drew me after her along the rope.
The void favours those who walk asleep.

LV

A sleepwalker's best friend is the roof.
At heights to disconcert an acrobat
You can see the young desert their garret-flat
Death comes to meet them, pointing them the way
And with a mother's hand leads them away.

LVI

Skywalking I conform to the dream-trope
Protected in a voidal envelope
Leoun too: while she cautiously outshines
The diamond fragments of the Heavenly Signs.

LVII

Does not the Great Bear pose some frightening equation?
What would the Sun convey by daily revolution?
And that pedant on the slate of the night-sky
With his freckled ciphering – what is he at? and why?
What of the Tree of Night with its cluster of bees?
These ear-rings and bangles . . . what of these?
And who spattered that fiery ink so high?

LVIII

Leoun pierced further under the soulless vault.
No landmark from the known world marked her route.
A hero lying asleep with his limbs straddled wide
Composed valley rock wood rampart and mountainside.
The swallows were nesting in the hollows of his arms.
For his arms flung apart left his armpits unarmed
And below in a tangled grove between his legs
The cockbird slept brooding on his eggs.

LIX

Leoun untouched by a grace so ignoble
Strode through his vineyard fallow-land and grove.
And I followed Leoun in my turn to trample
The body of the hero dismasted by love.

LX

'Twas Renaldo fallen prey to Armida's devices
Sleeping in the fragrance of his dewy fleeces.
Biceps shoulderblade breastbone thigh and hip
Littered the warm snow where the heroes sleep.

LXI

Armida in the veil of a lawful bride
And taller than a shot-tower surveyed fallen pride.
Chaste after love, her great body locked up,
She slept on her feet by her own true love.

LXII

Sure this group took form from a sea-billow swelling,
An erotic Atlantic of buttock and belly!
Now nothing is left in the wake of the wash
But a naked king lapped in the armour of flesh.
Like the fall of the angels lay this knight.

LXIII

Booted with ink are they that trample the wine-fat.
Likewise Leoun and I trample the sleeping king.
Will you reach haven you sleepers of my night's sleeping?
Suppose in your sleeping another sleeper should heave
And dream of a sleeper and he then dream of another
Shall I come at last after going from sleeper to sleeper
To the prison-wall and meet my firing-squad?

LXIV

Yet Naught hath Term. Even Mortality
Aspires to symbolise Eternity.
Dead dream of Dead and they of Dead the same.
Nothing breaks free of what informs our Frame.
Not so Leoun. Ignoring prison wall
She journeys to th' Incomprehensible
To her Companions and with Time and Space.

LXV

Look now, she pauses. Can it be she waits?
I halt. I tremble. If like Belphegor
(Whose deeds are in the Louvre) she does discover
That I am trying to foresee our goal . . .
Leoun sets off again and lifts her heel.

LXVI

I can see the flat of each heel disturb
The colourless fabric of the dream-robe.
One after the other her heels at the edge
Of the garment disperse Belphegor's image.
I used to love this part of the film when I was younger.
How do gates and fashions affect Belphegor?
She strikes with her hammer and the walls divide.
These murderers always have the public on their side.
There goes Leoun's heel, ah lovely, look!
High enough to see the sole of her foot.
The other takes its place and rises as high.

LXVII

Belphegor shook her hammer at the sky.

LXVIII

Each time a heel twitches her cloak awry
Does she think of striking at the spying fire?
God! Dare I impute to her any such desire?
Memories of some film were beginning to confuse...
Leoun is remote from the world that I prize.

LXIX

And yet the here and now is not my country.
I hope to have her for ever at the Dark Entry.
But still the separative chasms yawn.

LXX

Crime has revoked the Tables of the Law.
Where can I flee from Crime? which is the way out?
Now if there were some way and Leoun knew it
I should put a mammet of myself in the bed.
I should get Sleep framed for criminal neglect
I should make myself look so much like a corpse
That I'ld hoodwink the dream and run into port.

LXXI

Who sleeps dreams he flies. Thinks fate not so clever.
A fly-by-night flying and knowing the lever
Knowing how to manage the patent self-starter
Rising like Indian ink falling through water
Deep in an element furling and furled
Where flying is the lordliest ease in the world.

LXXII

Quite other to flit from the dream I enclose
Other than reveille may foreclose
Other to beat dawn with its comb like a cock.

LXXIII

When fanfaronading cock in farmyard crows
Shattered, my repose, attuned to slightest shock.

LXXIV

This thing subsists in me because I believe in it.
And yet a cock bonneted in raw meat
Crowing like the handle of a rusty pump
An old cock shouting like a market street
Can rout a royal ghost on parole from the tomb.

LXXV

Elsinor! Moonscaped and crenelated,
The other world your king had penetrated.
My shadow played Hamlet, Leoun played the King.

LXXVI

Would the poet blench before *a guilty thing?*
No. Leoun was adept at every illusion
Ever contrived in greenroom confusion:
Kings who go quietly at the Porter's knock
Kings whose marmoreal footfall sets the pavement rocking
Kings who fade *on the crowing of the cock.*

LXXVII

What time is it on earth where my stand-in plays for me?
Lente lente curritur noctis equi!
You cocks wake not the sick man from his slumbers.
Spare him his dreams. Draw not your golden sabres.

LXXVIII

I have said that your crowing is covered with rust
Your skin tettered yellow with a leperous crust
Your hat trimmed off with a star of red meat
That a beard of balls hangs down from your beak.
I have spoken.

LXXIX

For all that, your sabres are arms
Keen enough to kill our economy of charms
And decimate the camp of the angels of rest.

LXXX

Leoun went climbing from floor to floor
Of a sky-block with milk-light under every door.
I had to follow where Leoun chose to lead
Into a swarming hive of milk-white bees.
In cosmology this is called the Milky Way.

LXXXI

So blood riddled the walls of Troy.
So danced Saint Guy so danced Saint Elmo
Under the milky lustre-bough of mistletoe
So the fleur-de-lys on the banner of France.

LXXXII

The excited stars feigned indifference.
The farther Leoun led the nearer I came
The crueller their hard horrid eyes became.
They peer jealously for each other's disasters.

270

LXXXIII

Like sovereign states the stars hate their neighbours.
The will to battle sharpens their glances.
Some of them are raddled. Others pensive.
Some whose light waxes by self-destruction.
But all have hard hearts with swords for self-protection.

LXXXIV

I could no longer count the fever of their fires.
But the most inflamed of all were the dead stars.
News of their burning-out is slow to travel.

LXXXV

The chestnut tree of night made its chestnuts bristle
Sea urchins threatened in the deep sea of the night.
The peace that children worship with hands joined
Sparkled with pride explosives and points.
The sky like the sea must defend its fruit.

LXXXVI

I saw Leoun break out in a prismatic sweat.
A mimetic change Leoun then underwent.
Knife-like irradiations broke
From the pale folds of her cloak.
The threat of danger put her on her guard.

LXXXVII

Iron Maid of Nuremburg pointedly barbed
Madonnas radiating Spanish daggers
Sebastian and his tree shot down in arrows
Strands of barbed-wire, cactus, briar:
Leoun travels armed as you are.

LXXXVIII

Can I survive this? Or is this final?
How can I bandy stab for stab with this arsenal?

LXXXIX

Time was I saw women in opera-boxes eagerly
Await adulation of unarmed equerry,
Evening-dress a-bristle with fiery pins,
The Opera transformed to a plush pin-cushion
And burning lightning cauterising low-lit crimson.
Diamond bristles when woman turns.
If lover leaning over diamond hover
Diamond lunges and transpierces lover.

XC

Yes, I have seen some eminent duels at the Opera.
Cruel killers excited by lustre.
Too bad since the war those battles do not take place.

XCI

But these battles do take place in the world where I race.
I have no right to complain of their heart-plunging.
Who could prevent a star from lunging
Or the killers of heaven from stabbing out my eyes?
Any act affronts the proud walkers of the skies.

XCII

How is it with me? Limps my right leg.
Leaps my weak heart. My left leg drags.
Eye can scarcely see my hand upheld.

XCIII

Not too blind to know it's a hundred years old.
No need to finger my beard to know the truth:
I am old. Leoun has stolen my youth.

XCIV

I wanted to override the physical type
And wide awake outwit the wiles of sleep
Believe that our time and dream-time coincided.
See my raised hand? Forlorn hope exploded.

XCV

Pharaohs masked in gold gloved in papyrus,
Hands lay littering the sands of Egypt
When embalmers drained your branches of their juice.

XCVI

My cast-off hand littered the seeming track
Where no rash venturer's footfall leaves a mark:
Thus Pharaoh tries to hold the ages back
By challenging from his gay sarcophagus.

XCVII

Crossing their swords the stars feinted and thrust.
My severed hand lay at the end of my dead wrist.
A black bloody ivy bound a web of tendrils
Round a root with bones and finger-nails.
My hand dies first. But a star interjects.
Once my hand is dead, it kills me next.

XCVIII

Where is Leoun? Where the duel of arrogant stars?
It is my age, my city, morning in my room,
It is my own fatigue leadening my limbs
These are my own hands gauntleting my arms.

XCIX

Our unexampled city of flight-by-night and butchery
By night is like the statue of the Commendatorè.
Shadow-play and moon-play play trick by turn.
She is Commendatorè. She is Saint Petersburg.
(I speak of time past.) So I watched her go
Through my stereoscope in her amazing snow . . .
Paris walks beyond the marches of death.

C

And the Palais-Royal empty for Thermidor heat.
Its silence, haunted by the bluish flicker
Of lamps, passed back and forth between its two theatres.

273

CI

To the one dark couples went pushing and noisy.
The other bills Hugo and Alfred de Musset.
Racine was savage. Moliere blood-chilling.
Those circus games where Love does the killing.
The crowd stands waiting panting at the games
Under the vaulting of a snowbound maze.
The theatre-yard and antique taxi-cabs
No longer glimmer under mistletoe bulbs
While sheltering at every cellar-door
A beaver-hatted satin-slippered whore.

CII

Poets and actors are scared of little girls.
(In the Underground rages an autograph war.)

CIII

At the middle is a ghost shut in by the grills.
Frantically endlessly struggling, this ghost,
To climb on to the chair to take the oath
To hoist the Toothpick Lady to the balcony.
The universe conspires to give him the lie.
Here History lies dead. Her act is done.
Fenced in with golden grills as night comes on.

CIV

This place works by clockwork. It has lost its soul.
Its dream shelters behind a Chinese Wall.
Nothing sold here now but patent and Croix d'honneur.

CV

Palace of Don Juan Rampart of Elsinor
Your walking dead would leave me less dismayed
Than the Palais-Royal's girdling arcade
And less dismayed at your grandees from Hell
Than the familiar noise of its iron grills.
They pull them down of an evening. Raise them at dawn.
One of these iron curtains shattered my dream.

CVI

God! If one night in her magic world Leoun
Found an escape route from the eternal round
If she were only to mistake her way
If Fate restored her as Fate takes away
I should not again quit her solemn heels.

CVII

But for her walks she chooses other tunnels.
Those of the Palais-Royal might serve as frame
For her angelic swagger – after a dream-change.
There I might see her high-stepped heel again.

CVIII

I was day-dreaming. As afloat the swan
Offsets a ludicrous and clumsy walk
By neck's italic question-mark
So Leoun knows the world where she belongs.

CIX

For true Leoun is Leoun false.

CX

This night-song I write in chalks
On spiteful slate. Efface it, passer-by,
With tears of rage and bloody sigh.

CXI

How you astonish me, hairnets and leaves,
Girdles of bones and collars for cannibal chiefs,
On the purple knickers of the flayed-alive!
One flayed alive writes these naive
Verses where a fairground roundabout whirls on its axis
To utter disregard of the by-play of syntaxis.

CXII

The flayed-alive in skin reclad
Dies furled alive in his own flag.
He was asleep. He wakes. He writes a poem.
The poem – he knows – is not the kind to charm.
He does not wish to write it. Writes it all the same.
(So lovers write on walls.)
And so a hard-boiled Muse maltreats us all
The stuck-up bitch has no respect for anyone.
Leoun was the Muse or the Muse Leoun.

CXIII

Let me go: I shall write whatever I fancy!
Aren't you sick of pulling out my hair
And knotting it tight to the top of your lyre?

CXIV

Let me go! Let me go! I abhor your frenzy
My hair strung in hatred to the lyre
And the assizes where flayed I expire.

CXV

Ruthless Maenad you my daytime Muse
Leoun walks on remote from both of us.
Harrowing the internal world is what you like.
Automatically the mocker takes your side.
I know your tricks of sending your victims
To face the court and fork out for your crimes
Of twisting your lovers up like bits of wire
Of chaining bone to ghost and nerve to hair
Of leaving us half-dead – in fits of laughter.
You don't like what I write? Then do the other!
I know some chinks in your armour you can't hide.
I dare you.

CXVI

Sirs, what you write is a fraud

CXVII

Mirage Lady with uplifted scythe
Entering my theatre through the looking-glass
Will you take liberties like those astral tarts?
Will you torment me to catch me alive?
And if such be your plan, what warning will you give?
Dreaming is monstrous. Waking monstrous too.
Can I hope to find true peace of mind with you?
Shall I have to follow you through some worse complex?

CXVIII

Sleeping and waking have played me too many tricks
I long to break off and put paid to their rancour.

CXIX

If you are plotting my more ingenious torture
Can I sleep at the end untroubled by any dream?
You write? And your books are read, may I ask, by whom?
Does a world exist where I shall not have to speak?
Need I tremble there at Leoun and her panther-feet?
Need I tremble there at the Muse with claws like a lion?

CXX

Need I tremble there at the sky with its thousand million
Eyes intent on pulling our whole world down?
Your forbidden city is truly an open town
Where I can evade the shame of offering fight?
Someone is watching me.
                    Look out.
                              Keep quiet.

JEAN COCTEAU   ALAN NEAME
1942-44   1947-57

                                     (1960-61)

277

PAUL CELAN

Speak, you also

Translated by Michael Hamburger

Speak, you also,
speak as the last,
have your say.

Speak –
But keep yes and no unsplit.
And give your say this meaning:
give it the shade.

Give it shade enough,
give it as much
as you know has been dealt out between
midnight and midday and midnight.

Look around:
look how it all leaps alive –
where death is! Alive!
He speaks truly who speaks the shade.

But now shrinks the place where you stand:
Where now, stripped by shade, will you go?
Upward. Grope your way up.
Thinner you grow, less knowable, finer.
Finer: a thread by which
it wants to be lowered, the star;
to float farther down, down below
where it sees itself gleam: in the swell
of wandering words.

From: *Von Schwelle zu Schwelle* (1955)

(1971)

GIUSEPPE UNGARETTI

Contrite

Translated by Hugh MacDiarmid

I gang prowlin' roon'
My sheep's body
Wi' the hunger o' a wolf.

I am like
A wallowin' barge
On a tumultuous ocean.

Weep and Wail No More

Translated by Hugh MacDiarmid

Stop killin' the deid. Gi'e owre
Your weepin' and wailin'. You maun keep quiet
If you want to hear them still
And no' blur their image in your mind.

For they've only a faint wee whisperin' voice
Makin' nae mair noise ava'
Than the growin' o' the grass
That flourishes whaur naebody walks.

(1970)

DAVID ROKEAH

Mosaic

Chips of stone from Zovah for the mosaic.
Quartz spears from Mitzpe-Ramon in your heart.
Black shells from the sea near Achsiv.

Paint the night
which hunts a chestnut moon
between white mosque and copper dome,
eastwards, beyond the wall.
Paint the hour which joins no other hour,
the fevered silence

on the roofs of Sanhedria
rising to the moon like cracked vermilion bowls,
their pigment fading.

Chips of stone for the mosaic. The memories too.
Forsaken by love men curse the light

Decipher

Decipher the code of silence
earth did not break
in her geological pangs
and gather lost thunders
into stalactites.
At the mouth of the cave an old carob tree
flowers for the last time

Translated from the Hebrew by Ruth and Matthew Mead
in collaboration with the author.

(1979)

EZRA POUND

L'ultima Ora

from Montanari

When the will to singing fails
and there be left him no choice
but to rest without singing voice,
forever, unending, arms crossed,

Let it be by the roadside
where the ditch is wide and deep
and the smell of his fields, in sleep
can come to him, and the note of the robin,

And the elms can be there companionable
to him, as evening draws to its close
in the savour of spring time
melancholy a little, ending together.

(1964)

PART FOUR

Two Landmarks of Prose

T.S. ELIOT

Scylla and Charybdis

My writings, in prose and verse, may or may not have surprised other people: but I know that they always, on first sight, surprise myself. I have often found that my most interesting or original ideas, when put into words and marshalled in final order, were ideas which I had not been aware of holding. It is ordinarily supposed that a writer knows exactly what he wants to say, before he sits down at his desk; and that his subsequent labours are merely a matter of a better choice of words, a neater turn of phrase, and a more orderly arrangement. Yet I have always discovered that anything I have written – anything at least which pleased me – was a different thing from the composition which I had thought I was going to write. Perhaps I never quite know what I am saying until I have said it. Whether I have undertaken the particular task spontaneously, or whether it is a task set for me by circumstances, the element of the unexpected always plays a great part.

Hence the importance, at an early stage, of the title. One begins by choosing a title, in order to assure oneself that one has a subject: for a title is a kind of substitute or shadow of a subject. Now the relation of title to subject, and of both to the final composition, is, in the case of this address which I am at the moment delivering, a peculiar one. I am, as you may already have noted with impatience, curious about the process by which anything gets written: I am the more tempted to indulge this curiosity on the present occasion, because the Centre Meditérranéen is so closely associated in my mind with the name of the great explorer of thought, feeling and language who was Paul Valéry. So, in the first place, I will reveal that the title of this lecture not only preceded the subject, but was itself due to a misunderstanding. In correspondence with your President, M. Emile Henriot, I complained of the difficulties of deciding on what to talk about to an unknown audience; and I added, in a parenthetical and ejaculatory way: 'Scylla and Charybdis! to avoid both frivolity and dullness!' Your President, under the impression that I was offering this remark as a subject, replied at once that he thought it a happy idea, and that this title would be announced. I did not immediately correct him, because I wanted to wait until I had thought of something else. And then I said to myself: 'Why not?' The title is in itself a good one. The myth belongs to that Mediterranean world from which our culture springs; it refers to a well-known episode in Mediterranean pre-history; like other myths in the story of Ulysses it is what I believe Professor Jung would call a universal archetype of human experience. It responds to some of the deepest desires, and terrors of all human beings: it is the experience of life itself. It is applicable to almost any subject one can discuss. So, having had the title thrust upon me, I launched with zest into the exploration of my own mind, curious to discover what I might find there.

I turned then to consider the significance of Scylla and Charybdis in Poetry; for it is my experience that to enlist the attention of an audience it is best to begin from what one is generally supposed to know something about. It struck me at once that while trying to write a poem I am frequently in the position of the Homeric navigator in that particular difficulty. It is supposed that the poet, if anybody, is engaged in perpetual pursuit of *the right word*. My own experience would be more accurately described as the attempt to avoid the wrong word. For as to the right word, I am not convinced it is anything but a mirage. I will try to justify this opinion.

To take the problem first in its simplest form. The word which is the right word in one respect may be the wrong word in another. The *poetic* value, the poetic *meaning* I may say, of a passage of verse, depends upon three things: the literal meaning of the word, the associations of the word, and the sound of the word. The word with the exact meaning you want may be very far from euphonious in the context of the words among which it must be fitted. The word which has the right sound in that place may not mean quite what you want it to mean. Either choice means shipwreck. If the word makes the wrong noise, the surface of the poem is defaced; if it has the wrong meaning, the poem will not stand examination. In neither case, is the result poetry.

To illustrate this simple dilemma to you briefly and cogently, I should have to find instances in French. But few persons, and certainly not myself, know any language but their own intimately enough to be sure of themselves in choosing illustrations. So perhaps an insoluble problem which I encountered in the course of my own work, may suffice, as I do not need to quote the English line of verse. In one of my poems, 'The Dry Salvages', I had occasion to describe the sort of debris found on a sea beach, and among it the shells of a particular kind of crab. On re-reading the poem some time after the final text had been published, I was horrified to observe that I had referred to the wrong kind of crab – the *hermit* crab which has no shell of its own, but takes for a habitation the shell of some other deceased crustacean. The hermit crab, having no shell of its own, could hardly be identified by a shell on the beach; and indeed, I am not sure that I have ever seen a hermit crab. The crab I had in mind was the *horseshoe* crab. I knew the difference perfectly well: how was it that after spending months in re-writing and revising that poem, I had failed to notice that I continued to associate the name of one kind of crab with the mental picture of another? Simply because the sound of the word *hermit* fitted perfectly for my line, and the sound of *horseshoe* was harsh. In such a dilemma, there was only one choice: to put in the right crab, and sacrifice the sound.

In another situation, it might be desirable to take the other course and sacrifice sense to sound. Such dilemmas are frequent in the choice of words. Sometimes there is no one word which will do. The line of verse would be very much more effective if there was that word, but in its absence you must sacrifice concision and have recourse to a phrase or a periphrasis. In another poem, for instance, I found myself in great difficulties for a word to express *twilight before dawn*, as distinct and different from *twilight before night*. The word *dusk*, in English, means either: but its immediate denotation, to every English speaking person, is the evening. I suppose that is simply due to the fact that everybody is about in the evening, and only a minority of people are out of doors before dawn. (I have chosen this instance because I believe that *crépuscule* presents the same difficulty as *dusk*). I believe that I could have found one word meaning the dusk of morning, in one or more English country dialects, because country people are more likely to need such a word than townsfolk. But a dialect word – apart from the fact that its obscurity would probably have required a footnote – would have aroused the wrong associations. The scene I was describing was in a London street; the personages in the scene were not people who would express themselves in country dialect; and any dialect word would have been most unsuitable. So, after giving up the hope of finding one word, I had to try to find two words. The substantive word could only be *dusk*; there would have to be an adjective to indicate *which* dusk I meant; and if necessary I should have to support it with some other indication of the time of day. I first hit upon a word which seemed to me, for a short time, to be a real *trouvaille*: the adjective *antelucan* 'before the light'; in the great Oxford dictionary it is defined as: 'of or pertaining to the hours just before dawn'. Its meaning was exactly what I required, and I was much taken by the *sound* of the word. It is a word of Latin origin which appears to have been adapted to the English language during the Sixteenth Century, when a great many new English words – many of which have since been abandoned – were coined by scholars directly from Latin. As I do not find it in *Littré*, it does not appear to have been adopted into French. But here was a word with the right meaning and a very agreeable sound which nevertheless would not do. It is a rare word. Though its meaning is clear enough, such a word is appropriate only for an *ornate* style; and the passage into which I wished to insert it was in a very deliberately *plain* style: the word would have attracted attention to itself, and away from the task it had to perform. It might have been a suitable word if I had been writing in the style of Milton; but in my context it would have had the incongruity of a spectator appearing in full evening dress at a football match. So I had in the end to put 'waning dusk'. It was not what I wanted: but it was, I believe, the best that the English language could do for me.

I hope I have not taxed your attention too long with what may seem problems of interest only to those of the *métier*; because these reflections on the verbal difficulties of the poet lead up to problems of wider interest. My point is that the perpetual compromise with words, the necessity for vigilant attention to the literal meaning, the associations and the sound, has a bearing on the process of development of the original idea. In avoiding the several dangers of navigation, the poet cannot be too much concerned with the choice of the port which he hopes eventually to reach. It is necessary certainly, in a poem of any length, to have a plan, to lay a course. But the final work will be another work than that which the author set out to write; and will, as I have already suggested, be something of a surprise to the author himself. For the *idea* behind a poem will always be less than the *meaning* of the poem: the meaning depends upon the musical structure as well as upon the intellectual structure. In a poem, one does not altogether know what it is that one has to say, until one has said it; for what one intends to say is altered in the course of making poetry of it.

All this has a bearing upon the endlessly discussed problem of form and content, of *la poésie pure*, and of what is nowadays called *engagement*. The problem of Scylla and Charybdis is now appearing in the following form: should we regard poetry as a vehicle for the expression of our ideas, beliefs, emotions, observations and experiences, or should we consider these ideas, beliefs, emotions, observations and experiences simply as the material out of which we make a poem?

It is obvious that there are here two problems: that of the poet himself, and that of the reader of poetry. The poet may consciously intend to do one thing, and unconsciously achieve something else: the result may be something either better or worse than what he set out to do. In either event, he is judged by the achievement rather than the intention. The reader, however, who enjoys a poem under the impression that it is something different from what it is, is hardly to be congratulated upon his capacity for appreciation. Let us turn our attention, then, to the poem.

Here one would like to be able to give illustrations of bad poetry; and this is always difficult to do effectively. If the bad poetry one cites is unknown to the audience, the reference is ineffective. But the bad poetry of the past is soon forgotten by all but a few curious scholars; and to cite bad poetry of the present would be unkind to living authors. So I will ask you to accept my assurance that I have gained in the course of my life a very extensive acquaintance with bad and indifferent verse. It comes to me daily, from all quarters of the world; chiefly, of course in English; but in other languages too, and even in languages wholly unknown to me – for the last, I can only guess at its quality from the laws of probability. The worst, of course, is that in which the authors have nothing to say, and do not know how to say it. But the rest is divisible into two kinds: that in which the author has something to say, but does not make poetry of it; and that in which the author has nothing to say, but says it rather charmingly. At these two extremes we are exasperated or bored by the result: at the one, we are annoyed with the author who appears to be merely making use of verse, and exploiting its resources, for purposes of exposition or persuasion; at the other we feel that the author has been wasting our time with something trivial. In either case an imposture, conscious or unconscious, has been attempted: either to deceive us into believing that an idea has been transmuted into poetry, or into believing that a melodious arrangement of words contains an idea.

Between the extremes of two kinds of bad poetry, however, there is a range in which good poetry can differ widely. With some good poetry, we are, in reading it, more attentive to what the author is saying; with other good poetry, more attentive to the way in which he says it. For me, the poet who can make a fine poem with the minimum of the poetic, and at the other end of the scale the poet who can make a fine poem with the minimum of content, are always the subject of particular interest. At the one extreme, we might point to the *Divine Comedy* of Dante, and the poems of St. John of the Cross; at the other to some of the lyrics in Shakespeare's plays – notably those in *The Tempest*. But in choosing these illustrations I must make an important qualification. Dante may give the impression of being concerned with what he has to say, rather than with the way in which he says it: but we know perfectly well that no poet has ever given closer attention than did he to the technical problems of versification and language, or has ever attained a greater mastery of the *craft*. And as for Shakespeare's songs, though they are magical even when extracted from their context, they have a dramatic value also, which means that for their author they were a necessary detail in the structure of the scene in which they occur: their significance is due to the context in which we find them.

Let us try to find some other illustration, therefore, than Shakespeare's songs, of genuine poetry with the minimum of content. And here I must make a distinction. There are poems in which the content appears unimportant because the poem is a perfect and individual expression of commonplaces; there are others in which the content appears unimportant because we do not know what it is, and yet can enjoy and appreciate the poem without the necessity of knowing what it is. In my own enjoyment of poetry, at least, these are two distinct experiences. For the perfect and final expression of the commonplace, I can think of no better example than Gray's *Elegy in a Country Churchyard*. For those who do not know the poem, I will say briefly that it is, naturally, a meditation on mortality. The poet remarks that the graves are those of humble peasants who were once living and are now dead. In death we are all equal, and it does not matter very much whether we have an impressive monument or a plain stone. This leads to the conjecture that one or two of the obscure people buried here may have had gifts which would have brought them to fame and power had circumstances favoured such success. He ends with a rather improbable epitaph upon a young man, dead before his prime, who, one infers, might in other circumstances have become a distinguished poet.

I have alluded to this particular poem because it is a good

example of a beautiful poem which is nearly all platitude. Such poems are untranslatable: they can only be paraphrased by another poet of genius who can clothe the same international platitudes in the beauties of his own language. *'Rien n'est plus beau que le lieu commun'* says Baudelaire somewhere. From Homer to our own day, poetry has depended upon it. And we should be mistaken if we said that a poem like this, containing no strikingly original idea, was poetry of form rather than content. The content is never negligible. But we may say, I think, that the *idea* of a poem, or the ideas in it, so far as they can be expressed in words other than those of the poem itself, *must* be platitude, or rather, must belong to a genus of which what we call platitude or the 'commonplace' is a species.

Within this genus I include *The Divine Comedy*. What is the difference, with regard to the content of idea, between *The Divine Comedy* and Gray's *Elegy*? There is not merely a much greater number and variety of ideas, or a much more complex structure. The ideas themselves are more philosophic: that is, they are commonplaces for a much smaller number of people than the commonplaces of Gray's poem. That is the difference. The commonplaces of Gray are known to everybody and accepted by everybody: no mental effort is necessary to apprehend them. The commonplace is a matter of degree. It is when the statement is familiar to everyone – as, for instance, the statement that all men are mortal – that we say it is the form and not the content that makes that poem.

It is not only, however, the immediate accessibility and simplicity of the idea that makes us attend to form rather than content. The same thing happens in an antithetical case: when the idea is inaccessible. When a poem is so obscure that we do not know what the meaning is, or even what it is about, but when nevertheless it gives us enduring delight in a high degree, then also we are inclined to say that it is the form and not the content that matters. I pass from Gray to Mallarmé: no two poets, surely, could be more different. I have read, or attempted to read, a number of treatises written to explain the meaning of Mallarmé's poems. I am not prepared to deny the value of such investigation of origins; but I have never found that they enhanced my enjoyment of the poem. On the contrary, I have sometimes been tempted to say: 'if that is all there is to the poem, apart from a felicitous arrangement of syllables, it is not so fine a poem as I thought it was – perhaps I was mistaken'. But my mind obstinately refuses to believe this: I return to the poem, and I still enjoy it, after forgetting the explanation. Some of the 'explanations', indeed, set forth no more than certain accidents of circumstance which made the poem germinate in the poet's mind: these seem to me curious, but irrelevant. Others – especially when it come to *Un coup de dès* or *Igitur* – profess to set forth an underlying philosophy: but the philosophy, as expounded by the interpreter, never seems to me quite worthy of the poem. Yet I do not draw the conclusion, from the lack of concurrence between the interpretation of the poem and my enjoyment of it, either that Mallarmé's poems are meaningless, and consequently that it is not necessary for a great poem to mean anything, or even that I myself can enjoy a poem knowing that it has no meaning. A poem that means nothing must be trivial – and therefore cannot be genuinely a poem. It has merely given us a momentary illusion; but I am sure that, the moment we perceived an absence of meaning, we should all reject it. Mallarmé's poem is for me therefore at the opposite extreme from *The Divine Comedy*, only within these limits: that I can enjoy a canto of Dante while paying conscious attention only to what he is saying, and a sonnet of Mallarmé while paying conscious attention only to the way in which he says it. But this does not mean that the verbal genius and technical mastery of Dante, or the meaning of Mallarmé's sonnet, are not essential to my enjoyment of the poem.

I have held the view, and expressed it here and there in essays for many years past, that a poet does better to take over his 'philosophy' from the philosophers, than to invent his own. This comes down to a simple division of function: the genius for conceptual formulation and abstraction, which the greatest philosophers possess, and the genius for transmuting a philosophy into poetry, were in my opinion, quite distinct: it would be a miracle, and almost a monstrosity, for the two gifts, to the point of genius, to co-exist within the same mind. On this ground, I exalted the poems of Lucretius and Dante at the expense of the philosophical books of Blake; and I even went so far as to maintain that an inferior, fragmentary or chaotic philosophy could serve a great poet, in certain circumstances, as well as a more dignified one; for otherwise we should be obliged, for this reason alone, to admit the inferiority of Shakespeare to Dante.

I now believe that I have seen a little farther into the matter. I am inclined to think that we may mean two quite different things, when we speak of the 'philosophy' of a poet: first, a philosophy which he either takes over, or has attempted to devise for himself in the *language of philosophy*, and another 'philosophy' which can only be expressed in *the language of poetry*, and which is, in the truest sense, the poet's own contribution. Certain observations of Professor Pieper of Muenster, on the relation of the philosophic to the poetic activity, have encouraged me in this view. When we study the Aristotelian and Thomist metaphysic, for the purpose of understanding Dante better, we are increasing our knowledge, certainly, but it is knowledge of *origins*, of the material which went to form the poem. But the philosophy of Dante *qua* poet is a different matter from his philosophy *qua* student of the philosophers. If for instance we read certain of the more philosophic passages of the *Purgatorio*, translating them back into the terms of the *De Anima* of Aristotle, we may simply marvel that the poet has been able to make poetry of such austere and refractory matter. But the fact that it has been transmuted into poetry means that we are no longer in the same world of discourse as that of Dante's philosophical masters. On the other hand, this view of the matter explains to me my disappointment in the interpretations of Mallarmé. The philosophy of a poet cannot be translated into conceptual terms. What we do, when we apply the attempt to Mallarmé, is to reduce his poetic philosophy to an inferior conceptual philosophy. In neither case are we estimating the intellectual achievement of the poet.

By this statement, I do not mean to suggest, either that Mallarmé is as great a poet as Dante, which he certainly is not; or that it is worth while to discuss the work of every poet with reference to his 'philosophy'. It may be that I am risking confusion, in my own mind as well as in yours, by using the word 'philosophy' in two senses. In the ordinary sense, when we ask 'what is the philosophy of so and so?' – mentioning a poet, we expect the answer to be in terms of some philosopher or school of philosophers. If the poet in question is Dante, we answer 'Aristotle and Aquinas'; if Lucretius, we reply glibly 'the Epicurean philosophy'. Or, in the case of Goethe, we have to use a great many more words: we have to consult all of Goethe's writings, his letters, the reports of his conversation, trace the origin of all his ideas, and attempt to constitute them into an intelligible and coherent whole. But in either case, we are replying as we should to the same question when asked about any person with whom we are acquainted. When asked 'what does so and so believe?' we are usually satisfied if we are informed whether he is Catholic, Protestant, Spiritualist,

Theosophist or Rationalist, and at the same time are given the name of some political party to which he adheres. We are usually satisfied if we are told what the man *professes* to believe. If there is an evident contradiction between his profession of belief and his behaviour, we are reduced to conjecture. If we suspect the man of hypocrisy, we may make a likely guess; but if we suspect that his own mind is confused, and that he has not put his beliefs into order, we may say 'he doesn't know what he believes'. And in few human beings do we find a complete consistency of belief and behaviour; nor, in the greater part of life, is such consistency to be demanded: in one aspect, our beliefs are those ideas and principles which we maintain consciously throughout our life, and on the other hand, our belief at any particular moment is the *way in which we behave that moment*. Only, perhaps, in facing and accepting martyrdom, is a man's religious belief completely realised and authenticated.

The difference may be made a little clearer if I cite specifically religious or *devotional* poetry (Dante escapes from this category). In such poetry the commonest failure occurs when the author's conceptual philosophy is one which he *wants* to believe, but to which his intellectual assent is not complete. That is the most usual reason for the failure of would-be religious poets. Among the writers of good devotional poetry are those whose belief is genuine and passionate, but in whose work the personality of the author is essential: we share his feelings, we experience our exaltation through him. Of such is George Herbert. In another and higher category I should put St. John of the Cross, in whose poems the emotion is so directly the consequence of the idea that the personality of the author is, somehow, annihilated: in experiencing his poems we seem to be in direct relation with what he saw, without any mediation through the personality of the author himself.

It would perhaps be best to speak of the 'philosophy of the author' when we mean the philosophy which he either adopted from philosophers, or devised for himself *qua* philosopher; and the 'philosophy of the poem' when we mean what is found only in the poem itself and cannot be translated into concepts. It might be helpful if I recalled our point of departure. We started from the ordinary distinction of *content* and *form*, and noted that in common terms we may find ourselves enjoying one poem for what the poet is saying, and another poem because of the way in which he says it. In the one case we are inclined to consider the form of expression merely as *means*, in the other to consider the content merely as *material*. This is a matter of experience. At the one extreme, we have to ask 'why is this a poem, and not versified prose?' and at the other 'why is this not nonsense?' I am not here concerned with the limiting cases; but with the question: 'what is the relation between the value of a poem and the value of the ideas out of which it is composed?' And I ask this question because of my own experience, specifically as an instance with the poetry of Mallarmé. I do not feel, in reading Mallarmé's poems, that I am enjoying them because of their 'form' only: I find the content important. But I feel no impulse to try to explain to myself what a poem of Mallarmé is about; and, as I have said, when I have read explanations of their meaning I have always felt cheated. The Interpreter may be right, on his own plane of discourse; but what I am offered is something different from what I want. In the case of Dante it is something highly respectable in its own kind, a recognisable philosophy; in the case of Mallarmé it is something comparatively trivial. That is the only difference. And I feel that the poet has given me something which has caused in me an enjoyment which I cannot call simply sensuous: he has given me an intellectual exercise and an intellectual delight, which is different from that given me by the prose explanation.

Whether I am justified in referring to the cause of this intellectual pleasure as 'the philosophy of the poem' can only be judged by the reception of the phrase by my public – which is, first of all, yourselves: for, as I have warned you, these reflections have only come to me as the result of meditating upon my title, 'Scylla and Charybdis'. Obviously, the phrase 'the philosophy of the poem' is not equally applicable to every kind of poem. It is most relevant to the poems of those poets who, if they had not been poets, might have been philosophers. That includes poets who, if they had turned to philosophy instead of to poetry, might have achieved only a very modest place as philosophers. Among these latter, I do not disguise the fact that I include myself. (For I take it as inevitable, that when a poet theorises about poetry, the kind of poetry upon which his attention is centred is his own kind of poetry. And, as Valéry has said: '*il n'est pas de théorie qui ne soit un fragment, soigneusement préparé de quelque autobiographie'*.)

When I speak of 'the philosophy of a poem', then, I have in mind primarily a poem by a poet who has pursued philosophic studies, and who has even elaborated philosophic theories of his own. These have played an important part in his formation, and will make their appearance in his poetry, but in a form in which they are no longer maintained as theories, but presented as something experienced, and go to compose, together with his experience of life of all other kinds, the material of his poem. Different philosophies, or opposed philosophical opinions which cannot in the philosophical area of discourse be maintained at once, may thus be united and poetically reconciled. I should say, furthermore, that in this operation there is an intellectual work of organisation, which is analogous to the work of the conceptual philosopher. And I should maintain that the experience of the sensitive reader, in assimilating such a poem, is analogous in kind to his experience in assimilating the work of a philosopher. Only, *understanding*, with a philosophic work and with a poem, is a very different thing. It is owing to the misunderstanding of the fact that there is more than one kind of *understanding*, that we have inflicted upon us so many false explanations of philosophical poetry: those in fact, which reduce the philosophy of a poem to conceptual terms: whether of the poet's philosophical masters, or of his own thought when he was philosophising and not writing a poem.

With regard to the conceptual philosophy which a poet borrows from philosophers, or invents for himself *qua* philosopher, there are reservations to be made. The considerations I have been discussing are not, of course, equally applicable to every type of poetry, nor are they equally important in every poem of the same type. They are applicable to the degree in which philosophical ideas have contributed to forming the poet's mind and have been digested into (we might say *composted* into) that profound *couche* of experience which constitutes the soil in which the germs of his poetry are nourished. They are peculiarly applicable when the matter of a poem, rich with philosophical ingredients, is *organised* into a structural design. But neither the presence of such elements, nor their organisation, is a universal condition of *all* poetry. The *value* we assign to the poem in which they are found has no direct relation to our valuation of the original ideas in their conceptual forms: it is possible not only to make a bad poem out of the greatest philosophy, but a very fine poem out of a philosophy which, put abstractly, is almost negligible. Otherwise, we should have to assert, if we are Christians, that Dante is a greater poet than Homer or Virgil, Racine a greater dramatist than Sophocles; which would be manifestly absurd. The greatness of any particular poetry depends upon many things; among others upon the greatness of the language in which the poet writes; depends, therefore, upon the other poets who have previously written in the same language. It is hard, but I believe true, that some poet of limited gifts, who has the advantage of a great language, may be more important for the world than another poet, more richly endowed by nature, who has had to work in a language in itself of lower status in the world at large.

I come at last to a particular case of poetry which, in the sense which I have been trying to indicate, may be called philosophical. When I alluded, a little while ago, to Gray's *Elegy in a Country Churchyard*, that was not only for its illustrative value in that context, but with a view to a comparison I am about to draw. I cannot recall ever having read a comparative analysis of Gray's *Elegy* and *Le Cimetière Marin*, although I should be very surprised to learn that no one had yet drawn the parallel. An English poet of the Eighteenth Century, and a French poet of the Twentieth, have both written poems of meditation in a cemetery – each, the finest poem on this subject in its language. Each is a poem which anyone must know, who has any pretension to acquaintance with the poetry of that language. The comparison is peculiarly interesting in the present context.

Gray's poem is, of course, the perfection of an idiom and a versification which was a common style of poets of his time, and which had been brought to that point of excellence by a century of practice. Valéry's poem, on the other hand, is striking, from the first reading, by the triumphant boldness of its technical originality. I speak with diffidence, but I should suppose that in this poem of Valéry there is to be found a refreshment of French metric from Italian sources. I have spoken of Gray's *Elegy* as the distinguished expression of the commonplace. In Valéry's poem there are commonplaces – in what great poem are there not? – but there is a great difference between a poem in which commonplaces occur, and a poem based on the commonplace. Such a line as

La larve file où se formaient des pleurs

or even

Tout va sous terre en rentre dans le jeu

has all the force of the commonplace thought expressed in words which no one has found before: as with lines of Gray, I feel a kind of wonder and admiration as at a miracle of resuscitation of the dead. There are interesting differences on the same plane:

The breezy call of incense-breathing Morn

and

Les cris aigus des filles chatouillées –

there is more difference here than the difference between the Eighteenth and the Twentieth centuries, or even between what can be said in the two languages. But is there any important difference of type between the two poems?

The difference is fundamental. The content of Gray's poem, as I have said, consists chiefly of ideas which have occurred to all men in all languages at all times. Hence its structure is merely the plausible sequence by which one such thought leads to another. Valéry's poem has what I call the philosophic structure: an organisation, not merely of successive responses to the situation, but of further responses to his own responses. He has put more of himself into the poem – to that point at which the surrendering of the maximum of one's being to the poem ends by arriving at the maximum of impersonality.

Valéry solved the problem of Scylla and Charybdis in his own way, and because of his own peculiar combination of gifts. I cannot think of any other poet who could so certainly, if he had taken that course, have distinguished himself as a philosopher in the non-poetic sense. I can easily imagine him, had he made that choice in early life, as pursuing a course which would have led him to the Collège de France and such audiences as flocked, forty years ago, to the lectures of Henri Bergson. His parentage with Mallarmé seems to me exaggerated, or at least to be sometimes regarded as if he had no other lines of descent. His mind, in my opinion, was far more philosophical than that of Mallarmé, or than that of Edgar Poe to whom both poets have paid such generous tribute. Having turned to poetry, he achieved the miracle of writing poetry in which the approximation between the two modes of philosophising which I have tried to determine, the conceptual and the poetic, comes closer than in the work of any other poet. He remains a poet, because the translation of the content of any of his poems into conceptual terms converts it into something else – and *something else of less value*.

In remarking this unique character of Valéry's poetry I am not implying that he reached, or came nearer towards some goal towards which all poetry ought to strive, than anyone else. I have said nothing about his relative *greatness* compared to other poets. I only say of him that he explored what no one else has explored:

and if a poet gives us a few poems (for I rate *La Jeune Parque* and *La Cimetière Marin* as his triumphs) in which he has realised some potentiality of poetry as no one else has done or is likely to do, that, in itself, is glory.

Let me return to my two marine monsters. If a poet gives us the impression that he is employing his gifts to persuade us to accept a particular theory, or if on the other hand he seems to be exploiting, irresponsibly, a theory or a belief as material to make poetry out of, he will equally suffer shipwreck and destruction. The philosopher tries to make us *see* one aspect of reality; the poet tries to make us *see* another. These are two modes of contemplation: persuasion and propaganda belong to quite another universe of discourse. And yet there is one reservation to be made. Scylla and Charybdis cannot be escaped merely by having a good chart of the channel. Not all poets are equally conscious of what they are doing: and it may happen sometimes, that a poet succeeds in writing a fine poem with the wrong intentions. If his compass is in error, he may even, in laying his course directly for Scylla or directly for Charybdis, have the good fortune to pass triumphantly between them.

I should have liked to embark upon an examination of the Scylla and Charybdis of the dramatist – or even to proceed into more dangerous seas, and consider the Scylla and Charybdis of the politician which may be named *ideology* and *expediency*. But I must leave you to your own reflections on these matters, for I have, as lecturer, my own Scylla and Charybdis to avoid. I have escaped the Scylla of brevity, but I am in danger of the Charybdis of tedium.

February 1952

(1985)

DONALD DAVIE

Can Literary History Be Permitted?

In the grand project called 'history', literary history has never been granted more than a humble place. In the present century as literary criticism has demanded, and sometimes been granted, steadily more elevated status, literary history has lost what little esteem it had. And now when there are signs that literary criticism has overplayed its hand, so that its presumptions are seen to be indeed presumptuous, literary history has not benefited from the change. It is still seen as, if a discipline at all, a very shabby one.

In fact the project called 'history' is itself no longer grand. What we have been made to learn or to remember, not before time, is that what is called too loosely 'history' is properly 'historiography'; that all the books which offer themselves as 'histories' are in fact kinds of writing. No less than diplomatic or economic histories, literary histories are themselves pieces of literature, and of *imaginative* literature. No one doubted this, or made much of it, when Samuel Johnson printed his *Lives of the Poets* in 1779-81; it was only in the next century, when German savants floated the idea of a *scientific* historiography, that Johnson's sort of literary history fell into disrepute. If now one tries to write literary history on the Johnsonian model, one is bucking a consensus long established. But the truth is that, apart from Johnson's model, there is no other; every other seemingly available model in fact subordinates the chronicle of literature to economic or social or political presuppositions, if not (what in this field has proved the most rooted prejudice of all) *racist* presuppositions.

Kenneth Cox, a severe and admirably independent critic, has lately remarked of a would-be literary historian (myself): 'He posts himself at an imaginary point of vantage from where a question can be viewed under different aspects.' (*Agenda* 28.2) Cox's word is 'imaginary', not 'imagined' nor 'imaginative' nor 'imaginable'. The point of vantage which the historian occupies is thus declared to be, from the first, fallacious or fraudulent; and so the pretence that from that standpoint 'a question can be viewed under different aspects' is revealed as a bare-faced pretence indeed. Behind the threadbare illusion of impartial judiciousness, the historian is there in the middle of the *mêlée*, rigging the evidence, putting his thumb in the pan. Perhaps he deceives himself; the more reason that he should not deceive us. So the case for the prosecution unfolds. Yet consider... Samuel Johnson vehemently disliked republicanism, and that dislike colours his treatment of both John Milton's poetry and Edmund Waller's. All the same, the consensus over generations has been that, the prejudice once allowed for, Johnson's accounts of Milton and Waller still stand up, as judicious and even generous. In the sceptical and gibing climate of today, so determined to reduce all history not just to historiography but to partisan pamphleteering, that charitable option is no longer open: a literary historian averse to republicanism cannot (so the logic runs) be fair to republican poets. What looks like fairness on his part must be fraudulent. If Johnson's remarks on Milton and Waller still seem to have force, that forcefulness must be illusory, for otherwise we must suppose that Johnson transcended his ideological and social conditioning – a possibility not to be countenanced.

Let me come down to a specific case. Nothing that I have read of or about the late Hugh MacDiarmid (C.M. Grieve) persuades me that I would have found him agreeable, or even tolerable. He seems to have been a sort of person that I profoundly – and not just on ideological grounds – disapprove of. He figures however, quite largely, in *Under Briggflatts*, the chapter of literary history that I have tried to write. And he does so, not merely for the influence he has exerted, but for reasons more intrinsic. His writings, wasteful though they are, and dishonest, and self-aggrandizing, still add up to a personal witness unlike any other and not replaceable by any other. I rather profoundly disapprove of him, and (wearing my other cap as critic) I could confidently rubbish many of the passages of his writing that his admirers might put before me. But MacDiarmid's presence, though I find it so far from amiable, none the less imposes itself. Unable or unwilling to play the literary market-place, except very clumsily, MacDiarmid acted out one uncompromising way for life and art, under twentieth-century conditions, to work together. I do not approve nor recommend the sort of interaction that he practised. But I can, from a vantage-point very distant from his, applaud his conviction that such interaction there must be, and can approve his trying to implement it. Hugh MacDiarmid can indeed be, and must be, 'viewed under different aspects'. Those who want a quicker fix – 'Ranging shots', Kenneth Cox complains, 'leave a target located but unhit' – have come to the wrong shop; literary criticism may supply their needs, literary history can't. Ranging shots, bracketing the target, are what the historian's artillery is geared for; if you want a quick kill, look elsewhere.

On the other hand the historian is himself a killer. His lethal weapon is silence. To be left out of the record is worse than being pilloried therein; and whereas the critic may pelt the pilloried wretch, the historian need only pretend not to have noticed him. This looks like Olympian disdain; and no wonder it is resented. But this is one of those infrequent occasions in literary studies where totting up, and keeping a tally, has some point. In my history of twenty-five years of British verse I seem to have named with respect some fifty-seven verse-writers active in that span of years. To these Kenneth Cox adds seventeen more, whose names he implies are conspicuous by their absence. Thus the tally stands at seventy-four. But what previous quarter-century in the history of British poetry could be thought to have borne such abundant fruit? Does literary history, as distinct from bibliography, record seventy memorable poets between 1590 and 1615, between 1660 and 1685, between 1790 and 1815? Poetic talent, and the character that can harness such talent, are much rarer commodities than we like to remember when we look compassionately on our near-contemporaries. The historian, though he be the historian of his own times, has a duty to keep such statistical probabilities in mind. He will make mistakes, as Johnson mistook in attending to Elijah Fenton, Thomas Yalden, William Broome, Christopher Pitt. But there is no reason to think that the odds against poetry that matters are any shorter in the twentieth century than they were in the eighteenth. Many are called but few, very few, are chosen; it is a lesson that we are happy to learn about everybody's lifetime except our own.

But who is he to judge? Who appointed him? Thus the aggrieved cry of social democracy. And of course the question is unanswerable, in a social-democratic scheme of things. But that scheme has never applied to the world of the arts. The world of artistic aspiration and production is irremediably unequal, unjust. What gave Samuel Johnson the right to judge? Nothing, except his being Samuel Johnson who, though he was too compassionate towards Fenton and Yalden, Broome and Pitt, historically *placed* Milton and Waller, Dryden and Pope and Thomas Gray, with an acuity that we still have to weigh and accede to, or else quarrel with. Johnson's authority was not institutionalized; it was, as it still is, all *his*. What else should we expect, once we have acknowledged that literary history is itself a *genre* of literature? We know that literary history is possible because Johnson did it, he performed it. Others have done the impossible since: Sainte-Beuve, perhaps. But in English the monumental inauguration of literary history is surely Johnson's *Prefaces, Biographical and Critical, to the Works of the English Poets*. Literary history, we may say, should never have happened. But it did, and we inherit it.

What is intriguing, with a sort of intriguingness that confronts us continually with Johnson however we approach him, is that this founding monument of literary history appears just when other forces in what we call the Enlightenment had begun moving along paths that would ultimately reach the conclusion that literary history was disreputable, since it could never be other than a mask for other sorts of history, economic or social or ideological. Johnson, seemingly and chronologically a child of the Enlightenment, turns out to have been a very perverse and froward child indeed. In him the Enlightenment concocted its fiercest anti-body.

The literary historian cannot be, and must not try to be, impartial. If he models himself on Johnson, he will be conscious of his own partialities, will more or less boldly avow them, and then try to allow for them. Kenneth Cox discerns in me a partiality that I share with Johnson, when he lights on a passage where I write: 'We may hesitantly conclude that every poet's task is ultimately and essentially, if not mythopoeic, at any rate religious; and that it is dangerous for any poet to think otherwise'. To risk a hesitant conclusion is hardly the same as avowing a partiality, let alone (what Cox credits me with) an *obsession*. But he feels himself imperilled, and has me cast for the role of St. Dominic: 'The note of menace would be ugly if it were not absurd'. Literary history, always a faded and shabby endeavour and of late held to be groundless, can still, it appears, affect some readers as *threatening*. If literary history is a conclusively discredited activity, how can it still arouse such passions as are signalled by words like 'menace' and 'ugly' and 'absurd'?

I do not resent such words. I think they are disproportionate. But where's the harm in a little disproportion if it serves a good cause? And I think I can make it do so. For literary history is, undeniably, threatening. It threatens vested interests in the book trade, in various Chambers of Commerce planning 'Poetry Festivals', in academic institutions, in journalism, in manipulation of the public. This is so because it is, of its nature, inescapably *élitist*.

It declares, necessarily and of its nature, that most of the words uttered from public platforms in verse or prose, in syndicated columns and on TV programmes, are *lies*. This is what everyone knows, but no one will say. Literary history, if it is undertaken in a Johnsonian spirit, must say the unsayable: that most literary reputations, promoted and sustained by *hype*, are bogus; that the persons promoted as articulating our deepest sentiments are in fact articulating only the shallowest; that the best and most truthful writers of our time have, almost without exception, been sidelined, accorded at most a perfunctory respect. Literary history, conducted on these lines and by these principles, is therefore a deeply subversive activity – not because literary historians are congenitally bloody-minded, but because their training as *historians* leads them to think that our age, like all previous ages, will prefer the dishonest writer to the honest one; the slick tactician to the probing explorer; the comforting voice to the challenging one. (Of course the game-playing has become sophisticated: the comforting writer will 'come on' as challenging – particularly in the private and privileged area of sexual *mores*. But the literary historian is expected to see through such subterfuges.)

Why should anyone choose to play the part of literary historian? It is a very thankless office, sure to make many enemies and few friends. Perhaps there are people who perversely hanker for that equation. But more often the title is adopted by elderly people who reckon that at their stage of life they have nothing to lose. This may have been the motive of Johnson, who took on the chore of *Lives of the Poets* at the end of his long and bruising career in Grub Street, and was hauled over the coals for not joining in the adulation of Thomas Gray. A sort of coming clean is surely at the heart of it: at seventy a man or woman who has lived in the literary world has seen reputations come and go, has seen the frivolous writer preferred before the serious one (not always in the fullness of time to get his come-uppance), has seen the serious and disconcerting writer, as it might be Hugh MacDiarmid, shovelled happily into the margins as soon as he is dead, if not before. Doing justice, however belatedly, comes to seem imperative, a duty laid upon one's last years. If later and younger writers get less than justice, that is a risk to be run and a price that must be paid. There will be time for hasty verdicts on them to be reviewed. But for the dishonoured or inadequately honoured dead, if the claim is not acknowledged now, perhaps it never will be. That is the urgency which impels a literary historian of his own times. Even Felton and Yalden, Broome and Pitt, deserve to be remembered; and if Johnson had not remembered them, who but the bibliographer would now know even their names?

Thus literary history, we must agree, is anomalous. Its claims to be a scholarly discipline have been discredited, the grounds on which it claimed to stand have been shot from under it. However, both 'discipline' and 'grounds', in the sense I have just given them, hark back no further than to the eighteenth-century Enlightenment. 'It would be curious,' writes Kenneth Cox, 'if anyone expounding a theoretical subject should stray far from the vocabulary appropriate to it.' Now *there* is the dry and systematic voice of the Enlightenment. (For the subject in question, declared to be 'theoretical', is *buggery*). What impels literary history, and keeps it however frailly a going concern, depends on values that pre-date the Enlightenment, such values as we see honoured on gravestones in a churchyard. A keeping of the faith with the ancestors, even with the ancestors of no more than one generation before our own – this is what literary history, and perhaps all history so far as it knows what it is doing, recognizes as its overriding duty. Our responsibility as literary historians is commemoration, keeping in memory. If a post-Enlightenment morality does not recognize any such duty, that is too bad; it is a responsibility that, however anomalously, we shall, because we must, continue to discharge.

(1992)

PART FIVE

Essays

MOELWYN MERCHANT

The Coke Cantos

Now that we have all the *Cantos*, even to the *Drafts and Fragments*, it should be possible to match the final, massive achievement against the often-quoted projected summary: 'to write an epic which begins "In the Dark Forest", crosses the Purgatory of human error, and ends in the light' and to set this in turn against his description to his father, in a letter of 11 April 1927, of his plan for the close of the work: 'The "magic moment" or moment of metamorphosis, bust thru from quotidien into "Divine or permanent world", Gods, etc.'. Critics have in fact been reluctant to cope with the dilemma that the *Cantos* were consistently conceived by Pound as a unified whole but that to the very end of the work the 'quotidien' overlays the paradisal vision of 'the divine or permanent world'. In particular, the fact that the brooding presence of Sir Edward Coke, felt over some decades of creativity, should now emerge to dominate in full focus three of the final *Cantos* (107-109) has seemed so confounding that critics have seemed tacitly to ignore his presence. This is the more remarkable after the publication of the essay by David Gordon in *Paideuma* (Vol 4, Nos 2 and 3, 1975, pp. 223-299) in which the relation of Edward Coke to Confucian thought in Pound's work is magisterially explored. The continuity of Coke's presence, the congruity of his thought with other *personae* who dominate the *Cantos* is there wholly demonstrated. And yet Sir Edward Coke has seemed to fail to capture the critical imagination to the same degree as Adams or Jefferson, Malatesta or Confucius.

An obvious practical reason for this avoidance of a major issue is the difficulty of assuming Coke's assured significance in legal history. The last decade of Elizabeth's reign and the first two decades of the Stuarts' were seminal for the subsequent history of law and society in England; they were also turbulent and confused to a degree that is confounding to the legal historian. It is not the least of Pound's merits as an historian that both in the middle *Cantos* and in the closing sections of the work, he penetrates beyond the detail to the essential principles which underlay Coke's work. Nonetheless the story, as we shall see, is not clear and defies the neat categories which scholarship craves and which the earlier *personae* of the *Cantos* in large measure allowed.

But there is a problem beyond that of academic difficulty. Both latent and expressed, the parallels with the *Divine Comedy* have manifestly shaped much of the argument over the structure of the *Cantos*. Michael Alexander has succinctly expressed the analogy – and by implication the expectations it arouses:

> The *Cantos* are also arranged with some deference and reference to Dante's *Divine Comedy* – the gradual ascent to knowledge and illumination via Hell, Purgatory and Paradise. Again, the model is intermittently invoked; this *is a humanist Commedia* (*The Poetic Achievement of Ezra Pound*, Faber, 1979, p. 129).

True; and we should therefore expect illumination to lead to a transcending of the mundane; yet the 'quotidien' persistently intrudes; the harsh and all too mundane concerns of Coke in his confrontation with James echo the immediate concerns of Pound with the day-to-day. Is this an irreconcilable dilemma? Is the preconceived pattern, with its expectation of some kind of 'beatific vision' impossible in the very fabric of a humanist *Commedia*? and does the consequences of this dilemma define something of the tragic mystery of the last fragment but one?

> That I lost my center
> > fighting the world.
> The dreams clash
> > and are shattered –
> And that I tried to make a paradiso
> > > terrestre.

The last words of *Drafts and Fragments* assert the long-sought truth: 'To be men not destroyers', but over the closing years of creation there broods a darker matter, most movingly expressed in the fragment of CXX published in the latest New Directions edition of the *Cantos*:

> I have tried to write Paradise ...
>
> Let the Gods forgive what I
> > have made
> Let those I love try to forgive
> > what I have made.

Where in this final stage of the *Cantos* does Coke find his just place? Does his work in any way bridge the gap between aim and achievement? Have the *Institutes*, the massive commentary, 'Coke on Littleton', any key to this sense of final, if partial failure? Is a 'humanist *Commedia*' a 'paradiso terrestre' a self-defeating vision? or do the final *Cantos* and *Fragments* rather contain within their very fragmentariness a reconciliation, a conclusion which unites the visionary and the 'quotidien'?

We must return to Coke himself. Whether we encounter him in the pages of Holdsworth or in Catherine Drinker Bowen's *The Lion and the Throne* (Little, Brown, 1956), Coke is a protean figure, as complex as any in that complex age. His speeches and writings range from patient scholarly exposition to the vulgarest abuse (his academic butt, John Cowell, Regius Professor of Civil Law in Cambridge, became characteristically 'Dr Cow-heel'); scrupulous in his passionate defence of the Common Law against the invasion of Civil Law at the accession of James I, he was unscrupulous to an amazing degree in his manipulation of facts and authorities. Professor Samuel Thorne's Selden Society Lecture of 1952 demonstrates Coke's way with citation of authority:

> As a rule of thumb it is well to remember that sentences beginning 'For it is an ancient maxim of the common law' followed by one of Coke's spurious Latin maxims, which he could manufacture to fit any occasion and provide with an air of authentic antiquity, are apt to introduce a new departure... If I may formulate a theorem of my own, I advance this – the longer the list of authorities reconciled, the greater the divergence from the case cited.

But for all his dubious tampering with the historical evidence, Coke was clear that he stood for certain traditional liberties against the manifold encroachments upon them which he saw follow the accession of a Scottish king, trained in the tradition of Civil Law, to the English throne with its very particular relation to Common Law jurisdiction. Coke's struggle, single though it is, may be seen in many different aspects, all of them of the profoundest interest to us in elucidating Pound's interest in Coke and in his relevance to the last two centuries of American legal and social history. To the legal historian it is of prime relevance that Coke's highest office was Lord Chief Justice of Common Pleas and that both in this office and in his writings he opposed (in the event to his own downfall) the many manifestations of the Royal Prerogative which were undermining the structure of Common Law. To the social historian it will be seen as a matter of reverence for the

power of parliament and as a consequence, the legal administra-
tion of taxes. To the individual in society it will be seen as a strug-
gle over his right to scrupulous justice and the judgement of his
peers. These topics recur in many forms and combinations in the
writings of Pound, more especially and overtly in the late *Cantos*,
which move ever more closely to the detailed concerns of Edward
Coke.

His contemporaries were in no doubt concerning the signifi-
cance of Coke's work. Francis Bacon, his subtlest opponent,
wrote to the king at the height of the conflict in 1616: 'Had it not
been for Sir Edward Coke's *Reports*...the law by this time had
been almost like a ship without ballast.' Yet conflict was inevi-
table. The king's position was clear. Writing to Coke in April
1616, he set out his position plainly:

> Although we never studied the common law of England, yet
> are we not ignorant of any points which belong to a king to
> know...We cannot be contented to suffer the prerogative
> royal of our crown to be wounded...(We) who are head and
> fountain of justice under God in our dominions...out of our
> absolute power and authority we command you...

The struggle was one of mighty opposites, the Common Law
against the prerogative courts, of Star Chamber, the Ecclesiastical
Commission, Chancery and the others which were deemed to be
outside the authority of the Common Law. For the moment the
king prevailed and Coke was dismissed his office; but history –
and Pound's reading of it – was quite clear about the ultimate out-
come. In a letter to me, dated 17 September 1957, Pound anno-
tated his concerns with Coke's principles and conclusions and
vividly focusses their issue:

> Shx/ against Unlimited [Sovereignty]
> 33 years from S[hakespear]'s death to
> decapitation of Charlie

which appears significantly expanded in Canto 107:

> OBIT, in Stratford 1616, Jacques Père obit
> in 33 years Noll cut down Charlie
> OBIT Coke 1634 & in '49
> Noll cut down Charlie

The letter of 17 September mainly concerns items at the Folger
Library for use with the anthology, *Confucius to Cummings* but
ends with the sentence:

What about Coke as per enc/ IF you are
reading thru him.

The enclosure was a separate sheet dated '15 Sept' and the first
section reads:

COKE on PRINCIPLES
Jury trial/from Athens, by majority
Division of powers/Anselm vs. Wm Rufus
   at least from that time...
Nature of jury. Peers, i.e. capable of understanding the
  issues
    Vicinage, capable of understanding the
    circumstances?
SOVREIGNTY
Prerogatives: COIN, seals leagues
  Shx/against Unlimited.
  33 years from S's death to decapitation of Charlie

The topics are clear and inter-related: Jury Trial, Division of Pow-
ers, Taxation and Sovereignty. Later in the note there are two
significant entries which raise a teasing problem:

Various items raised in Adams cantos, but the above is useful
order in which to expose

and finally:

representation/responsible or not. geographic divisions or by
trades.
am totally ignorant of anything Coke may have held in pro-
posito.
Dont *recall* any item in Blackstone directly applicable.

The question raised here is that of Pound's direct knowledge of
Coke's actual writings and the period at which he obtained access
to them. The following extracts from letters I received from him
over the succeeding two months help to tease the matter out. On
1 November he writes, 'Coke's mind marvellous for lucidity'
(which appears in *Canto 107* as 'Coke: the clearest mind ever in
England'). On 7 November, in response to a question of mine in
conversation concerning the possibility of a hearing to secure his
release from S. Elizabeth's, he wrote:

Dear M/what to do? (Tuesday)
    Get the 'intelligentzia', i.e.

3 or 4 of 'em to FACE the issues, the reality
the problems of the ang/sax heritage.
IGNORANCE of Coke on MY part/known only in J. Adams
reference until 30 Oct. 1957...
I think my ten Adams Cantos were printed in U.S. in '39.
a few bits in earlier cantos/Jeffersonian until I found Adams/
Plea for Blackstone by Cairns, must have been Mich. Law Rev
about 15 years ago/
long silence...
Next job is to get Coke back into circulation/among other
items & that can hardly bring the FBI down on any innocent
enquirer...

It is interesting that this is no direct answer to my purely personal
question but shifts the focus to legal principles, which is empha-
sised later in the letter:

Are you trying to get a view of the situation/I mean in general,
the setting in which I or my 'case' occurs?
it covers from 1920 or thereabouts

and, pursuing the plea for critical thinking, he sees as the first
requirement

A census of men capable of grasping
a legal PRINCIPLE
in midst of pragmatic morass...
there is yr/ serious fellow parson, H. Swabey...
Will consider a serious idea and not try to dodge it.
rare bird...
horrible lack of intercommunication between clercs NOT
engaged in la traison...
benedictions, glad to have seen you/
cant get 40 years history in
one hurried hour...
Do you happen to know off hand if Mag Carta in Coke means
that the Hen. 3/ at Laycock (as was, now in Brit. Mus.) is ver-
batim as John's.

On 10 November Pound wrote:

that I got to Coke via the Sacred
Edict, a measure of decay in brit/and yank/ education

so that to this date the links and sources seem clearly to be refer-
ences in John Adams and analogies drawn from Confucian

thought, a confirmation of the argument underlying David Gordon's article in *Paideuma*. But on 12 November the tone changes dramatically:

> set of 4 vols of Coke, sighted in London/ also that C/ on Littleton fills the first

This is apparently Pound's first opportunity to read Coke at any substantial length and this when the Coke *Cantos* were steadily in the making. This may account in part for the tougher precision (in certain passages the clotted precision) of reference to the texts; the principles, the legal pattern and structure had been wholly assimilated from the unbroken tradition, in the years of the earlier *Cantos*; there was now no time for the digestion and assimilation at this stage of the vast quantities of matter in the Coke texts themselves.

Some tentative conclusions, then, present themselves. David Gordon summarises the historical significance of Coke's career in this note:

> Upon this thirteenth-century palimpsest of struggle for human rights is written a seventeenth-century struggle for virtually the same rights

and we may add that Pound felt himself engaged in precisely the same struggle, both objectively in relation to principles, as Coke was so engaged, and personally in his own circumstances, as Coke also became so engaged. For Coke the crux of the matter came in the definition of principles forced upon him by controversy with the civil lawyers. Cowell published his *Interpreter* in 1607 in which he defined the royal prerogative in terms which James would wholly approve:

> that absolute height of power that the Civilians call majestatem, subject only to God.

Coke retorted bluntly in words that were to come home to him with dire consequences in the final clash in 1616:

> The king has no prerogative but that which the law of the land allows him.

This radical difference in interpretation issued most critically in the matter of 'the reserve of power' and its relation to the judicial office and trial by jury in the courts. It was a common assumption that courts of law were an extension of the king's court as the source of judicial power – 'the reserve of power at the disposal of the king's personal entourage.' This is Shakespeare's assumption in both the tragic farce of the trial of Goneril and Regan in the third act of *King Lear* and in the Chief Justice's plea to Hal that his authority derived from the king's majesty:

> I then did use the person of your father;
> The image of his power lay then in me.

No-one denied that the judicial office derived from the king; it was, however, Coke's ultimate triumph that the independence of the judiciary once appointed, was firmly established in the English system of law after the seventeenth-century rebellion.

That these matters dominated Pound's mind in the closing months of 1957, when *Thrones* was nearing completion is clear from the above quotations from his letters. The key phrases are:

Division of Powers   Sovereignty   Jury Trial

and Coke would have responded warmly to Pound's definition of the nature of a jury:

Peers i.e. capable of understanding the issues
Vicinage, capable of understanding the circumstances

for Coke was rarely happier than when he was administering justice in his own 'vicinage', the county of Norfolk.

In purely formal terms Pound's *Cantos* come to no neat conclusion, no full close. It is true also that the last completely-wrought *Cantos* bristle with detail and that out of the broken terrain granitic passages obtrude:

> Nor can the king create a new custom
> in the fine print (*Canto 107*)

But the *Drafts and Fragments* with which the whole work ends have a different kind of conclusion, a new emotional and visionary pressure, a gathering of themes which defy formal coherence. The previous three *Cantos*, 107-109 (the 'Coke *Cantos*') constitute one entire statement of argument which crowns the intellectual structure of the *Cantos* as a whole: that law is over-riding; that particular laws are manifestations of the universal rule of law, through which alone justice, order, the decencies of daily living can be achieved. A richer and more tranquil mind than Coke's and contemporary with him, expressed this insight in its fulness; Richard Hooker's *Ecclesiastical Polity* comes to its most lyrical conclusion in a vision of the universality of law:

Now if nature should intermit her course, and leave altogether, though it were but for awhile, the observation of her own laws ... what would become of man himself, whom these things do now all serve? See we not plainly, that obedience of creatures unto the law of nature is the stay of the whole world?

To this Pound would have assented, indeed did assent in *Canto 107*, with Confucian reference and English particularity:

> That is our PIVOT
> Statute de Merton.

To all these insights set out in the Coke *Cantos* the *Fragments* are a lyrical coda, in which there is also found a place for passages of tragic backward-looking. There is no *Paradiso* here, nor even a *Paradise Regained* but an entirely new vision which is both terrestrial and celestial, the city achieved and realised: 'a city remaineth', 'a Body politique'. It is perhaps not too much to say that Magna Carta is the final concrete embodiment of the whole structure of natural law which the *Cantos*, in their long exploration, were seeking, a structure by which the city is walled, itself a metaphor of the cosmic order. The fragments that remain, gathered in the profound silences of Pound's last years, point the joy by means of the tragic undertones, the regrets, the omissions, the mistaken by-ways. Had the *Cantos* been theologically motivated, had the main trend of Pound's long search been that of Dante, the closing beatific vision could have excluded in ecstasy the memory of error and failure. The *Cantos* could come to no such comforting end; this 'humanist *Commedia*' had to take into its fabric, to our enrichment, the tragic tone of recollection, a tone which enhances the moments of lyrical vision. Mary de Rachewiltz writes of the presence of her father: 'He brought with him a dimension of – no, not stillness, but magnitude, momentum'. Nowhere is this magnitude more amply shown than in the transition from the gritty understanding of Edward Coke to the resolution of the *Drafts and Fragments*:

> seeing the just and the unjust,
> tasting the sweet and the sorry.

(1979)

TOM SCOTT

The Poet as Scapegoat:
Ezra Pound & Politics

Julian Cornell: *The Trial of Ezra Pound*
Michael Reck: *Ezra Pound, A Close-up*
Harry M. Meacham: *The Caged Panther*

These books all concern the worst literary scandal of the century, if not of all time, the US treatment of its greatest poet since Whitman, from 1945 to 1958. The present reviewer's apology for commenting on the momentous questions raised here is that in a democracy every man has a right and duty to have his opinion and to express it.

The first of these books, by Julian Cornell, who was Pound's lawyer during and after his indictment, is mistitled; Pound was never tried, and if he had been, no genuinely objective court, in my view, could have found him guilty of treason. Perhaps Mr Cornell means 'trial' in the religious sense, or as a synonym for 'ordeal', both of which glosses would have meaning. This book is not one for review in the usual sense: it is a presentation of the relevant documents and there is no alternative to reading it. The horrors (surely entirely illegal savagery to a civilian?) of the Pisan cage, the drafting to the US, the indictment and court procedure, the hair-raising psychiatric mumbo-jumbo, the fear of the vindictive mood of the times putting Pound's life in danger, the life-saving plea of insanity, the whole staggering circus, all are here. They even tried to smear his intelligence by declaring how he did in IQ tests which no doubt were valid for school-children. As to that, Bernard Shaw well said somewhere that he never yet saw an intelligence test that didn't make him out to be a moron, and he left it to his reader to guess whether that reflected on him or the testers.

It is clear that Mr Cornell did his duty by his client, as far as was possible, in the heated atmosphere of the time, and all of us, and Americans in particular, owe him a debt of gratitude. The atmosphere was full of repressed hatred and lust for revenge: scapegoats had to be found for the worst evil in history – otherwise we had to face the intolerable fact that we are all guilty. Hence the Nuremburg travesty of justice, hence the judicial murder of

William Joyce for treason against a country not his own, hence the hysteria over Ezra Pound. I remember a poet friend of mine, just returned from the US at the time saying that popular feeling would hang Pound if it got its way. I mentioned this to Rachel Annand Taylor, who said 'Hang Ezra? Nobody would be so ridiculous as to hang poor Ezra – he's just not that sort of person.' She was a far left-winger, loathed his outlook, but meant that he was not capable of crime. Like most good poets, Pound was, in fact, an innocent, a Don Quixote with Pegasus instead of Rosinantes for a steed, where political reality is concerned. I have never met a poet whose politics are to be taken other than poetically, that is to say in terms of his vision of the coming of the kingdom of poetry on earth, the divine harmony, and not in terms of power-politics. A poet's politics are visionary, not political.

The central issue of the whole tragedy of Ezra Pound is the place of the poet in presentday society, that is to say in an antipoetic one. The US as a comparatively young and inexperienced society was particularly vulnerable here, and is due a measure of our pity and sympathy for the albatross round its neck. I have been inclined to think that to those traditional oppressors of the poetic mind, the games master, the drill sergeant and their like, has been added the psychiatrist, the soul-shrinker, the man who thinks that the soul is a disease of what otherwise would be a sound machine, the body. But there is little doubt that here the psychiatrists were all, to a degree at any rate, on the side of the angels, or at least of the muses. The myth that Pound was insane may indeed have saved his life, or at least prevented his subjection to even more brutal treatment in prison.

Mr Cornell's book must be read, for the unique evidence it marshals on the indictment.

Mr Reck's book brings evidence of a different kind to bear on the whole Pound case, particularly on the later years of his life in the asylum for insane criminals where he was incarcerated for twelve years, and on his release. It is a biography, the latter part of which is drawn from personal knowledge, and the author succeeds in bringing the human being out of the legend: and a warm, generous, patient, heroic, deeply concerned and responsible human being he is, arrogant and idiosyncratic, but sane. There is no trace of persecution mania, let alone paranoia, no power-lust, no avarice – a man remarkably free of the deadly sins, with the possible exception of pride and anger, and they are controlled: for his hard-hitting uncompromising assertiveness is a different thing from pride, being a tool designed to get things done.

Pound in fact is something of a saint, as testimony by various famous men has long made clear: more precisely, he is an innocent, for his virtue is of nature rather than of grace and laboured discipline. He is a man who behaved from the first as if there had never been a Fall. The young man who was bewildered when a publisher told him, in London, that Palgrave's *Golden Treasury* held sway not because of taste in poetry, or because people didn't know better, but because So-and-So & Co made a living out of it, is the real and abiding Pound. He never accepted that the world suffers not through ignorance, but through sin, because he doesn't know what sin is. For him, to know the good is to do the good, an assumption that only a kind of saint can make. Ideas go into action – they are not just interesting possibilities – and opposition to right action comes from ignorance, not from the ill-will of vested interests. This is the key to Pound, and Mr Reck brings out the invincible integrity of the man even in the appalling and long-drawn-out degradation his country awarded him for the sin of being not only good but truthful. His fate has some parallels with that of a certain Greek corrupter of the young, Socrates; and with that of a Hebrew stirrer-up of the people against authority, asserting the true tradition against the corruptions of priests and quislings, one Yeshua of Nazareth. Like Socrates, he might have suggested that his punishment should be a life-pension from the country he has dignified by his work. And if he was not exactly crucified, he had, like Yeshua, much gross mal-treatment by his countrymen to forgive.

Mr Reck also makes some telling comments on the work, gives the Fenellosa translations and what Pound made of them, and asserts the primacy of the ear in approaching a poet who has the finest ear of the century, and of any American ever. A good, decent book.

Finally, and best, there is Harry M. Meacham's account of how the 'caged panther' was at last released: like Prometheus from his thousand years on the Caucasian rock, and the attentions of Jove's American Eagle. Mr Meacham is a very American pheno-menon, a high-powered business-man who is also a man of cul-ture, a consumer, and in a minor way producer, of poetry and literature. This combination, plus tact, shrewd social chess-play, determination, and (a quality which informs all the others but might embarrass him), a genuine love of the poet, allowed him to play a central part in Pound's release. I mention the love, because

Pound has always had the ability to inspire such love in people of all sorts and in the most unlikely circumstances: and that speaks volumes.

Mr Meacham destroys the myth, fostered by Robert Frost among others (including Mr Cornell; and Mr Reck seems half sold on it), that Robert Frost got Pound out of St. Elizabeth's. The real heroes of the case are, as one might have imagined, Archibald MacLeish, T.S. Eliot, and Ernest Hemingway; and of these Mac-Leish was the director-general, the man on the spot, the man watching for his chance, the man informing the others, deploying his troops at the right time: the least of these troops being, at the last moment, Frost. Another name in the role of honour is Dag Hammarskjöld, who tried to get Pound the Nobel Prize for literature. Hemingway played a waiting game, and when he saw his opening, struck hard: he announced, when receiving the Nobel prize, that it ought to have gone to Ezra Pound. Mr Meacham himself seems to have been a sort of liaison officer in the quiet campaign, and an effective, first-rate one at that, not only keeping clear the lines of communication, but supplying some of the ammunition and will to fight. Pound touchingly acknowledges this debt to him in letters quoted in this book, and the rest of us can only record our own share of gratitude to him.

Other people mentionable in the roll of honour are e.e. cummings, who not only was a faithful friend throughout but sent Pound a cheque for a thousand dollars he had just got for one of his paintings; Professor Giovannini of the Catholic University; and Wytter Bynner. One of the most significant stories is that Hemingway sent Pound a cheque for 1500 dollars, which was not cashed, though desperately needed, but framed. Most writers were of course sympathetic, the remarkable exception being Robert Graves. Among officials it is probable that more people were sympathetic – there is evidence of this in the book – than were able, or felt able, to do anything. For instance, Pound was released only five months after William P. Rogers became secretary of State. A great fuss seems to have been made about Pound's supposed influence on the racist agitator (allegedly so) John Kasper. Indeed, a cynic might suggest that Pound was eventually released on condition, or tacit understanding, that he got the hell out of it, for he was too hot for the US to hold even in a lunatic asylum. All that Pound did, apparently, was recommend Kasper to read Confucius and Agassiz: not exactly subversive material. There is one thing Pound can never be accused of – inconsistency.

Having got together with great labour, his main points of doctrine, he hammers at them ceaselessly, with relentless single-mindedness.

Both Meachan and Reck bring out one most salient but least commented upon feature of the case: the position of Mrs Dorothy Pound. She followed him from Italy, handled his affairs, lived in squalid circumstances all the years of his incarceration, her money blocked by various governments whose inhumanity will become legendary; visited him daily, made heart-breaking decisions involving his life, his freedom, and her own happiness – all without complaint. None of the usual sources of money for impecunious writers which America spends so generously seems to have been available for her greatest poet and his wife. Meacham quotes an interesting letter on the subject (p. 184).

These books, then, are required reading for all educated persons who, being educated persons, must think out the implications of the Pound case.

What was it all about? I won't go over the charges, but think aloud. The broadcasts in question were patriotic defences of the American Constitution as interpreted by Pound, and allegations of Roosevelt's betrayal of it. He is no bully, he doesn't pick on little guys. They were not made for the Fascist government but for America, by an American patriot. He was not and never was a fascist; he was not and never was a traitor. It was Pound propaganda, and behind it was the anxiety of a sensitive man to save life and blood – particularly American life and blood. The question of whether his views are right, were right, is irrelevant. I think not, but the matter of opinion is not at issue, only certain facts. It was stated before each broadcast that he was working within his rights as an American citizen loyal to his country and its Constitution, which he was defending. He saw the Europe he loved suffering a second disintegrating war in twenty years. He felt that he knew the causes of these wars and that it was his duty as an American citizen to tell his countrymen what he believed they were. They were pretty wild broadcasts, fired with anger, but they wouldn't have corrupted anybody. The British might have arraigned Bernard Shaw on much worse charges, of inciting the troops to mutiny, when he said at the beginning of the war that his advice to service men was the same as in the first war – shoot your officers and go home to your wives. The same Shaw, incidentally, used to say that Mussolini was giving the Italians as strong a dose of socialism as they could bear, but nobody called him a fascist. P.G. Wodehouse might have been in trouble, too, had not good sense prevailed. Why then the extraordinary panic and vindictiveness over Pound?

There was the charge of fascism – it won't hold. There was the charge of anti-Semitism – more difficult. The Jews have historically a foremost place in the rise of usury, as Shakespeare, and Dante among others believed. But to blame the Jews for that, or identify tham with it, is as crazy as to blame the French for alcoholism because of their role in the wine trade. One of the evils stemming from Hitler's 'final solution' is that even a lifelong Zionist and friend of Israel scarcely dare mouth a normal criticism of certain faults evident in certain Jews for fear of being branded anti-Semite. It is unhealthy. Pound is not an anti-Semite in the racialist or religious sense, but a critic as outspoken of certain Jews as of other people – Americans, for instance. But he didn't always make the necessary qualifications and particularisations. He regarded anti-Semitism as such as 'unscientific' and 'unAristotelian' – his own words. The fault is more in the abnormal situation than in the man: I've heard worse things about Jews from Jews: of course.

Not enough there to account for the vindictive attitude to Pound.

Pound's 'economic theories', as the fly-boys put it, like puppies sniffing round a hedgehog? These 'theories' seem to me to hold a lot of sense. He is right that you can't create money out of nothing, unless you are a forger: therefore the Bank of England, among others, was given a forger's charter. Value is created by producers of goods and inheres in goods, and money is only a way of circulating goods and equivalents, and clearly ought to be controlled by the producers of the goods for the benefit of the community. That private bankers have control of the community's money, with power to inflate or deflate it as they choose, is gross infamy and fraud: what is worse, it is ultimately so incompetent that it cannot be allowed to go on creating wars, crises, and hell on earth. This is where we are to-day – the world's financial system has got to be changed and brought under genuine democratic control. I don't say that Pound is right on all money matters, or any other matters, but he is unlikely to be all wrong either. In any case, he puts forward arguments that ought to be discussed by intelligent people, not dismissed.

Here I think we are onto something. Literary men with no knowledge of economics often describe his monetary theories as crazy, but at the same time there is a strange silence about them. If Pound had put forward the theory that the moon was made of green cheese, would people have been defensive about it, fearful of it, out for his blood because of it, afraid to argue it out with him? They are afraid of his 'theories' precisely because they are *not* crazy but make good sense, at least in certain fundamentals. So do the theories of Douglas and other men who have been treated only less oppressively than Pound. The very publishers that have the honour to publish him in Britain have not had the common decency to publish his 'theories', although they are essential to an understanding of the *Cantos* and his whole position: they even allude to them slightingly in the blurb of the Cornell book.[1]

Fascism has nothing to do with Pound's maltreatment by the US, which has never been notably hard on it since the war: alleged anti-Semitism has something to do with it: and the 'economic theories' have quite a lot to do with it. The abuse has the mark of fear all over it – fear of the truth. It is very dangerous to tell the truth. Not one of the authors under review has the guts or grace to give an account of, much less discuss, Pound's views on money. They bow low before Mammon. None of them seems to be aware that Pound's fight for financial reform and against the tax system shows a more practical concern for the just distribution of wealth, and for freedom, than the vague 'socialism' of so many English poets in the thirties and since. He attacked the problem of inequality and social injustice at its root – that is, in the means of distribution itself – the issue of money:

> Infantilism increasing till our time,
> > attention to outlet, no attention to source,
> > > That is: the problem of issue.
> Who issues it? How?   (Canto 87)

It is clear that, though the situation has improved in some respects since the thirties, the present financial system is out of date and totally ill-equipped to deal with the needs of the modern world. The century has gone from crisis to war to crisis every year or so in a series of stop-goes, deflations, inflations, devaluations, slumps, booms, revolutions and counter-revolutions. Britain has devalued twice at the command of non-elected international financiers who produce nothing, but who own all production, means of production, and producers from the cradle to the grave:

---

[1] Some of this material was subsequently published by Faber in *Ezra Pound: Selected Prose 1909-1965* (1973) Ed.

De Gaulle's giant strength has been shaken to its foundations by the same vested interests, while the labour government of to-day like that of Ramsey MacDonald before it, has been ham-strung and made to reverse its policies, swallow its promises, and pay respect to the same financial oligarchy who effectively control policy, except in certain limited areas, whatever government is in power. Therefore anybody, a Douglas or a Pound, who offers some explanation and constructive criticism, is surely at any rate entitled to serious and respectful consideration. Ninety-nine per cent of us have nothing to fear from such airing of these basic facts.

Pound's 'monetary theories', then, have too much truth in them for the comfort of the financial minority who enslave the human race (and are themselves enslaved by their own machinations); but the silence or denigration they meet with is probably due to general 'ignorance of coin, credit and circulation' rather than to any conspiracy – they are certainly not enough to account for the outrage. Other people have fought for monetary reform, but they were easily contained by the financial grip of the means of communication, and more or less gagged. Douglas was not allowed to advise the Alberta government in 1935 (there is still a conspiracy of silence about the success of even a gelded social credit system there and in British Columbia), and all the normal channels of communication were barred against him and Soddy: but they were not martyred. What is it then, about Pound? What does he symbolise to the American average man? Clearly, despite the rational weakness of the case, it is treason: and since it is not a legal treason, it must be some other kind. Could it be cultural? Pound is the last of the great American Europeans, the cultural self-exiles, like James and Eliot, whose preference for 'civilised' Europe may be seen as an affront to Americanism – a cultural treason. Also, perhaps, he stood for the recently discredited isolationism, in another sense, politically, wanting America to stay out of the war. The kind of Americanism which in fact runs through the whole of the *Cantos* is antipathetic to the Roosevelt-Democratic prevailing trend. Pound therefore was unlucky in being a screen for various projections: a Europeanised Yank who is also a political isolationist in American politics. The fact that there is more American history, and conscious, intelligent Americanism, in the *Cantos* than in the whole of Walt Whitman or any other American poet, is irrelevant. The scapegoatism depends on only a vague notion, or total ignorance of and indifference to the poetry. I predict that the next century will see, even be dominated by, a dialogue between the US and China in which Pound's poetry will take on an importance and weight not obvious at the moment: that not only has he woven a new wholeness, or at any rate potential wholeness, out of European and American, but also of Chinese, elements. But all that can't be seen by the man in the street, for whom Pound's very apartness from his own time is itself a kind of treason. At a deeper level, there is of course the suspicion, hatred and fear felt by the ordinary philistine of a philistine age for any poet: it is hard to resist the conclusion that Pound, in fact, was victimised not for this or that reason but simply because he was a poet, and a big enough one, on a heroic enough scale, to be cast in a tragic role in the popular mind.

Given this basic mistrust of the poet as such, the other projections can be seen as merely aggravational. Yet another of these must be mentioned. Pound savagely attacked Roosevelt, and when a great fatherfigure dies, the folk-mind sees it as a magical killing demanding revenge. Some 'bad' son or other must be blamed and sacrificed for the death of the father, so that the general guilt-feelings may be assuaged: a scapegoat is needed. Then there was the feeling of guilt about the bloodshed of actual sons by actual fathers – of GIs sent into war by their elders, demanding the sacrifice of a 'bad' father-figure. Thus, true to the irrationality of the unconscious, Pound was able to serve both as bad son and bad father; and however flimsy the legal case against him, the mythopoeic one was colossal: it is from this that the psychiatry brigade, knowingly or not, tried to save him. An ordinary man would have been in little danger (most of those actually tried for treason in the US were found not guilty, and two lightly sentenced), but Pound was a poet, a fitting scapegoat for the 'bad guy' heroic role.

All these elements play a part in the appalling story of Pound's ordeal. Even now people of high cultural status talk about him in terms of 'he was punished enough', not that he was innocent: unless indeed a man should be punished for being a poet, for speaking his mind, for telling the truth as he sees it, for asserting the freedoms accorded him by the Declaration of Independence and the Bill of Human Rights. But in that case the suicide of the human race is inevitable.

The day is far hence when the place of the poet in society will be re-defined and accepted, even welcomed, as jesters once were by kings, as a necessary professional and permanent opposition judging the things of time by the standards of eternity, the relative by the absolute. The United States of America are leading the way in this direction: their generous encouragement of the arts since 1945 all over the world is already legendary and has put us all in debt of gratitude to them. How odd, then, how ironical, that history must record their unparallelled meanness to their own greatest poetical son. Pound should be cleared of all dishonour, for the good name of the United States: it would be an act of large generosity entirely in keeping with the American character, always big enough to acknowledge a mistake when it makes a mistake, and offer generous amends.

(1969)

HENRY SWABEY

The Just Price

As a student at Durham in 1935, I was puzzled by the poverty so marked in this distressed area, for Britain itself produced a variety of goods and was backed by an enormous empire. Ezra Pound, then known as a poet-economist on both sides of the Atlantic, kindly responded to my enquiries and indicated his own *ABC of Economics* together with Silvio Gesell's *Natural Economic Order* and the Social Credit ideas of Major C.H. Douglas.

Pound gave lucid definitions in his book and Gesell analysed the monetary system with great clarity, and Douglas deplored the existence of Poverty amid Plenty due to financial restriction.

These authors showed that money is not a commodity – like a heap of gold – but is largely a system of book entries supplemented by cash, which is a kind of ticket. If goods be visualised as theatre seats, then the seats will not be claimed if too few tickets are issued, while an excess of tickets would cause confusion. It could not be beyond 'the wit of man', said George V, to devise a system of distribution; nor, of course, was it. Unfortunately the banks held the monopoly of credit and were able to regulate distribution. Yet credit relies on the belief in future production and is based on the country's abilities and resources, so that society has credit and it belongs to that society.

Douglas further demonstrated that the money system never generated enough purchasing power to meet the prices charged for goods and services. We can see that today in the vast debt on credit cards of various kinds, which shows that the goods are available but the money to pay for them is only supplied *in advance*. Moreover an increasing number of businesses are going into bankruptcy and before the war the charts for bankruptcies and suicides varied in close proportion.

As a solution, Douglas proposed a compensated price, which he called a Just Price, together with the distribution of a National Dividend; and the amounts of these depended on the productivity of the country and on the improvement of process.

Pound further suggested that I should connect the insights of the new economics with the thoughts of the past, and indicated two kinds of enquiry: into the bishops' mints and into mediaeval economic doctrine. These mints, at Durham and various other centres, supplied currency to meet local needs until suppressed at the Reformation, and minted the silver for a modest fee.

The mediaeval system sprang from the ideal of the Just Price and distinguished between Usury, payment for the use of money, and Partnership when both risks and profits were shared. Further refinements dealt with loss sustained through making a loan and profit that was lost. The Just Price (*justum pretium*) linked up with Douglas's exposition of the Just Price in the twentieth century.

The Church of England, I found, vigorously, even luridly, proclaimed the condemnation of usury until the time of Cromwell, while David Jones enunciated the last condemnation from St. Mary, Woolnoth, in 1690, and seems to have lost his living for this temerity.

In between the two systems, Bishop Berkeley appeared and in his *Querist* of 1750 he asked whether it was not a great privilege for a banker to create £100 with the stroke of his pen. This shows that the banks create the means of payment out of nothing, and it has taken two further centuries for people to realise that the money system does not rely on the amount of precious metal available. The fact was known centuries before Berkeley, for Langland mentions 'letters from Lombardy' in *Piers the Plowman*.

Rectification, in the form of a national credit office and the realistic issue of credit and cash, has unfortunately not followed on the enlightenment given by Pound and Douglas. Alberta, for instance, which elected a government to implement social credit, was denied access to its own credit. In fact Douglas always stressed the danger of centralised power – the pyramid system – and used for his quarterly the text from Micah: 'They shall sit every man under his vine and under his fig tree; and none shall make them afraid.'

He wrote (April 2nd, 1949), 'In effect, if not in technique, money must originate in the individual so that the central power has to come to him for it.' And on October 13th of the same year he stated that 'It is clear beyond all question that the gates of hell are wide open, and the torrent of evil will sweep away anything not intrinsically stronger than evil... You know that long-distance air pilots mark on their course charts the point of no-return where you must go on, because you can't turn back to your base. The devil has passed the point of no-return and we had better recognise it.'

These insights show that the author of Social Credit penetrated to the roots of human motivation, as surely as the sixteenth century prelate who called usurers the 'wringers and stringers of our very souls'.

(1985)

TWO TRIBUTES TO EZRA POUND
ON HIS EIGHTIETH BIRTHDAY

Robert Lowell

A TRIBUTE

Ezra Pound's writings belong to the moment of experimental explosion – Stravinsky, Schoenberg, Picasso, Rilke, Joyce, Eliot, Proust. His work, like theirs, is alive with a radiant daring, we now seem to have lost. As a man, he had the surpassing generosity of his sure, discovering eye. How often he encouraged other artists at the risk of breaking and dispersing himself! His translations have a glory of music, freshness of idiom and something exuberant, indefinable and personal that make others seem joyless and soiled. His *Cantos* are heroic, a poem as long as a long novel, written in a time when it seemed as if only prose fiction could bring off anything extended, important and readable. And yet the Cantos are not metered fiction, nor do they go against the grain of what is possible in poetry. I want to hail my old friend on his eightieth birthday, and reverence his courage and humor – a great, jagged, far-shining splendor!

Marianne Moore

A NOTE

Pound is the most contagious teacher I have known – deadly in earnest, at the same time, indigenously piquant. 'You might have more fun with rhymes', concerning a flat line as equivalent for a French one. How indesputably right: 'consecutive work toward an avowable end'. 'A coherent paragraph in plain English. The rule? Subject, predicate, object.' AND, 'ask the solid of yourself; the trifle of others.'

(1965)

STUART PIGGOTT

David Jones and the Past of Man

In the summer of last year, when in Vienna examining the great national prehistoric collections, I was given the opportunity of seeing for the first time the original of the famous Upper Palaeolithic sculpture usually kept in the museum safe, and known as The Venus of Willendorf. And as I held this numinous figure, the first words that flashed into my mind were not technical archaeological reflections on Gravettian *art mobilier* of 20,000 years ago, but a quotation –

> Who were his *gens*-men or had he no *Hausname* yet
> no *nomen* for his *fecit*-mark
>   the Master of the Venus?
> Whose man-hands god-handled
> the Willendorf stone
>   before they unbound the last glaciation.

The Anathemata had bitten deeply into the consciousness of at least one archaeologist.

I suppose it is because I am a prehistorian that my most immediate contact with David Jones's work was made by the impact of this poem. I had read *In Parenthesis*, and had been delighted and moved by his paintings and engravings, particularly the *Ancient Mariner* set, but with *Anathemata* I suddenly found that far from us having, in the phrase he has quoted from C.S. Lewis, 'unshared backgrounds', by a quirk of circumstance his emotive referrents were so often my own, from Mesolithic to Mabinogion.

The 'devoted things' of the Greek title are the latent and underlying realities of the past of man, all the more real for being so often unperceived by prehistorian and historian. He defends the choice of the word as title with the support of Homer and St. John Chrysostom, but there is yet another significant instance of its use, almost too apt to be true. The Greek geographer Hecateus, writing in the fifth century BC, is reported to have said that the Hyperboreans, a mythical northern people but located by him in the British Isles, had a notable circular temple dedicated to Apollo and adorned with *anathemata*. It does not matter whether or not Stonehenge or any other known and surviving prehistoric monument is referred to, but by Middle-Sea and Lear-Land were these devoted things brought by matlos of the Maiden to Pretani shore? At all events some people in Greek antiquity thought of *anathemata* in a British shrine, and it is in Britain that David Jones has made his offering of things loved.

The past of man is something continuous, and one can never be certain that it is really past, and not present or even more disconcertingly, future. Part of the excitement communicated by David Jones's poetry is the ambiguous position in which he puts his readers, disturbing their neat and safe chronological proprieties and the pedants' division of culture and creed. The archaic smile of the Kouros is on the face of the 'numbed and scurvied top-tree boy' on the ship bound for Albion from Corbilo, and a sea shanty swings us past Langland's Rose dish-seller and the Cockney Lady of the Pool to the ultimate mysteries of the Mass. And one is carried along, association linked to association so that one happily moves from the 'oral gloss from a Heidelberg gaffer' to the words of Pilate in

> the empty time
> after tiffin
> and before his first stiff peg.

At the opening of *The Anathemata* there is a magnificent panorama of geology linked to humanity, where 'nine-strata'd Hissarlik' is but a part of the great aggradations and deposits of history, one with the 'microgranites and the clay-bonded erratics wrenched from the diorites of Aldasa' embedded in the strata of the glaciations. Even as an archaeologist (or because I am one) I should hardly have thought the Quaternary Period a subject for more than the most disastrous and pedestrian verse. 'I once did hitch the syntax into verse', Calverly made Browning say in his parody of *The Ring and the Book*: David Jones has transmuted the Pleistocene into pure poetry.

Perhaps it is not for nothing that 'deposits' is a favourite word of his, both in poetry and in prose. 'Deposits' are an essential part of his poetry. 'I believe that there is, in the principle that informs the poetic art, a something which cannot be disengaged from the mythus, deposits, *matière*, ethos, whole *res* of which the poet is himself a product.' It is a significant and revealing word. Deposits may imply a slow historical process of accretion, stealthily forming silts, slow strata, the layers of a pearl; or again, they are the man-made caches and hoards – hidden treasures; votive, ritual and foundation deposits, and the last great deposit of all, the body in burial. Medieval (and indeed modern) Treasure Trove law turns on the question of the *animus retrovandi*, the intent to recover which was in the mind of the man who made the deposit. Was the treasure buried with an intention or at least a hope that it would again be retrieved by the owner or his heirs? But whatever the *animus* may have been, its aspirations were not always fulfilled, and the treasure lay unregarded and lost. David Jones does not let poetic treasure trove go unclaimed: like the Crown in law, he steps in as *ultima haeres* to the deposits, and brings them splendidly to light. He explores poetic deposits with the anxious care of the good excavator (far better than Schliemann 'who digged nine sites down in Helen's laughless rock'), alert for the unexpected feature, the illuminating oddness, the links that bind culture to culture.

To words themselves he applies a process of inspired nuclear fission. As you read, the simple-seeming syllables, in the context of their deposits, explode in a radiant and beneficent blast of highly charged meanings, associations and what the seventeenth century liked to call 'correspondences'. As a bard should, he displays his word-hoard, but the words are radio-active with history. Some of the scintillations may miss us, but enough hit their target to start up in ourselves a chain reaction of generated excitement. The words themselves will never be the same to us; they have been enriched historically until each is a piece of history itself.

Prehistory imperceptibly becomes history, and with David Jones this half-historical world of transition lies in Wales. Here again I find myself, almost by accident, sharing a background. Not perhaps so much because I am half a Welshman, though who knows what obscurely unconscious promptings may not have led me to early Welsh poetry, near-ignorant as I am of the very language? Few enough read Old English (even if far more than those who can master early Welsh), yet Beowulf and Caedmon are not so wholly strange to the educated reader as are the Gododdin or Llywarch Hen. The Saxons have had a temporary victory over the Celts here. But for those who have a frame of reference, here lie links from prehistory to Arthur, to the Grail, to the Church. Here too, among the perils and horrors of the haunted Celtic woods, lurks the persuasive demon of sentimentality. If he ever even risked an encounter with David Jones he would have been instantly repulsed by such a vehement Welsh-accented *Retro!* that he would have not left even a flickering shadow of a barbed tail.

'It is next to impossible for us' he writes of the early Celtic church 'not to feel "romantic" *about it*' but this, as he says very firmly, is not because it *was* 'romantic' in itself. The early monasteries 'bear the mark of tribal man'; 'there is in the whole Celtic thing an elusive hardness'; he doubts 'if the virtue of tolerance can have had much place' in this ancient society; above all, it would be a grave error to sentimentalise it as 'kindly, tolerant, freedom-loving and romantic'. To be intensely poetic about the past without any lapse into sentimentality is no easy thing. It can only come from an intellectual honesty leading to a determination to try to see each aspect of the past in its own terms, and not in the false terms of one's own presuppositions, which reduce the past into something safe and ordinary, instead of extraordinary, diverse and challenging. Henri Frankfort, a great ancient historian, deplored this tendency to 'project the axioms, habits of thought, and norms of the present day into the past, which, as a result, seems to contain little that is unfamiliar to us. It is remarkable how rarely historians of ancient or alien civilizations have guarded themselves against the danger'. We must, Frankfort said, try to find out what he called the 'form' of a civilization or a culture, the unique qualities which made it a valid entity among other communities, and having perceived this 'form', we must assess things in terms of this framework. David Jones has been wiser than many historians in his approach to the past of man.

(1967)

335

SAUNDERS LEWIS

A Note

(Translated from the Welsh. Originally printed 'by way of Preface' to the catalogue of the retrospective exhibition of 1954-5 at the Tate Gallery.)

It is a grief for David Jones that he has no Welsh. He reads what he can get of competent English translation of early Welsh verse and prose. He corresponds with scholars about the Ancient Books and old tales and the myth and Matter of Wales, and he treasures the grains thus garnered. He feeds his meditation and his imagination on the Welsh past; it is a key to his work as English poet and as painter.

Another key is the Faith. Observe the inscriptions, phrases from Introit or Gospel, shown here with the pictures. It would be a blunder to pass them by with merely a glance. The artist worked long at them, praying them to their shape on the paper, building them up with brush-work around and within them, even as pious Welsh mothers used once to embroider the Promises into samplers on cottage walls.

There's a passage in Part 4 of *In Parenthesis* where Dai boasts in the trenches of France; it borrows its plan from a poem in the *Book of Taliesin*:

> This Dai adjusts slipping shoulder straps, wraps close his misfit outsize greatcoat – he articulates his English with an alien care.
> My fathers were with Black Prinse of Wales
> at the passion of
> the blind Bohemian king.
> They served in these fields,
> it is in the histories that you can read it, Corporal – boys
> Gower, they were – it is writ down – yes.
> Wot about Methuselum, Taffy?
> I was with Abel when his brother found him,
> under the green tree.

That is how David Jones, poet and painter, sees things and paints them. Doric and Ionic and Corinthian columns, all the ages of Greece and Rome, are a background to the parenthetic travail of Aphrodite. The past is all a now, the eternal in the petal, tree branches in the clay of the teapot and in the brittleness of glass. The earth itself in her alert pain dreams of the hand that has shaped her. Nor man nor place stands alone. The scapegoat of Israel is caught in the barbed wire of 1915 and the trees of the field walk in through the windows of your house. David Jones is an artist who affirms that the vision in the final canto of Dante's *Paradiso* is an ever-contemporary fact.

(1967)

KATHLEEN RAINE

Tom Scott and the Bardic Lineage

Although the word 'bard' in current usage is no more than a perhaps jocular term for a poet with a certain stance (no-one I think would apply the term to the lonely stamped-addressed envelope generation) it still carries, in Ireland and in Scotland, the echo of an older social order in which the role of the poet was clearly defined. 'Self-expression' was no part of the poet's art, which was a public, not a private function, essential to the cultural coherence and continuity of clan or kingdom. It was the office of the bard to relate the deeds of king, chieftain and warrior, to transpose events of this world into the enduring records of the imagination, to awaken in clan or nation the sense of glory. Theirs was the art of enchantment through the use of the enhanced and structured language of verse, usually sung and accompanied by the harp or some other stringed instrument. (The 'harp' of the bard still clings in association with the otherwise empty word.) Although the office and the word belong properly to the Celtic races the bardic view of poetry lives on in Scotland as a whole. Sorley MacLean, who writes in Gaelic, is a true bardic poet; but the bardic memory is also very much an aspect of the revival of lowland Scotch ('lallans') in this century. One thinks of Hugh MacDiarmid; and of Tom Scott, than whom no poet has better served the Scotland of the Imagination.

The bard was part journalist, part historian, for it was in bardic poetry, memorized and transmitted within an oral tradition, that notable events were recorded. It was for the bard to praise and enhance the dignity of kings and heroes – women also, Maeve and Helen of Troy are bardic queens. Satire too was a bardic weapon, and to receive a 'bad press' from the bards was much the same as the supposed office of a 'free press' today. Verse and music helped the bard to memorize and transmit the cultural treasury of his people. I am old enough to remember old men and women in the Highlands and the Western Isles whose memories were treasuries of the words and music of hundreds of songs, and stories also, mainly historical, but with recent additions, for the unwritten Book of the People had not ended in a world where literacy had no great importance. Many of these would have been lost – many more have been lost – but for the collections made by such scholars as John Lorne Campbell of Canna, Margaret Fay Shaw and Hamish Henderson now preserved in the archives of the School of Scottish Studies. Now in those kitchens where the songs were sung and the stories told, the all-obliterating television-set channels in the ephemera of a world that has lost its memory.

Oral poetry (when did academics begin describing poems as 'the words on the page'?) would of course have kept the words of the language burnished, as the spoken word resonates and is received with its full freight of meaning and sound by the listener. To this day in India the sound of the mantra (and this term includes poetry) is held to be powerful in raising the consciousness of the listener. Words spoken and sung carry the full quality of human experience, feeling is never absent. The 'words on the page' can be stored in dictionaries and computers, but not the words of song. The English of England today is a half-dead language, but north of the border it is otherwise. Reflecting on what it is that makes Tom Scott so fine a poet I am led back to the language that has made him, and that he has served so faithfully in all his works.

Tom Scott has conducted a life-long love affair with the Scots language and its rich vocabulary fitted to every aspect of human life – earthy humanity, noble pride, scathing contempt and withering ridicule whose rich vocabulary Shakespeare's Kent (*King Lear*) might have envied. 'Flyting' is in Scotland a poetic genre of its own, in which Tom Scott himself excels. Every situation from carnality to the dignity of religious devotion lies easily within the compass of a language spoken by a whole nation. Humble or heroic, love and war, lament for the dead or bawdry and drinking, whatever lies within the range of the human heart has found words in the speech of Scotland. Nor is it only a few poets who savour those spoken words, the poet only reflects a sort of national solidarity which takes pleasure in a speech that defines Scotland to itself. Edwin Muir has somewhere written that whereas the best English poetry is the work of the upper, educated classes, in Scotland this is not so – the finest poetry of Scotland comes from, and addresses itself to, the poor and proud people of croft and bothie, albeit bearers of proud ancestral names. The terminal state of the English language one can see as the inevitable result of the rise of the working-class, whom two or three generations in industrial cities have deprived of any rich local culture their forefathers may once have had, so that current

English is now a demotic language with an ever diminishing vocabulary of words shorn of ancestral resonances such as, across the Border, are embodied in the spoken language of a whole people. This may in Glasgow and perhaps elsewhere be subjected to influences similar to those in England, but hitherto national pride has preserved the language. Words, like people, don't thrive when they are not loved. They need to be spoken, and above all to be sung, for song is the language of love. Tom Scott had when he was younger a fine tenor voice, and his fine sense of music informs all his verse.

A life-long socialist, a one-time Marxist, but with a fullness of the sense of human values that can only be called Christian, Tom Scott is a bard of the common man and woman, of the stone-mason Brand the Builder. His father was such a man, and *Brand the Builder* is a celebration of his father and grandfather and all those anonymous builders of towns and houses whose good work we inherit. If as a bard of the working class we compare him with, say, Tony Harrison who in England has attempted to speak for a working-class in search of a soul, all the advantage of language is with Tom Scott. Harrison's deliberately demotic English is without music, or nobility, and works against his intention. This is perhaps inevitable, for the 'two cultures' goes back to Shakespeare and perhaps beyond, whose noble characters speak one language, his clowns another, a common speech always intended to raise a laugh, as in English music-halls down to Frankie Howerd's *Up Pompeii*. You only need to put something into cockney or Yorkshire to preclude the proud, the tender, the noble and the subtle – these dialects are apt only for wit and earthy comedy. William Barnes will no doubt be cited as a solitary swallow who does not make a summer, but Thomas Hardy (unfortunately perhaps?) did not write in his native Dorset speech but in a self-taught and foreign English; not even John Clare, 'the peasant poet', (the very phrase suggests the rarity of such poets in England) gloried in his language as do the poets of Scotland and Ireland.

What the bards did for their chieftains Tom Scott has done for Brand the Builder, man of the people but glorified in his full human dignity. For the luxurious and blind civilization of Western materialism his scorn is eloquent in *The Ship*, the Titanic of modern civilization sailing on its fatal voyage. He has also written some of the most beautiful love-poems of his generation, for whom indeed erotic love itself has suffered from the split between the carnal and the spiritual, inherent in the English tradition, which set D.H. Lawrence in pursuit of obscene words which he vainly hoped would serve the purpose of reconciling the heavenly and the earthly Venus, which Tom Scott so easily accomplishes:

> The efterstang o love in the dainshoch hert
>> Mony a love-maik fyles.
> Baith lad and lass ken weill the broddan smert
>> That stogs throu lovers whiles
> As, spelder-haughed, they dwaum in ilk ither's airms,
> The grieshoch aye alunt in lends and thairms.
>
>> But whaur's the lad or lass
>> Because of this
>> Wad ettle to bypass
>> Love's beild o bliss?

– or the contempt of 'A Writer's Conference':

> Douce Embro fowk are in a steir,
>> For meetin aa in quorum
> A wheen stray dogs hae gaithert here
>> And pisht on their decorum

There is no poetic mode in which Tom Scott is not a master-craftsman. He is, besides, a fine translator, with some splendid translations of 'Maister Francis Villon', from Dante (all too little), from *The Dream of the Rood*, from St. John of the Cross, from the Anglo-Saxon *The Seafarer*, from Baudelaire.

What English translation of Villon can match the grim grandeur of the language of Scotland: (from 'Ballat o the Hingit')

> We hae been washed and purifee'd by rain.
> The sun has tanned our hides a leathery hue.
> Craws and pyes hae pykit out our een
> And barbered ilka stibble chin and brou.
> Nae peace we ken the twenty-fowr hours through
> For back and furth, whiles braid-on, whiles askew,
> Wi ilka wind that blaws we twist and slue,
> Mair stoggit nor straeberries, and juist as raw.
> See ti it ye never mell wi sicna crew
> And pray the Lord shaws mercie ti us aa.

Tom Scott has all the proud independence of his race that in itself has kept the language from that loss of dignity that is eating away at contemporary English, as verbal hooligans delight in vulgarizing and desecrating our greatest national heritage, the language itself. I remember at some function at Edinburgh University Tom Scott deliberately standing outside the door of the room where the guests were assembled, and I came out to talk with him bearing my glass, since he refused to set foot inside. After a brilliant university career (as a mature student, following a time at Newbattle Abbey under Edwin Muir) the post of 'poet-in-residence' was suggested, which he took to be a tempting of the muse. Certain it is that he held it a disgrace that Edinburgh University had a department of English but not Scotch. Either way it provided an opportunity to adopt that Scottish stance of proud independence and scorn for the 'establishment' which came as naturally to him, and became his tall lean red-bearded form as it would have come to his poetic forbears the bards, creators and custodians of the heroic virtues of their race.

T.S. Eliot supported him, doubtless recognizing in him that devotion to 'the language of the tribe' Eliot and Pound respected and themselves exhibited. And he has done what few in this country have even attempted in this century, left the language of Scotland richer and in better shape than he found it.

> I maun confess't, I am nae mair
> Nor a bardie singin oot on a limb
> But o yae thing I am sikkar suir
> There's nane can say the same o him.

'On a versifier who caa'd me "only a singer".'

(1993)

342

HEATHER BUCK

Geoffrey Hill

Among the other reminders of the holocaust at Sue Ryder's war museum in Cavendish, Suffolk, is a tin labelled Zyklon. Instantly it brought to mind Geoffrey Hill's,

September Song
born 19.6.32 – deported 24.9.42

Undesirable you may have been, untouchable
you were not. Not forgotten
or passed over at the proper time.

As estimated, you died. Things marched,
sufficient, to that end.
Just so much Zyklon and leather, patented
terror, so many routine cries.

(I have made
an elegy for myself it
is true)

September fattens on vines. Roses
flake from the wall. The smoke
of harmless fires drifts to my eyes.

This is plenty. This is more than enough.

This short poem crystallises what makes Geoffrey Hill for me the most important poet writing in English today. It embodies his passionate voice of warning for our torn and broken world, anger for the selfish indifference towards violence and suffering, as well as affirmation of the beauty of the natural world. These twin themes are threaded throughout the whole of his work, in the succession of soldiers, martyrs and writers imprisoned or put to death for their particular vision whom he holds up for our gaze, coupled with his celebration of the natural world in image after image of astonishing beauty. Nowhere is this contrast more vividly evoked than in *The Mystery of the Charity of Charles Péguy*,

where images of war alternate with stanzas recalling the pastoral
beauty of France, e.g.

> among the beetroots, where we are constrained
> to leave you sleeping and to step aside
> from the fleshed bayonets, the fusillade
> of red-rimmed smoke like stubble being burned;

or in contrast,

> Yours is their dream of France, militant-pastoral:
> musky red gillyvors, the wicker bark
> of clematis braided across old brick
> and the slow chain that cranks into the well
>
> morning and evening.

His is the haunted voice of the seer. It is inevitable that such a
voice should attract an avalanche of words, but luckily what he is
saying, and the way that he says it, is too important to be eroded
by the smoke and stridor of contemporary criticism. There is
nothing 'difficult', 'cold' or 'tight-lipped' about his poetry; sev-
eral re-readings of any page of the *Collected Poems* will yield all the
passion and beauty one could desire. Let us pay this great poet,
living and writing among us, the tribute of reading his work.

(1992)

ALAN MASSEY

Geoffrey Hill

The self-evident excellence of Geoffrey Hill's poetry must have left many a commentator stuck for adequate expressions of praise. To welcome this book – the first 'Collected' of many, one hopes – I shall attempt an ideogram of sorts, a grid of quoted generalisations. I shall try to press it inwards to indicate Mr Hill's particularity; full justice to that particularity would call for something more rigorous.

Let Confucius supply the first strand. The translation is by James R. Ware (Mentor Books, 1955):

> When substance overbalances refinement, crudeness results.
> When refinement overbalances substance, there is superficiality.
> When refinement and substance are balanced one has Great Man.

It fits; I would add only that part of 'substance' is language, part of 'refinement' subject-matter.

Strand two is from David Jones (*Epoch and Artist*, Faber, 1959):

> The artist, no matter of what sort or what his medium, must be *moved by the nature of whatever art he practises.*

That is from a man who knew what he was saying, and doing, if ever a man did; also a man whose 'Yet he's plenty breath for bawling / as if this were his Latin spring, / this calcined waste his lapsed *vervactum*'[1] is as palpably Jonesian as are palpably Hillian the lines... but open the book where you will. As volumes of collected poems ordinarily go, this *Collected Poems* comes over as well clear of the ordinary. In one respect it reminds me also of Sir Thomas Malory's prose book: I mean – open it where you will and you will find something to stop you in your tracks, something to do with the artist's acute sense of the medium.

T.S. Eliot contributes strand three (*The Use of Poetry and the Use of Criticism*, Faber, 1933):

> The ordinary reader, when warned against the obscurity of a poem, is apt to be thrown into a state of consternation very

[1] From 'The Agent'; see David Jones, *The Roman Quarry* (Agenda Editions, 1981).

unfavourable to poetic receptivity...There is such a thing as stage fright, but what such readers have is pit or gallery fright.

Relevant in excelsis. How often reviewers and critics have told us how difficult Geoffrey Hill's work is! And the current widespread indifference to poetry – in England of all places – an indifference as painful as it is frightening – is at least partly attributable to decades of academic harping on the difficulty of modern poetry in particular. Of course much of the best modern work is difficult; it is not so difficult that only an Einstein or a Wittgenstein could hope to grasp it. Of course Geoffrey Hill is a poet's poet; so is Shakespeare, so is Chaucer – who for centuries have managed to reach English-speaking people at large. One reason for welcoming this paperback 'Collected' is that it has a chance of going relatively unmediated to the reading public.

The fourth and last strand is Pound's (*Literary Essays*, Faber, 1954):

> Beauty in art reminds one what is worth while. I am not now speaking of shams. I mean beauty, not slither, not sentimentalizing about beauty, not telling people that beauty is the proper and respectable thing. I mean beauty. You don't argue about an April wind, you feel bucked up when you meet it. You feel bucked up when you come on a swift moving thought in Plato or on a fine line in a statue.

I would bracket this with strand two, stressing the nature of the art. Also I shall risk a step beyond 'beauty' and say 'glamour'. There is an unmissable, unmistakable comeliness about the finest work in any medium. Tippett's music has it, the Gauguin detail on the cover of the book under review has it, the poetry between the book's covers has it. An older word than 'glamour', which dates only from 1720, might have been preferable, though it does hark back via *gramarye* to a hypothetical Anglo-Norman form *glomerie*. I am further indebted to the Oxford Dictionary of English Etymology for what is, given the present context, an irresistible bonus: *magister glomeriae*, 'title of a former official in the university of Cambridge'.

Quite simply (and to say nothing of rhythm or of 'music') it is Geoffrey Hill's *language* that lifts him out of the ruck: much as the presence of unusually good looks has an outshining, even eclipsing, effect. This may seem bad luck to those less liberally gifted, but the best of them are not resentful; you could argue of some that the fault is theirs for not 'making more of themselves'. There are time-hallowed poetic recourses and resources. Poets who do not acquire these assets 'by ear', by osmosis, from the masters of the past, are at liberty to labour at them. Syllepsis, meiosis, oxymoron, hyperbaton, paranomasia, etc.; they are to be found in dictionaries and in such works as Fowler's *Modern English Usage*. Classic onomatopoeia opens Hymn XVI of the *Mercian Hymns*: 'Clash of salutation. As keels thrust into shingle...' Each of these devices has a will of its own and will not be applied like a plaster or taken like a pill. C.S. Lewis wrote of courtly love (*The Allegory of Love*, OUP, 1936): '... only the courteous can love, but it is love that makes them courteous.'

Becalmed in the generalising area of my chosen quotations, I have scarcely gestured towards the poet's individuality. The four strands of my curtal-ideogram apply to all of our best makers, past and present; my point is precisely that he is of that company. What can we hope for but that the best language will seep into the national consciousness? The best language sings from a very small number, and Geoffrey Hill is our most noteworthy *rara avis*.

(1985)

PART SIX

A Reconsideration

JONATHAN BARKER

A Land that is Lonelier than Ruin

L.M. Findlay, the editor of Algernon Charles Swinburne's *Selected Poems* (Carcanet Press), talks in his introduction of the 're-habilitation of Swinburne' telling us that this 'is inevitably an uncertain enterprise', obviously unaware that all serious readers of poetry know *Itylus, The Triumph of Time, A Leave-Taking*, the first chorus from *Atalanta in Calydon, The Garden of Proserpine*, and *A Forsaken Garden*. It is a mystery how Findlay intends to bring about this 'rehabilitation' without including *Itylus* in his selection of poems, but exclude it he does thereby robbing us of a poem of rare memorability and rhythmic sweep:

> Swallow, my sister, O sister swallow,
>> How can thine heart be full of the spring?
>> A thousand summers are over and dead.
> What hast thou found in the spring to follow?
> What hast thou found in thine heart to sing?
>> What wilt thou do when the summer is shed?

One of our better critics, Michael Schmidt, has pointed out that 'that first line is one of the most curious errors of taste in English poetry'. Looked at from one angle much of this poet's work can be made to appear absurd, for the simple reason that if we go to Swinburne looking specifically for qualities he does not possess we will find little but such absurdities.

Before we apologise for or criticise Swinburne's faults we would do well to enjoy his strengths. And, as L.M. Findlay is aware, these strengths are at variance with our own preferences in poetry today. In the main post-modernist readers have ceased to associate Swinburne's mellifluous musicality with the language of poetry, or the metrical swing of his rhythms with the rhythm of poetry (Auden, Betjeman, Kipling and Causley would be exceptions of great distinction). It was the same in 1918 when Ezra Pound noted that 'Swinburne's art is out of fashion' and went on to put his finger on what we find wrong with Swinburne:

> He neglected the value of words as words, and was intent on their value as sound. His habit of choice grew mechanical, and he himself perceived it and parodied his own systemization.

His self parody 'Nephelidia' is included in this selection and it proves Pound's point, while also revealing a previously unacknowledged sense of humour:

> Surely no spirit or sense of a soul that was soft to the spirit and soul of our senses
> Sweetens the stress of suspiring suspicion that sobs in the semblance and sound of a sigh;

Pound's observation that it is the 'systemization' of Swinburne's verse which makes it unpalatable is linked to an observation made earlier in the same essay:

> He habitually makes a fine stanzaic form, writes one or two fine strophes in it, and then continues to pour into the mould strophes of diminishing quality.

This is apparent even in 'By the North Sea', one of Swinburne's best poems, which in its opening lines describes the bleak grandeur of Dunwich in Suffolk:

> A land that is lonelier than ruin;
> A sea that is stranger than death:
> Far fields that a rose never blew in,
> Wan waste where the winds lack breath;
> Waste endless and boundless and flowerless
> But of marsh-blossoms fruitless as free:
> Where earth lies exhausted, as powerless
> To strive with the sea.

The stanzaic pattern is a frame rigidly controlling the language and feeling of the poem. The first section of the poem repeats the pattern and effect systematically for fifteen verses in the same stately, and eventually tonally repetitive, dactylic metre. The concrete particularity of this poem contrasts with the often generalised nature of Swinburne's language, as shown in the magnificently sustained 440 lines of the earlier 'Dolores':

> Could you hurt me, sweet lips, though I hurt you?
> Men touch them, and change in a trice
> The lilies and languors of virtue
> For the raptures and roses of vice;
> Those lie where thy foot on the floor is,
> These crown and caress thee and chain,
> O splendid and sterile Dolores,
> Our Lady of Pain.

Pound's observation on Swinburne neglecting 'the value of words as words' is noticeable here. At the same time the poem's effect owes more to the lyric singing line of 'Itylus' than, say, the longer narrative movement of a poem such as Robert Browning's 'Childe Roland to the Dark Tower Came'. Swinburne needed space to express himself and that length called for a 'systemization' which eventually, through monotony, wearies the reader. The problem of the long poem was first noted by Edgar Allan Poe in his essay on 'The Poetic Principle':

> I need scarcely observe that a poem deserves its title only inasmuch as it excites, by elevating the soul . . . But all excitements are, through a psychal necessity, transient. That degree of excitement which would entitle a poem to be called at all, cannot be sustained throughout a composition of any great length. After the lapse of half an hour, at the very utmost, it flags – fails – a revulsion ensues – and then the poem is, in effect, and in fact, no longer such.

In Swinburne, as in Poe, we have a lyric sensibility married to a mathematical delight in repeating patterns, with subtle changes within a stanza form. The original impulse for the poem metamorphoses from feeling into a patterning of words.

Another interesting comment on the sheer volume of Swinburne's poems can be found in T.S. Eliot's essay 'Swinburne as Poet' still a key text on the poet although it was first published in 1920:

> The words of condemnation are words which express his qualities. You may say 'diffuse'. But the diffuseness is essential; had Swinburne practised greater concentration his verse would be, not better in the same kind, but a different thing. His diffuseness is one of his glories. That so little material as appears to be employed in *The Triumph of Time* should release such an amazing number of words, requires what there is no reason to call anything but genius. You could not condense *The Triumph of Time*. You could only leave out. And this would destroy the poem; though no one stanza seems essential.

And so it is. Swinburne's lack of proportion and sense of scale are certainly wearisome at times, but as Eliot observed, are at the same time 'one of his glories'. As long as the reader of 'Dolores' maintains the requisite speed the poem will lift off the page and live; but it will fail as an entity as soon as the reader stops to examine a specific image in detail:

Thou shalt blind his bright eyes though he wrestle,
  Thou shalt chain his light limbs though he strive;
In his lips all thy serpents shall nestle,
  In his hands all thy cruelties thrive...

As with Byron's *Don Juan*, we need the speed of reading in order to create the poem's unmistakable effect and atmosphere. We have to read Swinburne in a way which he dictates, just as we have to read *The Waste Land* in an unusual way to experience its qualities.

There are two great successes in this extended lyric style in Swinburne: 'The Triumph of Time' (a poem ironically letting us know in its title that time is a theme implicit in the length of the poem) and 'Félise'.

'The Triumph of Time' disproves Eliot's point:

The poetry is not morbid, it is not erotic, it is not destructive. These are adjectives which can be applied to the material, the human feelings, which in Swinburne's case do not exist. The morbidity is not of human feeling but of language.

In fact, 'The Triumph of Time' is itself a great ocean of feeling, and progresses from distress to acceptance of loss:

I will say no word that a man might say
Whose whole life's love goes in a day;
For this could never have been; and never,
  Though the gods and the years relent, shall be.

Recognisable feeling and emotion served by language, without what Eliot calls 'the hallucination of meaning', can be found later in:

And grief shall endure not for ever, I know.
  As things that are not shall these things be;
We shall live through seasons of sun and of snow,
  And none be grievous as this to me...

Here we find the true voice of feeling accurately expressed within a poem which does not always maintain such felicity of statement. But even the ending keeps close to the reality of human loss:

I shall go my ways, tread out my measure,
  Fill the days of my daily breath
With fugitive things not good to treasure,
  Do as the world doth, say as it saith...

354

Even the Browningesque 'Félise' manages to express loss accurately and recognisably:

> Live and let live, as I will do,
>   Love, and let love, and so will I.
> But, sweet, for me no more with you:
>   Not while I live, not though I die.
>   Goodnight, goodbye.

And, finally, 'A Leave-Taking' expresses feeling in a restrained and accurate language reminiscent in its concrete precision of Hardy or Herbert:

> Let us go hence, my songs; she will not hear.
> Let us go hence together without fear;
> Keep silence now, for singing-time is over,
> And over all old things and all things dear.
> She loves not you nor me as all we love her,
> Yea, though we sang as angels in her ear,
>   She would not hear.

Compared with Ernest Dowson's marvellous 'Non Sum Qualis Eram Bonae Sub Regno Cynarae', it is Dowson, not Swinburne, who looks antique and vague in meaning, although here with a rhythmic subtlety quite beyond Swinburne:

> Last night, ah, yesternight, betwixt her lips and mine
> There fell thy shadow, Cynara! thy breath was shed
> Upon my soul between the kisses and the wine;
> And I was desolate and sick of an old passion,
>   Yea, I was desolate and bowed my head:
> I have been faithful to thee, Cynara! in my fashion.

A plainness of language and an eye firmly trained on the object can be found in Swinburne's 'The Sundew':

> A little marsh-plant, yellow green,
> And pricked at lip with tender red.
> Tread close, and either way you tread
> Some faint black water jets between
> Lest you should bruise the curious head.

This poem on a carnivorous plant is reminiscent of D.G. Rossetti's 'The Woodspurge', but outdoes that fine poem in its clarity of observation:

The hard sun, as thy petals knew,
Coloured the heavy moss-water:
Thou wert not worth green midsummer
Nor fit to live to August blue,
O sundew, not remembering her.

The famous mood-paintings of Swinburne are represented best by 'On the Downs' and 'A Forsaken Garden'; neither quite maintaining the authority of their first stanzas, as Pound pointed out was generally the case:

A faint sea without wind or sun;
A sky like flameless vapour dun;
　　A valley like an unsealed grave
That no man cares to weep upon,
Bare, without boon to crave,
　　Or flower to save.

starts 'On the Downs', while another symbolist landscape, 'A Forsaken Garden', commences magically:

In a coign of the cliff between lowland and highland,
　　At the sea-down's edge between windward and lee,
Walled round with rocks as an inland island,
　　The ghost of a garden fronts the sea.
A girdle of brushwood and thorn encloses
　　The steep square slope of the blossomless bed
Where the weeds that grew green from the graves of its roses
　　Now lie dead.

'By the North Sea', one of his best poems already partly quoted, most successfully of all merges the inner mood of the poet with the actual outer landscape. The poem employs a winning variety of stanza forms which manage to break the patterned regularity which creates the monotony of Swinburne as in:

The waves are as ranks enrolled
　　Too close for the storm to sever:
The fens lie naked and cold,
　　But their heart fails utterly never:
The lists are set from old,
　　And the warfare endureth for ever.

III

Miles, and miles, and miles of desolation!
　　Leagues on leagues on leagues without a change!

Sign or token of some eldest nation
  Here would make the strange land not so strange.
Time-forgotten, yea since time's creation,
  Seem these borders where the sea-birds range.

Surely, with Crabbe's *The Village*, one of the most impressive mood-paintings of the Suffolk coast in our literature.

So we have several Swinburnes, and not just the obvious mixture of classicist and satyr. Swinburne was the poet who extended the lyric poem into hundreds of lines all of which aim to sing not argue. Also he was a symbolist poet working contemporaneously with his continental peers creating mood pictures of imaginary or real places corresponding to the inner emotional and imaginative life of the writer. We have Swinburne the startling poet; the arrival of whose poems Thomas Hardy said were as if 'a garland of red roses/Had fallen about the hood of some smug nun' into Victorian England. Or, alternatively, as Ifor Evans put it 'It was as if a satyr had been let loose in a Victorian drawing-room'. But Swinburne was also a poet who could write objectively about things seen or felt in a wide variety of ways, including the marvellous self-parody already quoted, and 'The Higher Pantheism in a Nutshell', a parody of Tennyson:

One and two are not one: but one and nothing is two:
Truth can hardly be false, if falsehood cannot be true ...

God, whom we see not, is: and God, who is not, we see:
Fiddle, we know, is diddle: and diddle, we take it, is dee.

We have Swinburne the writer of the unsuccessful Shellyian spiritual autobiography 'Thalassius', and the exceptional translator of Villon's 'The Complaint of the Fair Armouress':

Though I gat bruises green and black,
  I loved him never the less a jot;
Though he bound burdens on my back,
  If he said 'Kiss me and heed it not'
  Right little pain I felt, God wot,
When that foul thief's mouth, found so sweet,
  Kissed me – Much good thereof I got!
I keep the sin and the shame of it.

Elsewhere in the poem he makes the wonderful line 'And sweet red splendid kissing mouth'.

From *Songs Before Sunrise*, the political antithesis to *Poems and Ballads* first series, L.M. Findlay includes the tiresome 'The Eve of Revolution' and leaves out the mechanical 'A Watch in the Night' while sadly missing (perhaps on grounds of space) 'Siena', a poem praised by Pound as one of the 'few rallies of force' after *Poems and Ballads*. 'Siena' offers the reader a rare glimpse of Swinburne's middle style, conversational, relaxed and again permeated with a sensitivity of feeling:

> O gracious city well-beloved,
>   Italian, and a maiden crowned,
> Siena, my feet are no more moved
>   Toward thy strange-shapen mountain-bound:
> But my heart in me turns and moves,
> O lady loveliest of my loves,
> Toward thee, to lie before thy feet
> And gaze from thy fair fountain-seat
> Up the sheer street;

The exclusion of this poem is a missed opportunity.

The linguistic masterwork of this large and well-produced selection from the poems is clearly the late 'By the North Sea'. The bleak resonance of this poem convinces the reader that he is in the presence of a particular sensibility which here recreates the mood of a particular place. Certainly anyone who knows Dunwich cannot help but approve of this work. It takes several readings to see the originality and success of the poem, but once perceived fully it can be seen as some of the best of Swinburne. In the notes the editor quotes Swinburne enquiring of Lord Houghton:

> Do you know the 'dead cathedral city' which I have tried to describe . . . Dunwich, in Suffolk? The whole picture is from life – salt marshes, ruins, and bones protruding seawards through the soil of the crumbling sandbanks.

The poet's eye is held close enough to the place and the sense of place for him to evoke its spirit and atmosphere through both detailed and generalised description. The cold, external beauty of this poem contrasts interestingly with the rich hot-house blooms of the better poems from the first series of *Poems and Ballads*, and adds another dimension to the poet's work.

But elsewhere Swinburne's over great rhythmic facility in shaping language creates his main problem; that of an emotional thinness. An emotion is often spread too thin over the wide area of a poem to satisfy a contemporary taste for compression, complexity of surface and ambiguity of meaning. 'By the North Sea' on the whole avoids this thinness.

The movement of Swinburne's writing career is away from life and into literature. The emotional disaster portrayed in 'The Triumph of Time' and 'A Leave-Taking' led to Swinburne's perverted and wrong-headed assumption that love and pain were intimately related. In 'Dolores' 'Our Lady of Pain' is accordingly seen as 'O mistress and mother of pleasure'. This correlation can be seen again in the superb lyric 'A Match' which throughout prefaces opposites with the hypothetical 'If':

> If you were queen of pleasure,
>   And I were king of pain,
> We'd hunt down love together,
> Pluck out his flying-feather,
> And teach his feet a measure,
>   And find his mouth a rein;
> If you were queen of pleasure,
>   And I were king of pain.

The love/hunt metaphor used so often in Petrarchan love poetry here achieves a personal meaning for the poet; that of forcing something wild and free into a discipline, 'a measure', as Swinburne trains language into complex verse patterns rather than uses it to say things plainly.

The pain and trouble of lost love in turn led to Swinburne's poem 'The Garden of Proserpine', the first of Swinburne's gardens, and one which led him away from the real world of emotion and sight into a symbolist inner world in which feeling is isolated from the reality of pain and suffering. Unlike the 'here' of Keats's garden poem 'Ode to a Nightingale' which signifies our given world, the 'here' of Swinburne's 'The Garden of Proserpine' is a metaphor for a state of mind:

> Here, where the world is quiet;
>   Here, where all trouble seems
> Dead winds' and spent waves' riot
>   In doubtful dreams of dreams . . .

Elsewhere the poem is reminiscent of Tennyson's 'The Palace of Art':

> I am tired of tears and laughter,
> > And men that laugh and weep;
> Of what may come hereafter
> > For men that sow to reap...

Swinburne's fellow man is not seen through the pronoun 'who' but through the impersonal 'that' as if an object, showing already a dissociation from fellowship and the enthusiasm and vitality evident in 'Itylus' and the choruses from 'Atalanta in Calydon'.

If 'By the North Sea' is Swinburne's late masterwork, then his early masterwork must be 'Félise', a long poem which shows his fatalistic withdrawal inwards away from outward action and effort:

> We know not whether death be good,
> > But life at least it will not be:
> Men will stand saddening as we stood,
> > Watch the same fields and skies as we
> > And the same sea.

Later Swinburne was to return to this theme in his other garden poem, 'A Forsaken Garden', a poem which can be read as a revisit to his own deserted emotional life, ghostly fronting Swinburne's constant obsession, the sea. All vitality has gone from the garden as it has from the poet's heart, and as it had from the prince in Edgar Allan Poe's similarly symbolist poem 'The Haunted Palace'.

'At a Month's End' also returns to an old passion with great effect:

> So to my soul in surer fashion
> > Your savage stamp and savour hangs;
> The print and perfume of old passion,
> > The wild-beast mark of panther's fangs.

In the poem Swinburne describes himself as 'your light white sea-mew' implying that the violent panther might threaten to devour him. In these poems Swinburne makes interesting poetry from his personal autobiography. 'Thalassius', which expresses the same things differently ('with too long strong stress of grief to be/His heart grew sere and numb'), he writes weak poetry hardly worth the name.

The fact that desolation of the emotions and landscape is the theme of his best poems seems to prove Pound's observation that 'Swinburne was actually broken by a real and not by a feigned emotional catastrophe early in life', although surely Pound's belief in 'his later slow decline' can be seen to be wrong when we read 'By the North Sea'.

This selection is an extremely wide ranging one, including poems from all periods and not particularly favouring the better known poems. L.M. Findlay has clearly read his way steadily through all the poems, selecting those which will most effectively aid that 'rehabilitation of Swinburne' he so wants. But the list of poems wrongly excluded from such a sizeable collection must be noted by the reader coming to this poet for the first time: 'Itylus', 'Faustine', 'The Leper', 'A Ballad of Burdens', 'August', 'After Death' from Swinburne's best single book *Poems and Ballads*, first series; and the systemized but effective 'A Watch in the Night', the undervalued 'Siena' and 'The Oblation' from *Songs before Sunrise*. And surely at least one of Swinburne's baby poems should appear to represent another, admittedly linguistically thin, side of his work; and to admit a little love and light into this, in many ways, loveless and lightless book. 'Babyhood' or 'A Child's Laughter', sentimental as they are, should surely have struck a chord in the editor who could have related that sentimental affirmation to other, colder sides of Swinburne.

Far from being a profound thinker (indeed some would defensibly argue that he hardly thought at all!) Swinburne was primarily a *literary* poet in that he saw the manipulation and control of language as the poet's particular skill. In one way his facility with language led to his downfall, in that as long as he kept pouring words into stanzas he felt he was expressing what he had to; while, alternately, this same facility (called appositely by T.S. Eliot 'such an amazing number of words') created his very best poems. Surely Swinburne's failing lies rather in his inability to admit other people as objects of real affection into his poems. When other people enter they do so as inhuman symbols (Dolores, Proserpine), or heroes (Mazzini, Victor Hugo), or fictions based on unhappy love (Félise) or as babies, not adults.

His body of work is a lonely one, at its best when expressing isolation within a specific landscape. Always allied to his best poems is the sea, 'the great sweet mother' constantly celebrated by Swinburne, as by Byron, as a metaphor for personal and political freedom:

> ... shoreless waves whose glee
> Scorns the shore and loves the wind that leaves them free,

Strange as sleep and pale as death and fair as life,
  Shifts the moonlight-coloured sunshine on the sea.

As those lines from 'A Swimmer's Dream' show, Swinburne could only find happiness in such solitude.

We should not dismiss Swinburne's writing career as a complete decline after a strong, if not totally original, start. (We can see the influence of Keats, Browning, Landor, Rossetti, Tennyson and Shelley in *Poems and Ballads*, first series.) As Findlay has found, there are poems throughout Swinburne's writing career which reward reading and rereading. All poetry lovers at some time read Swinburne with real, even intense, pleasure, and without his work English poetry would be the poorer. A fine tide of feeling sweeps through Swinburne's systemized imitations of classical metres; and, if that feeling is expressed more through rhythm than actual meaning, and, if at times we find that feeling thin or repetitive, then we should accept these as the unavoidable failings of a lyric talent which also needed, indeed felt compelled, to write at some length.

(1983)

PART SEVEN

Two Memoirs

BASIL BUNTING

Yeats Recollected

A lecture to the Yeats Society at Sligo, 1973.
(I have left this lecture exactly as it was delivered, a mere may-fly some trout might take, and no hook in it. 1974.)

I have been trying to solve a conundrum: why should people like you, who know all there is to be known about William Butler Yeats, ask me, who know so little, to talk to you? Certainly, the number of people who knew Yeats diminishes year by year, but there are still many of them left. Fewer, no doubt, remember him as long ago as I do, and perhaps you have listened to them all in turn at your meetings in Sligo and call on me merely so that you can tick my name off the list, without any vain hope that I might tell you something you did not know already. I am as ill-fitted for the task as any man could be. I like to mind my own business, so that I have never inquired into the lives of the people I know. I haven't the least idea whether my friends beat their wives or how they go about the mysterious feat of getting enough to live on. I don't suppose Yeats beat his wife: she was too active, but if you put me on oath I dont know that I could swear to it.

As to getting a living, Yeats seemed pretty comfortable to a young man as hard up as I was, but he once told me he was sixty before he earned £200 a year by writing. I've remembered that because it filled me with gloomy and far too accurate notions about my own future. I dont think it throws much light on his finances, and it may not even be true, since men use good round terms when they advise younger men against writing for a living. They are engaged in advocacy, not history, and dont expect to have their summary accounts audited.

I have confessed that I am not curious about other men's lives, so that I haven't much to remember. Now I must add that I dont study to remember, because I have always found Memory to be a cunning and persistent liar, which no doubt explains why the Muses, her daughters, are so unreliable. Whenever accident enables me to check the facts, memory seems to be wrong. If I consider Yeats, as you have obliged me to, I begin to wonder whether God had any hand in the man I remember at all or whether I have created him all by myself. You will understand why I prefer to see poets only through the print on the pages of their collected works, with no intervening memories, not even their own. My shrivelled remains of a conscience reminded me of this before I accepted your invitation to talk about Yeats, but, as I think Shaw said, every man of forty is a scoundrel, and a man as old as I am is more than a match for whatever conscience he has left.

The printed mentions of me that Yeats has left are not at all flattering. In one place – I cannot give you the reference – he shows some alarm at the prospect of meeting one of the wilder disciples of Ezra Pound. At another – *Pages from a Diary*, on the seventh page – he shows himself disturbed by my conversation, though he is also kind enough to say that he had admired my verse. The conversation was about God and the church, and young men are apt to be very summary in their judgements of such matters, and crude in expressing them. I wonder whether Yeats ever discovered that I was a Quaker, if not in intellectual persuasion, at least by temperament and education. However that may be, he got used to me. I witnessed his will – the next passerby would have done as well for that – and I was sent to Switzerland to collect his children from their school and conduct them by easy stages to Rapallo.

It was at Rapallo that I met him. I dined or lunched or supped or underwent some similar formal presentation in the flat he had taken at the top of a big modern block overlooking the bay. I remember nothing about it, but a little later at some similar meeting he astonished me by reciting to his guests the whole twenty-eight lines of one of my poems, word-perfect, though to me, at first, almost unrecognisable in his hieratic chant. I dont know whether this was an extreme case of the common politeness of getting by heart some quotation from the poet you are entertaining and uttering it at the first plausible opportunity, or whether he really liked it. Perhaps he did, for it was written when I was under the spell of Mallarmé and might have sounded like an echo of tunes he had been familiar with in his youth. I dont recollect this out of pride, for Yeats admired and praised some poems I would hate mine to be ranked with, but because it seemed a very handsome amends to make for his initial distrust. From then on he talked freely with me whenever we met.

That was not so often as might be imagined, because Yeats was ill a good deal of the time. He had the disease which was called, in those days, Malta fever, because Maltese were said to catch it from the goats whose milk they drank; but it had been called

relapsing fever, a better name, since patients are continually get-
ting better and then suddenly showing all the symptoms again as
badly as ever or even worse. At one time Yeats certainly thought
that he was dying, and that is why Ezra Pound and I were sud-
denly called to witness his will. However, he got better again and
again and relapsed again and again. At one time he would be
strolling about the town – a little town still in those days – and at
another he would be what the hospitals now call 'serious'. This
went on so long that he began to think he had been bewitched, so
that the doctors were helpless: what he needed was a powerful
and well-disposed wizard. But for magic he had only himself to
rely on in that time and place, and he was often too ill even to
think fruitfully about magic. However he did at last convince
himself – perhaps I ought to rephrase that – he did at last manage
to humbug himself into believing that his illness was caused by a
certain ring he wore, and the next time he was strong enough to
venture out, he and Mrs Yeats made their way to the end of the
mole and cast the ring into the sea, with the appropriate formula;
and it seemed to work, for that time he did not relapse, which
confirmed him in his half-belief in magic.

Yeats's illness is also connected with the story of the suicidal
cat. In those days there lived, in a fantastical villa at Zoagli, near
Rapallo, an Italian dramatic poet called Sem Benelli of whom I can
say very little except that his work answered well in the theatre,
so that he grew rich, ran his own theatre company, and enjoyed
the society of extravagant beautiful actresses. His current mis-
tress lay in bed to all hours of the day, caressing an exceedingly
fine white Persian cat, until another play was ready for produc-
tion and Sem Benelli's company had to set out on tour. Then they
were puzzled what to do with the cat, till Sem Benelli's secretary,
who was a friend of mine, remembered that I was living alone in
a flat above Rapallo and might possibly welcome the cat's com-
pany, but he was not sure, so he never asked me. He went about
things in a less simple style. One day I heard a sort of scuffle on
the stairs, and then a knock at my door, which I opened just in
time to catch a glimpse of petticoats whirling as some peasant girl
ran away. I couldnt chase her, because I tripped over a basket that
had been left on the threshold, and the basket mewed. When I
opened it and saw the magnificent cat, I couldnt imagine where
it had come from or why it had been left at my door, but I was
rather pleased than otherwise. I gave it milk, and went out to get
fish for it, and the cat made itself at home immediately. The girls

from next door came to see me a little oftener because of the cat. But my satisfaction didnt last long. The cat was used to being stroked and petted all day. It would never leave me alone. If I wrote, it came and sat on the paper. If I typed, it tried to sit on the typewriter. Whenever I put it down it complained, and looked so hurt that I had to stop working to comfort it, and thus I grew more and more exasperated and left off considering the cat's feelings. At last one day when I had put it down, it jumped onto the window-sill, called my attention with a prolonged miaow, struck a melo-dramatic attitude (I assure you) and leapt down three stories into the garden. Perhaps it got rid of one of its nine lives, but in veteri-nary terms it only dislocated its shoulder. I had that put right, but as soon as the cat was tolerably active again I determined to get rid of it. By that time we had found out where it came from, but Sem Benelli's house was closed and very likely the actress who had fondled the cat had been succeeded by another. I couldnt just return it. I thought of leaving it on somebody's doorstep, as it had been left on mine, but Ezra Pound suggested Yeats. He was ill, too ill to work, but restless, and he might as well fondle the cat; and its attempted suicide was certainly something to ponder on: so the cat was solemnly presented to the great poet and its beauty made it welcome. For a time. Unfortunately – that seems the wrong word – but unfortunately for the cat, Yeats got better and tried to work, but the cat wouldnt let him. While it was with me it had become expert in every means of sabotaging work that a cat is capable of and it toiled with desperation to prevent Yeats think-ing of anything whatever except itself. At last it had to be shut out on the balcony, where it lept onto the balustrade, cut an attitude, proclaimed its intention of suicide, and jumped down, four stories this time, to the pavement. It broke a leg. No one but the vet could take any satisfaction from that, and by now the cat had only seven lives left, so there had to be councils to decide what to do with it. At last it was given to Ezra Pound's father, and there, I believe, it found lasting content, sitting in the sun with that kin-dest of old men.

I dont know whether Yeats ever alluded to this cat. It seemed just the sort of creature to furnish him with symbols, but I cant remember ever seeing anything I could trace to it. Perhaps, like me, he had a guilty conscience for driving the poor animal to suicide. Anyway, that is the only thing I can tell you about Yeats that is likely to be new to many of you. He strolled sometimes alone along the promenade in a long overcoat and a broad brimmed hat, with his hands often behind him and his eyes on the ground a yard or two in front of his toes, as though the exterior world were as narrow for him as for Wordsworth's Old Cumberland Beggar; the very picture of intent poetic reverie, filling whatever spectators there might be with awe and admiration. But those who got close enough might have seen that his eyes were not fixed on the ground at all. They were darting from side to side, looking for someone to gossip with, and if he spotted an acquaintance – Ezra or George Antheil or me for instance – sitting in the cafe he lost no time in crossing the road to sit with us. You are bound to ask me what his conversation was like and what it was about, and I have to confess that I cant tell you. We enjoyed it, it must have been good conversation, but it had no such marked characteristics as stick in the mind, such as Ezra Pound's lightning and unexpected wit, or the marriage of paradox and commonsense in Shaw, or the belligerence of Wyndham Lewis, or Ford's story-telling. He liked argument so long as it was not too cogent, about religion and the wilder sort of metaphysics – Plotinus, for example. Sometimes he was willing to discuss the technical side of poetry, but on the whole it seemed as though he felt technique to be too intimate a matter for much public discussion. Most of all he loved gossip, current gossip for preference, but old gossip too, as though nothing were ever altogether past and done with. If conversation were in any danger of flagging, you could always revive it by a reference, in any context, to George Moore. Yeats's invective about Moore was always as fresh as though their difference had happened only yesterday. He said he disdained Moore, yet he could never let the subject alone, never dismiss it in weariness, never remember how many years had gone by since Moore's offence.

Fortunately, one of the first pieces of literary work I ever did had been done for George Moore, so that the bait was always at hand and the big fish always rose to it.

Another conversation with Yeats has provided a line for Ezra Pound's *Cantos*. We were sitting inside the cafe on a wet afternoon, eating cakes, George Antheil and I, when Yeats joined us. He must have said something about Shelley, when I, intending to wave a red rag at the bull to liven up the afternoon, announced that there was no good in Shelley whatsoever, except perhaps that he had recommended incest, which, I said, must be the best foundation for domestic tranquillity. Yeats did not bother to come to Shelley's rescue, but began considering my proposition about incest in detail. I forget what he had to say about it, but presently he said: 'Ssshh! If the general public could overhear the conversation of poets, they would hhhang the lot of us'. This was reported to Pound, and it was not wasted on him.

Sometimes he tried to convince me that magic, theosophy, and the rest of his paraphernalia were not just a subjective source of symbols for him, but were real, objective happenings. He gave me some notion of Madame Blavatsky, and her mixture of obvious charlatanry with feats which he thought she really believed, and which he was, provisionally, willing to believe. I had met Annie Besant and been impressed by the force of her personality, but Yeats said she was not to be mentioned in the same breath with Blavatsky. But at this date I could not possibly separate what he said about the formidable woman from what he has written about her, and that you know already. Altogether I think he preferred the wizards of his youth to contemporary wizards. He was not inclined to bother with Gurdjieff, for example, and was uneasy about Aleister Crowley, though eager for all the details of the latest scandal from Crowley's Sicilian den. That kept me in the conversation, because Mary Butts, who had been horrified at Cefalu, had told me all about it when she paused in her flight at Genoa, while it was fresh in her memory and before her memory had had much time to embroider it. There was something about Crowley trying to push somebody over a cliff, though whether the pushing was done physically or by suggestion I'm sure I cant remember now. And something that Mary didnt like, had happened to a goat, and I hadnt collected enough details about that to satisfy Yeats. Sometimes his pleasure in scandals which must have been terrible to the people concerned rather disgusted me, but this is not the occasion to dwell on that.

In other ways, Yeats was kind and thoughtful of other people. His children possessed a very splendid Wendy-house, but had grown out of it. He handed it over to my little daughter and she and the dog wore it out in a year or two. It must have been troublesome to arrange its transport to Italy. We could never have afforded such an expensive toy. Also he put up with the presence of Antheil or myself at times when he must have found us intrusive, merely because the young learn from the old and the old must let them. Now that I am old myself I realise how much kindness was necessary to show such tolerance.

He had a mint set of the new Irish coinage, with the animals on it, a perquisite of his senatorial labours, and took great pleasure in showing it to us. On the other hand, the Abbey Theatre, his other continuing public activity, did not seem to give him much satisfaction. When Lennox Robinson came to Rapallo to consult him about it, Yeats grew agitated and irritable. I haven't the faintest idea what the trouble was. Perhaps he was just tired of the stage by then.

That, I am afraid, is all I can now remember about Yeats. Of course, there are plenty of general impressions; but they are neither factual nor precise, and I daresay they are derived as much from his writings, and even from other people's talk about Yeats as from genuine memories, accurate or inaccurate. Many of you are probably much better qualified than I am to form such impressions; however, here are some of them, for what they are worth. Some of you probably know better, and some may be annoyed, but I think my impressions are founded on fact, however much they may have strayed in more than forty years.

I am often asked whether Yeats actually believed in magic. 'Belief' is a difficult word, covering everything from immediate conviction, such as comes from what a man sees for himself or similarly immediate experience, to the results of self-hypnosis. Yeats was interested in any evidence he could find for a world that goes beyond the matter science can investigate. He knew by experience that a great deal of what is alleged to be such evidence turns out to be deliberate fraud, but could not give up hoping to find evidence that could not be contradicted. I think he kidded himself that he had found such evidence, and I think he was more than half aware that he was kidding himself. Magic, Rosicrucianism, theosophy, even plain free-masonry, provided him with symbols he could use to build poems with, symbols which had not been overworked by generations of previous poets, which were harder for imitators to acquire than the Irish mythology of his youth, and which could be made to mean almost anything he chose or to mean half a dozen things at once. It was too handy a store to be sacrificed to scepticism. Yet I think scepticism was there underneath. He talked about his theory of the mask: if you wear a mask long enough your own features come to resemble the mask, till it is hardly possible to know for sure whether you are wearing it or not. I think that was his frame of mind about magic. He had made a habit of it which was useful both for writing poetry and for escaping from the materialism of socialists and capitalists, and he felt that if he investigated the origins of his habit too closely he might lose those advantages. A great many people who have

371

what they call religious beliefs have no firmer foundation for their faith than Yeats had for his magic; but their faith is not that of the mystics who have seen God nor the philosophers who have invented him. In most cases I think it is merely self-indulgence, and in others, as with Yeats, a utility, a means to perfectly human ends.

About 1930 I had gone to Siena to look at pictures and stumbled quite unexpectedly on the writings of St Catharine of that city. That very hardheaded and formidable lady drew no line whatever between her dealings with unsatisfactory popes and emperors and her dealings with God. Indeed, she was as tart with one as with the other. Writing political letters and holding the Infant Jesus in her arms were all in the days work for her. It is impossible to know what she meant, but impossible to doubt that *she* knew, quite clearly. God was as much a part of her daily life as dishwashing, and just as concrete and real to her. I was, and still am, greatly impressed. But St Catherine didnt impress Yeats. His mysticism was not of that kind. His God was not real, but an escape from reality. He was impatient of discussing St Catherine, as he was impatient of discussing George Fox's very immediate dealings with God. Compared with these, Yeats's mysticism was trivial. If he believed at all, he believed it for his own ends; he sought it, it was not forced upon him.

Magic is primarily a means of exerting power or persuading yourself that you can. Would you rather win the football pools or be granted the cloak of invisibility? Yeats's magic was never as crude as that, but there was something of that sort in it, beyond the help it gave him in writing poetry and the means it gave him of evading materialism. I dont know whether he ever suspected that this third motive might have something to do with his cultivation of theosophy, of Plotinus, and of other anti-rational shortcuts to power. Faustus was damned, mainly, I suppose, for his vulgarity, and Yeats hated vulgarity too much to suspect that a trace of it might linger somewhere in his unconscious motivation. Yet love of power underlines a great deal that is not even superficially mystical in his poetry. He thought of himself as one of a governing class, with obligations, but with privileges too. Disdain of shopkeepers, readiness to snub stone-breakers with political opinions, contempt for the mob, even when the mob was an abstraction, show clearly enough that Yeats felt he had a right to power that he did not share with the greater part of mankind. If you have none of the real power of armies and police and huge fortunes, magic is an unsatisfactory, but often irresistible way of pretending to yourself that you have an equivalent.

Perhaps by now you think that I have forgotten that we are discussing a great poet. Yes, but you have asked me to discuss the man I knew, rather than his poetry. Yes, again, but it is now generally admitted that Yeats was a great poet, nobody needs convincing of that. Rather, it is time to begin considering what his limitations were, so that we can, sooner or later, consign him to his place in the succession of great poets in our language. The young are getting impatient of him, as when I was young we had got impatient of Tennyson or of Swinburne. The young are apt to say that Yeats was an old square, or even a fascist beast. Such criticism may be irrelevant to poetry – I think it is – but it is as well to get it out of the way if possible. There were plenty of other fascist beasts about in the thirties, and among the poets, Yeats's close friend Ezra Pound is the most obvious. Eliot is another, the more insidious for being disguised as an English gentleman. What these poets and many other writers really had in common was a love of order. With order in society it matters little whether you are rich or poor, you will not be harassed by perpetual changes of fortune, you can plan your life's work within known limits, not felt as limits because they are as unavoidable as the limits imposed by our physique or the duration of human life. Whether an orderly society ever really existed or could exist is beside the point. Plato planned one, in our own day the socialists have proposed half a dozen different models for one, and in Yeats's youth William Morris had imagined yet another Utopia and made a great impression with *News from Nowhere*. Yeats went further than the rest when he called for ceremony, manners as elaborate as those he imagined in the Byzantine court. All such fancies assume tacitly that the regulations and ceremonies are made by extremely wise and perfectly unselfish rulers, not by Stalin or Hitler or even Mussolini, and none of their proponents, not Plato himself, pauses to consider where and how such rulers are to be found. The maxims given to guide the wise rulers are plausible and disastrous. You are told how blessed the ruler is who will make two blades of grass grow where one grew before, but never reminded that the people may not give a damn about blades of grass. They may, like the Arabs in Libya and in Palestine, prefer a desert, and there may be good reasons for preferring a desert. Abdulaziz Ibn Saud might have listed them. The blades of grass maxim is the standard excuse for imperialism, and

I think Yeats would never have used it; but it lurks under all utopian dreams of order.

Weighing this up, if it is worth weighing at all, you must of course allow for my own conviction that 'God is the dividing sword', and that order is no more than a rather unfortunate accident that sometimes hampers civilization. But my purpose is only to remind some critics that Yeats's love of order is something he shared with Dante and Shakespeare and probably far more than half of the world's great poets, as well as with nearly all the philosophers and historians. His way of expressing it was his own; he took his instances largely from the world around him, that of the Anglo-Irish gentry, which differs in personnel from the hierarchy of the church or of business management or of the civil service, but does not differ from them in principle. He was much nearer to Bernard Shaw than he would have liked to think.

Still, if Yeats's political thought hardly differed at bottom from what was current all around him, if his philosophic, theosophic, magical quasi-religion was trivial and by origin insincere, politics and religion were not his business except in the sense in which they are everyone's business. He was a poet. It is true that he loaded his conception of being a poet with all manner of lofty moral responsibilities, which seemed to claim authority in politics and religion. He wrapped an invisible bardic cloak around him whenever he uttered a line of anyone's verse. His determination that poetry should be noble rather starved his own of the humour which was part of his conversation. But for him, at least in middle-age, poetry needed no formal thought, no logical theory. It was in him. Just as we say some painter thinks with his brush, so Yeats thought with his pen, and if his pen ever misled him on purely poetical matters, it was so rarely that I cannot think of an instance, though perhaps a search through his volume might bring a few to light. I don't suppose that he was born that way. So far as my experience goes, poetry is a craft hard to learn and only acquired by long apprenticeship. In these days, of course, there is no one for a man to be apprenticed to except himself, so that diligence is more necessary than ever. Yeats was diligent. He must have taught his ear to attend to rhythm and vowel sequence and what the Welsh have codified but the rest of us grope for to hold the sounds of our verse together; yet he learnt all these so early that people who are content with inaccurate phrases would say he was born with them.

What did he read? What lines echoed in his mind? Perhaps

some of you know. I don't. I only see that already in 1889 *The Wanderings of Oisin* gave notice to those who had ears to hear that a great poet had arisen in Ireland. It is a young man's work, not quite autonomous. There is a surrender to sound which must owe something to Swinburne, and, through Swinburne, you can hear now and then a hint of Tennyson's trickiness. There is an evident intention to vie with the swift course of William Morris's best work, and some miscalculation in this, for Morris's had, in, say, *The Defence of Guenevere*, matter enough to keep the poem tearing along at a great pace, but the story Yeats had chosen is short of incidents. It would languish if he did not keep it alive by tricks of sound. All this granted, Oisin is still a poem that holds its readers, and here and there in it are lines which go so straight to the point that neither Tennyson nor Swinburne could ever have written the like. I don't mean a logical point, nor even a narrative point, but lines which convey an entire atmosphere in four or five words, or set the pace of a whole episode. There are vivid lines that contrast with the dreamlike confusion of other passages, and make the dream endurable that would bore us but for these interruptions of its mistiness. The onomatopeic skills of Oisin are as well worth investigating as the symbolic intricacies of Byzantium.

(1974)

375

NORMAN REA

9.9.42 HILL, Geoffrey W.

I expected changes, of course. It would have been altogether too much to presume that forty years of speculative development would leave the area untouched. There was little hope that the market town would be now as it had been then when we were at school. I knew too that the school had gone, Bromsgrove High School, the town grammar school, sometimes the County High School and never once confused with the minor independent, that is private, school on the far south side of the town which was called, simply, Bromsgrove School. I had watched the change in the Year Book of local education authorities, which is a kind of Wisden for unreconstructed schoolmen, as it moved in the sixties to College Lane and the concrete, glass and flat roof so instantly recognisable as the style of that best forgotten decade of architecture. The present head of the school, now North Bromsgrove Comprehensive School, in recognition of its change of site and status, summed it all up wryly when we talked about current educational change: don't opt out, with a sixties building and a flat roof, the bonus won't meet the cost of repairs. He was an intelligent, humorous man and I liked him even when he laughed as I told him my college was opened in 1965 and had a flat roof. I am sure that it was not simply his age and mine that made me feel he was different, a welcome difference, from the head that Geoffrey and I had known fifty years before – Dr Baron, a hard, unbending, austere and seemingly humourless man, though not without kindness, as I learned in later years.

I had contacted the school in an effort to trace the records of the grammar school, of Geoffrey, of the staff, and, I suppose I have to confess the self-interest, some whisper of myself in the rapidly changing history. The welcome and the help I was given was generous but it was perhaps not surprising that I wanted to visit the site of the old school on the Stourbridge Road first. There was no intention of churlish behaviour, it was a reaction to nostalgia. The buildings are still there. The school had gone, disappeared these thirty years, but the solid Victorian virtues of red brick and softening limestone remain just as they were, with the lawn, the gardens, the sweep of unused drive at the front, and still the Scots pines by the windows, tall above the roof-tiles now. From deep within memory I suddenly see two cartoon pictures on the wall of the Baron's study, a green crocodile depicting the daily procession from the annexe in New Road, next to the Public Library, up to the main school, and the other, a boy flying through the air to land in one of the pines. Satchwell, I think, who in a mad game had pretended to dive through the window fully intending to catch the sill as he went through and stop his headlong flight. He missed. His neck and life were saved by the comforting needles of a large Scots pine. The boys' entrance was to the left nearest to the town, the girls' to the right up the Stourbridge Road. A mixed grammar school was unusual then and despite the efforts of Fanny Baxter, the Senior Mistress, to segregate and regiment, it remained resolutely mixed. I walked up the drive to the archway entrance, ahead of the playground and the sportsfield, right into school, left down the steps to Leeson's empire of fears and tears, the woodwork room, the only teacher to so intimidate me I absconded rather than go to his classes. Just through the archway on the right I remembered the lavatories. It was not so strange that it should be so because they figured in my first memory of the school, even before I became a pupil, from the day I went to sit the entrance examination, the Scholarship, what I later knew as the 11-plus, the selection test for grammar school where failure led to the secondary modern school however education officers tried to placate with honeyed phrases about no pass or fail only finding the right place. There were, I think, still some fee-paying students lingering in the school in the forties. I had no fears about the selection day, not through self-awareness, some accurate assessment of my ability to gain a place, the confidence of understanding my ranking, but rather the opposite, total ignorance of the system. I had no conception of what was taking place but happily went along with the suggestions of my teachers at my primary school, as did my parents, neither of whom had a grammar school education anyway. My mother was a scullery maid at the age of fourteen. It was clear that this happy ignorance was not the case for some, for among the abiding memories of that day were the boys being sick as the tension of expectation overtook them and overpowered them. One poor soul whose control had given way altogether stood at the top of the steps crying and pissing himself, the wet stain growing at the crotch of his short grey trousers, the sobs convulsing him. I remember the teacher in charge, Eddie French, later my Maths teacher, taking the boy away with a kind of brusque efficient sympathy which characterised his style of teaching. I knew it was fear that did it though I wondered why the experience of the day should bring it on. We all knew that fear. I guess that most of us had pissed ourselves in fright when the bombs dropped on us.

There was fear, too, or perhaps apprehension that first day of school. In the last weeks of the primary school we had been told all the horror stories, of how the new boys were taken one by one and thrown through the hedge on to the nettle patch, how we would be made to run the gauntlet of boys armed with plimsolls battering our backsides. None of the stories were true. We were, on the whole, kindly received by pupils and staff alike, with one or two exceptions who sometimes slip back into the mind when the night is quiet and still, when sleep will not come. I suppose we feared the head, the Baron, the good doctor, for he carried power and authority with him. He had a cane too and he was known to use it and that was more important. He would sweep into the school drive via the girls' entrance in his dark Prussian-blue Lanchester to park in the small court near the school hall and stride into his office at the T-junction of the school, brown trilby hat, grey double-breasted suit, thick glasses and the battered face of Bulldog Drummond. He could make his voice heard from one end of the corridor to the other but rarely did because we froze on sight of him in case we should be singled out. I still hear his voice sometimes in my head, the rich chesty sound that only later I realised was the tar clogging his lungs, for he smoked at least a pack a day of 'Three Castles' cigarettes.

The buildings are still there. The school has gone except where it lives in the shadows of my mind and stirs now and then into the light.

I went back to the road and realised what was missing: a feature of the end of afternoon school was the rush for the buses. No school buses then, just the service run by the Midland Red. The Rubery, Rednal, Longbridge group had to go into town for the 144 and 145 but those who lived in the villages along the Stourbridge Road, Catshill, Fairfield, Belbroughton, caught the 318 right outside the school gates. The bus stop had gone with the school. As I stood there thinking of the characters as they made their way to the top deck of a Midland Red double-decker, Jim Wilkes up to Catshill, Geoffrey to the Police House at the end of the village at Fairfield, and Tolley and the rest of the wild Belbroughton country crew on beyond, a new 318 went past, a kind of demented van with windows, and I felt sad with a sense of loss. No doubt it was more economically and environmentally sound but I still felt sad.

I walked to the top of the High Street, passing the notices pointing me to the Housman Heritage Trail and Safeways Supermarket and up the road to the 'new' school no more than four hundred yards away. The staff were, as I have said, kind, helpful, generous, gave me a room to work in and trundled in the boxes which contained the archives of Bromsgrove High School: three small cardboard boxes. I read somewhere once that the whole of the accumulated palaeontological evidence for the descent of man would fit in three small cardboard boxes on a kitchen table. It was, nonetheless, a shock. An admissions register, some school magazines, a roll or two of school photographs, detailed plans of the current school and newspaper clippings of its opening. The buildings were still there. I had just left them. The school had gone and all that remained of Bromsgrove High School was in three cardboard boxes.

I flicked through the admissions register which had been meticulously kept in a copper-plate hand by the various school clerks and secretaries over the years. Date of Admission, Name, Boy / Girl, Date of Birth, Father, Father's occupation, Address. Then a set of letters, a cryptic with no code available and difficult to decipher. I looked for Geoffrey first: 9.9.42 Hill, Geoffrey, W; B. 18.6.32; W G Hill; Police Constable: The Police House, Fairfield, Nr Bromsgrove. I turned the pages idly, catching other names and looking for my own, David Jones, Peter Stevenson – that must be Rocket Stevenson who played Brittanicus in the school play! – Alan Stephenson, the Head Boy the year I went to school, Sam Summers, Peter Kelly, Glenda Ince, Patricia Mutlow, Janet Luscombe, Fred Holliday who became Vice-Chancellor at Durham. I stopped after a while and went back to Geoffrey's entry and carefully noted down the details including the cryptic Stat. W.SP NF. No clue was given, no guide, no explanation from the current staff who couldn't understand it either – I guessed it had something to do with his status as a 'scholarship boy' who would pay no fees and the fact that he was a young for age entry to the school, a boy of special promise. It was an explanation sufficient to satisfy me at the time.

For some reason I went back to the beginning of the register and found I was looking not so much for the names but the occupations given for the father. It was clear from the occurrence of labourer, road sweeper, farm-hand, factory worker amongst the

379

bank-clerks, shopkeepers, managers and teachers that there was a good smattering of pupils from the working class even before the war. It looked about one in five. During the war years it was difficult to place the social strata because so many were simply registered 'HM Forces' but after 1946 it became clear the the predominant social group in the school were first generation grammar school working class boys and girls. I checked back again and the swing was clear: in the post war period, even given the rather crude analysis I made as I ran my finger down the pages, there was little doubt in my mind that the largest proportion of pupils were from working class families. I wished I could photocopy the register and take it to place in front of the insufferable student with the faked drawling tones of the working class as he imagined it, coming from an impeccable diplomatic background, a minor public school, who informed me in his tutorial that grammar schools were middle class institutions and in response to my query, as I had queried his essay, replied that they were full of middle class pupils who kept out the working class. I did mildly remonstrate that personal experience, though not always generalisable, suggested otherwise. It became apparent, though, that like many before him he had pirated and parroted the phrase without knowing what it meant even to its originator. We did go on to talk about prefects, house systems, the games and athletics tradition, the team. Bromsgrove High School had a prefect system, a head boy and head girl and an equal number of prefects from boys' and girls' sides of the school. All the prefects wore black gowns like undergraduates then, but not the bum freezers, for they reached at least to the knee and had full sleeves and served to keep you warmer in winter, to be worn at all times in the school.

There was a house system too. It was a very strong feature of the school in which victory at the end of the year was achieved not only from points won in inter-house sports but accumulated from the contribution of every single pupil on a credit / debit system, marks for work, behaviour and achieving standards. Appleby, Hibbins, Sailman; staff passed on and now remembered only as the names of the houses.

I was sure that there would be reports on the Houses in the School magazine. There were surprisingly few magazines in the boxes and I went through each one trying to place them chronologically. At first in the earlier of the magazines it seemed they were simply a diary of the school year, a record of events, the official report of speech days and the lists of prizewinners and prizes. I saw that Geoffrey had won the Governors' Prize three years before me. I had not known that. He won the Upper-School English prize too. And just as well. But then there was a change and this simple reporting gave way to a more lively style. Criticism appeared, stories, poetry. There in 1946/47:

1   *Fishing*

If you find that this life with its day-to-day strife and its
bustle and buzz is depressing,
Then go with your line on the first day that's fine and yield
to the river's caressing.
Quite heedless of squirms, take a large tin of worms and
pick out the fattest for baiting;
When this has been done, just lean back in the sun with
nothing to do besides waiting.
As your eyes fondly dote on the little red float, you will
certainly find yourself wishing
That in this world's hustle, its hurry and bustle, there was
more time in which to go fishing.

2   *Boating*

When it's cold, you desire an arm-chair by the fire and a
mere glance outside makes you shiver;
But when summer returns, then your numb body yearns
for a day in a boat on the river.
So an ex-Oxford Blue takes his place in the crew (and at
pulling stroke-oar he's a master);
Thus you look a fine show as down river you row – but the
little trip ends in disaster;
For you say that you're near, so you think, to the weir, but
the cox at the stern won't believe you;
Then you find you can't stop and go over the top – so there
for the present I'll leave you.

3   *Football*

You wait in a queue for an hour, maybe two, to pass through
a gate with your ticket;
Having entered, you then wait till twenty-two men come
out with a football and kick it.
You shout and you cheer (it's a funny idea, but somehow
you can't quite resist it).

So when they all yell, then you shout out as well 'It's a goal!
no, it isn't, he's missed it!'
Having kept up this roar till your throat is quite sore and the
players have finished their caper,
You go home to tea to sit reading, maybe, accounts of the
match in the paper.

Geoffrey W. Hill, Form IV L.

These were a surprise. I do remember Geoffrey playing football
once reluctantly in a house team I think, and his interests may
have stretched to watching Bromsgrove Rovers or Stourbridge
United (though not as stretched as his artistic licence, for in the
case of either team waiting for two minutes to get in would be a
trifle excessive, let alone two hours). It is possible that he fished
and enjoyed it. There were certainly plenty of streams and ponds
to while away an afternoon, around Fairfield and Belbroughton,
though I would guess that he would even in those days be more
absorbed by a book than a little red float. But what was immedi-
ately evocative was 'Boating' because there were echoes of days
on the river at Stratford upon Avon. One of the great joys of
school was the passionate interest of the English staff in taking us
to live performances. As pupils we were taken to plays at Birming-
ham which was close and particularly to the Shakespeare
Memorial Theatre at Stratford where the theatre visit was often
made into a trip which enabled us to go on the river, picnic, visit
the proper historic sights and round off the trip with a play. It is
difficult now to communicate the magic of those visits to the
young people today for whom such events are commonplace,
indeed so common that they often have little regard for them;
they have become blasé about the opportunities which they have.
It was not like that for our generation. The English staff at school
recognised the need, the hunger for live performance where we
could watch, engage, savour. For our experience was one where
the war years had forced us into a huddle round a crackling radio
to listen to plays and music. The chance to watch a play unfold
was an enchantment beyond words for us. Fortunately our
teachers saw further than that and, whilst they delighted with us
in that new found pleasure, they pushed us on and encouraged
us to talk, to discuss, to write about the experience and some of
what we wrote they were prepared to publish in the school maga-
zine because they knew too that publication is a great stimulus for
a young writer. Thus a visit to Stratford 30th April 1948. The

Merchant of Venice, Robert Helpmann as Shylock, Diana Wynyard as Portia, Paul Schofield as Bassanio and with Esmond Knight, Noel Willman, John Kidd, Mairhi Russell. Geoffrey had never seen it produced and was enthralled. He was not alone. There were many of us for whom this was the first live production. He wrote about it soon after and it was clear his critical faculties had not been left behind. There were details which irritated him: three caskets sit centre stage for the scene at Belmont and are still there for the next scene in Venice thirty miles away. He was deeply impressed, moved, by Helpmann as Shylock:

> Oh yes, Shylock raved and ranted and whined and wept, as any crafty villain should, but underneath it all lay great dignity. I shall never forget my last glimpse of Shylock, broken, ruined, ill, he stumbled from the courtroom with the crowd jeering and laughing at his heels. Then, at the top of the steps, he straightened up and looked round with such fierce pride that the crowd was hushed as he continued down the steps and away.

The staff, and it started, probably with Mr Lloyd and Miss Gledhill, were not content for us to engage with the performance of others. Even where this involved discussion and writing it was for them still passive and more was needed – for us to perform ourselves. The staging of *Caesar and Cleopatra* was a massive affair for the school with a huge cast, many costumes and changes of scenery and demanded an organisation that ran on silvered ball bearings. These productions are common now but this one needs to be placed in context for in that immediate post-war period it needed imagination, courage and great faith to stage the play. This was the height of post-war austerity, the worst winter in living memory made desperate by the miners strike, no fuel, food rationing, clothing coupons and for everyone, hardship. It was against this that Mr Lloyd decided to stage this marvellous spectacle. It was an act of triumphant defiance which in the end set standards for school productions for many years. I enjoyed it enormously. It was my first part in a production, as Ptolemy, King of Egypt, it gave me a taste for the stage and gave me too the opportunity to get to know one of the spear-carrying centurions well – Geoffrey Hill. Lloyd and Gledhill left the school for other posts shortly after, Lloyd, I think, to become a headteacher and Gledhill one of his senior staff. We all wondered who would follow this remarkable pair and all of us were convinced that a golden era just begun was over as soon as it started. We were all unprepared. At first it appeared that there could be no greater contrast, even physically: Lloyd was small dark (and greying at the end) a stocky bespectacled Welshman and now in his place was KHM Curtis, tallish, thin, blond curly hair with a side parting, moustache, and quickly dubbed Flying Officer Kite, or just plain Kite. The first lesson with him did not go well. We were talking when he came in and continued when he had himself started in his quiet unhurried voice. Not for long. He stopped, lifted the lid of the desk and slammed it down with such force and noise that classes a block away stopped in shocked silence. He then raised his voice, told us precisely what he thought of our ill-mannered behaviour which was not, and would never be, acceptable to him and then he walked out, leaving us to think about it in silence. Three or four minutes later he reappeared at the door, walked to the desk and began again as though nothing had happened. It was a splendid performance. It was only after years that we realised how alien, though effective, that kind of action was to that essentially shy man. He was the most extra-ordinary motivator of young people, kind, gentle, good-mannered and generous. His shyness sometimes made him appear aloof but he was never that, for the warmth of his concern always reached you. He was always encouraging; it was not that he eschewed criticism; on the contrary it was by his careful criticism that he encouraged our own critical faculties and nudged us to our new creative efforts, above all developing a passion for literature, for the arts, which has stayed with many of us who were fortunate to come within his influence. He quietly took over the school productions and widened their scope, Restoration Comedy (with Geoffrey now a drunken fop) Northanger Abbey, Lady Precious Stream, each to allow us to come to new understandings of style and performance. It was an exhilarating time. Auditioning for a part once for him I chose foolishly to read part of 'How Green was my Valley' where news comes of Dada's death in the pit. My Welsh family background gave an edge to it that carried me away. When I had finished and mopped away the tears he said very gently 'There's no Welshman in Lady Precious Stream, I'm very sorry to say, but I would like you to do two things. Would you be a kind of Chinese horse and would you read your pieces to 3LP tomorrow?' I did both. He was instrumental in ensuring the involvement of pupils in running the school library, not just carrying out the clerical chores, the administrative tasks, but helping determine library policy, suggesting books for purchase and experimenting with projects. It became the sixth form study and one of the liveliest places in the school with many of us staying long after school hours to discuss poetry and politics, the latest books, films, plays under his benevolent eye. Only the birth of his first child curtailed his devotion to us, just a little.

It was his encouragement of writing that became one of his greatest gifts to us and his lasting memorial. I am not sure even now, after years of thinking about it, just how he did it. Of course we wrote in class, we wrote for homework and he encouraged us to write for the magazine. It was more than that. I do know that within a short time we were showing him pieces that we had written, essays, stories, poems, and he would take them quietly, read them at home and come back to us with them, going over them with great care, suggesting here, questioning there. Always he seemed to have time for us and we trusted him. I have no doubt that KHMC was a prime motivator in developing Geoffrey's work. His poetry changed from the humorous juvenilia of fishing, boating and football and within the year the school magazine had published

Pylons
Will no one befriend these strange newcomers?
Awkward and gaunt, yet half-defiant
Of our rootedness; we count their summers
And find them few, yet will not love these giant,
Narrow-chested oaks that trail their queues
Across the meadows and the torrent's roar,
But only sneer and say they spoil our views,
Or pass them by with curling lip. Therefore
Across their scarecrow shoulders I would place
A smock of aged respectability,
And in their gaping mouths a pipe of briar,
That they might wear some semblance of a face
To demonstrate a mute servility,
And touch their buzzing forelocks to the squire.

G.W. HILL (V.L.)

There was a new power, a sense of imagery in the poetry now which suggested a leap in maturity from that only months earlier.

The school magazine was edited by pupils with Ken Curtis as a member of the editorial committee. The head would never have allowed it to continue without a staff presence for he was much too cautious for that, but somehow Ken Curtis never seemed like an imposition, a dead authoritarian weight, and no-one was the slightest concerned at turning to him for advice and listening to his cool voice of reason. But where Geoffrey's poetry was concerned we had no need to listen to him, for by 1949 and the publication of 'Fotheringhay 1587' it was clear to all of us who cared to read, what had been apparent to Ken Curtis for some time – that Geoffrey Hill was a major presence in our literary world and was developing as a very good poet indeed.

Fotheringhay, 1587

i

The rain-flaked sky-wheel rubs the
Dove-tailed shingle off the stall,
The pied mare heaves and moans in foal.

The iron Keep's scaffold hubs the
Whirling circle of the wall.
Out of its orbit shoots the soul.

Circles start and stop in pain,
    But I –
Until the axe-arc fall again –
    Am whole.

ii

Morning moved the image nearer
To the constant queen, and clearer
Came the rays of life to sere her.

Praying gave the image grace,
But dread of death usurped its place:
Fear wiped its hand across her face

And passed; for dying on the bleak
Scaffold, she saw what all men seek.
But then it was too late to speak.

The elder doffed its cap of mist. The wind
Drummed through the snaring branches of the wood
Till the black-laced birches bobbed on their toes
Like eager children at a festival.

And craning forward they saw the sun, mounting
With firm step to her expectant zenith, poise
At the turn of the stair and brazenly
Lean on a bannister of cloud, waiting...

Waiting until her desire died. Lust waned
With the wind, and the drooped birches dozed as
The moon crept like a little dog to lie
Between the head and shoulders of the earth.

The last of his poems in the school magazine came in 1950 as he left.

Pastorals

I

The cherries stitch a crumpled lace
Of blossom on their skirts, and face
The orchard with unwitting grace.

But then falls Winter's final blow
And they must bend their heads, as though
To shield their eyes from their own snow.

II

As cock-fowl that have fought their feathers off
Totter apart, lacking the emphatic
Gesture of plumes, the trees in Winter file

Across the field. These, forced by frost to doff
Their skin of leaf, lay bare the static
Bone, firm, behind the switchings of the smile.

Geoffrey Hill

It was there I stopped. I sat in the little room where I was work-
ing, the cardboard boxes at my side. There was a stillness, a quiet,

there in the hub of the school. I thought about Geoffrey, I thought about KHMC. I repacked the boxes. I tidied my notes. I made my thanks and my goodbyes. In my head as I walked back to find my car I could hear again the sound of the hall at the old school filled as always at the end of term with the traditional hymn 'Lord dismiss us with Thy blessing'. I knew before I reached the car that I wanted to go on, to find Ken, to talk with him again. I traced him down to Epsom. Too late. He died two years ago.

I went to Bromsgrove to look for Geoffrey Hill. I found him. 9.9.42. Hill, Geoffrey W, Born 18.6.32

But I found KHM Curtis too. I somehow don't think that Geoffrey would mind.

(1992)

PART EIGHT

A Closing Miscellany

W.H. AUDEN

On Technique

On hedonistic grounds, I am a fanatical formalist. To me, a poem is, among other things, always a verbal game. Everybody knows that one cannot play a game without rules. One may make the rules what one likes, but one's whole fun and freedom comes from obeying them.

There are a few poets – D.H. Lawrence, for example – whom one feels had to write in free verse, but they are the exceptions, not the rule. Those who do must have an infallible sense for line endings. So often, when reading 'free' verse, I can see no reason why a line ends where it does; why the poet did not write it out as a prose-poem.

At any given time, I have two concerns on my mind, a subject which interests me and formal problems of metre, diction, etc. The Subject looks for the right Form, the Form for the right Subject. When the two finally come together, I can write a poem. For example, a few years ago, I was preoccupied with the, to us, strange and repellant ways of the Insects. At the same time, under the influence of Goethe in his middle 'classical' period, I was wondering whether it would be possible to write an English poem in accentual hexameters. The outcome was a poem about Insects in hexameters.

A pause should *always* be made at the end of a line, longer if there is punctuation at its end, shorter if there is enjambment without punctuation.

When writing a poem based on syllable count alone and ignoring stresses, I usually, but not invariably, follow the latin habit of eliding contiguous vowels separated by *h* or *w*. But in reading the poem aloud I pronounce them both. Thus *now imagines* I count metrically as three syllables, but I pronounce them as four.

I have written one or two short poems based, like some of Bridges's, on vowel length not stress. But because of the uninflected nature of English, which is always making vowels long by position, it is impossible to write a poem of any length in this way without resorting to fancy diction.

I don't bother about the visual appearance of a poem on the page, except in one respect. If it is written in long lines, the printer must so set it that there are no run ons.

(1972)

BASIL BUNTING

Hugh MacDiarmid Lost

Driving home after a visit to Wylam we paused for a sandwich and something to wet it at Moffat, taking care to avoid the tourist traps with which Moffat abounds. The bar was long, dark and rather forbidding, a place for covenanters, it seemed, or equally contentious, stubborn people. A tableful of workmen eating their bait began to stir ominously as soon as we sat down, as though trouble might be brewing. While our sandwiches were cutting and the whisky barely tasted the largest workman rose frowning and came to our table; but what he said was: 'Is it no the great poet, Hugh MacDiarmid?'

Chris said nothing. I doubt if he heard. So I answered: 'It is.' On that all the workmen, six or seven of them, got up and stood around us. 'Ye'll drink on us', they commanded, and drink on them we did until every man of them had paid a round, while they expressed their admiration, quoting his poems, asking his opinions on this and that, from whisky to Clydeside MP's. They would remember that day, they said, all their lives.

Luckily the road from Moffat to Biggar carries no traffic whatever, much of the year, so that I got him home dazed but safe and Valda had a word or two to say about it.

What other poet is there, or has there been these many, many years, who would be recognised and spontaneously honoured by men of no education and no pretension whatever? It was not MacDiarmid's politics that attracted them; the poems they quoted were not political. It was not even the sound of their native dialect, for some of the poems they admired were in English. None of MacDiarmid's poems were simplified to aim at the poor, they were written for a hard intellectual audience. Their candour, their lack of side, the feeling that he meant what he said, with or without occasional stumblings of technique, these carried through the printed page to the least literary of men.

We had been recognised and stood drinks already once on that journey, but by middle-class reading men whose enthusiasm was real, no doubt, but not half so fully felt as that of the workmen at Moffat.

I do not think it is an exaggeration to say that Hugh MacDiarmid's death is a rare loss, one such as we have not suffered for a long time and are unlikely to suffer again for as long.   (1978)

GEOFFREY HILL

'The Age Demanded' (Again)

Humphrey Carpenter: *A Serious Character: The Life of Ezra Pound* (Faber, 1988)

To begin with civilities. Mr Carpenter is plainly an honest and industrious professional who, having received a commission, labours to meet the demands and fulfil the obligations of the task. Though possibly too modest to lay personal claim to that 'greatness' which the age confers on its most successful literary realtors, he nonetheless enjoys his share of their power, the power of the genre. This is the lustrum, if not the decade, of the 'masterly' biography and even the modest practitioners must relish playing maestro to the mere *fabbro*. They are our patrons.

It is not inevitable that a patron will patronize. Mr Carpenter does so, on occasion, with a genial imperceptiveness that can be more damaging than cruel intent. I see little or no evidence that he understands how poetry is made, what its unique difficulties might be, or how one might speak cogently about it. Canto XLV (the 'Usura' Canto), he says, 'would be a magnificent, perhaps unflawed piece of work, were it not for the uncomfortable fact that it is a hymn to an obsession' (547). This 'uncomfortable fact' is no such thing; it is a patronizing fancy. At this level of discourse, Shakespeare's *Sonnets* 127-152, *Astrophil and Stella*, Coleridge's 'Asra' poems, and *Finnegans Wake* are equally hymns to obsessions and serve equally to indicate the inanity of his remark.

Carpenter's scrutiny of the handling of Pound's case between 1945 and 1958 draws in part on archive material at St. Elizabeth's Hospital and elsewhere. This section of the book is not without value and, as an article of eight or ten thousand words, could have enlivened the pages of some journal of psychiatry or jurisprudence. But assiduous research is not an automatic guarantee of intrinsic value and there is a considerable amount of excess baggage in this weighty volume:

> After an hour's wait, to no purpose that I could see, we took off again for Brussels, arriving at approximately 1700 hours. The wait there, also, was to no purpose that I could discern. No petrol was taken on and we were not permitted to leave the vicinity of the aircraft to go to the lunch counter, which was

some distance away. We took off in about forty-five minutes and arrived at Bovington approximately 1830 hours (GMT) . . . (695)

This is from three pages of recollection by a member of Pound's military escort from Italy to Washington. I fail to see how the integrity of the narrative could have been in any way damaged by the judicious trimming of such details. It is possible to be at once scrupulous, immensely industrious, and too easy on oneself. Some eight pages (863-870) are taken up by quotation and para-phrase from Donald Hall's 1960 interview with Pound for *The Paris Review*. Carpenter fully acknowledges the debt, but that is not my point. The interview is not only copiously used; it is also diffused, dissipated. Carpenter is interested in vignettes of character; he shows little concern for the heart of the matter, the intensity and quality of the technical and moral debate in which Pound and Hall were engaged.

I have recently received a leaflet advertising the forthcoming 'Armistice Festival' in London and Oxford. Notice is given of the inevitable Poetry Competition in which 'Competitors from schools, colleges and universities are invited to write the poem they think Wilfred Owen, Rupert Brooke or Edward Thomas might have written on war and peace, had they survived to the age of fifty, seventy or a hundred years of age'. Do the organizers of this foolish contest really suppose that they are honouring the achieve-ment of those poets by so assaulting them with notions of rele-vance and empathy? In the end I feel no more kindly towards *A Serious Character* than I do towards the efforts of these misguided people. The literary industry, which requires each of its products to be equally worthy of purchase and which understands little but occasion and opportunity, cannot admit the suggestion that Owen, Thomas, or Pound may, in the context and texture of their work, have done something out of the ordinary. (Pound's extra-ordinariness is trivialized in the Faber blurb, whose author appears to have misread the second sentence of Carpenter's Preface). I have acknowledged Mr Carpenter's conscientious professionalism. It seemed to me, even so, as I reached the end of this volume of a thousand pages, that the age has demanded the wrong kind of covenant once again: a covenant not so much with Pound's crea-tive achievement, or even with the exemplary tragedy of his life, as with what was once called 'temporall besynesse' and the unre-gulated din of 'education' and commerce.

(1988)

394

PETER LEVI

Penelope Palmer

The Lamp, A Selection of Poems by Penelope Palmer (Agenda Editions, 1982)

There is a kind of modern poem where the verses have a strong and delicate individual outline, like a drawing in which every stroke of the pencil was exact. There is another kind in which the air seems to melt around the edges of the verses, almost of the words. It is as if every sentence had been meditated until it was spoken with an inner resonance. Of these two kinds of poem the first is commoner in English, the second in Italian, but some poets combine them in this or that proportion: Larkin for example and Montale. They come together particularly happily in a fresh and brilliantly promising first collection of poems by Penelope Palmer, *The Lamp*.

Penelope Palmer had already published a novel when she was twenty-five, but in November 1981, before these poems had appeared, she died aged thirty-seven. What does promise mean in those circumstances? Promise is always a sense of a fresh wind, a new taking hold of the technical means of poetry by young and strong hands. But it is more than that, a glimpse of a personality, or of a certain depth of spirit or a new style of thought, which is already present when it is scarcely revealed. In this more important sense which I intend here, the Eclogues of Virgil must have been the most promising first book ever published.

These poems make a far stronger impression as a collection than they did when some of them appeared here and there in periodicals. But Penelope Palmer had already created the special appetite for the special taste of her poetry; they lingered in the memory and one wondered who she was. Taken together, they mingle their influences of intelligence and warmth and of stony confrontations of death and other such realities. The effect of individual poems is of power modestly reined in. Taken together, the power intensifies. Individual poems are restrained by precise subject: a shut chapel at Herculaneum, the portrait of a dead young woman, flowers, an evening. Even so, the meaning soars like a sunset far beyond the conventional garden walls of each poem. But taken together there is more passion and more reason than anything but poetry could express.

What is said is governed by modest intelligence, irony, our education nowadays, a morality of restraint; this carapace fits her strong womanly and personal feelings well, particularly in those places where the carapace cracks a little. Her observations of love, – 'This is a poor way to love' in one poem, '(this isn't love)' in another – are scrupulous and moving. Characteristically 'God is conspicuous by his absence'. One can be certain only of the dog and the cat and the baby tortoise. But the lyrical tone is unmistakable and quite convincing. It was an achievement that must have taken many years, and which has not been easy for any modern poet. One of the most accomplished of these poems most exemplifies it, a poem dazzling in more than one aspect, called Charles Morgan.

In a time when other poets of different kinds have been emerging thick and fast, like hares out of the corn, Penelope Palmer belongs to no school, only to a tradition which is roughly Larkin's and that of the very early Sylvia Plath. Her poems are not showy, only extremely able, moving, engaging, gripping. This is a book for grown-ups, not for professors. It is about love, life, balance, God, grown-up matters. God knows what poetry ought to be, but if it is like these poems it will still be the most beautiful and serious use of the breath of mankind. Without any 'ecstasy of affirmation', Penelope Palmer was a Marvellian poet. These poems, as poems, constitute the best first collection in a number of years. Ave atque Vale.

(1982)

JOHN BAYLEY

Death and the Captain

Thom Gunn, *Collected Poems* (Faber, 1993)

In a recent piece in the *TLS* Donald Davie touched in a new way on the old question of the 'truth' of poetry. Forcefully, as in every-thing he writes, Davie asked why professors of Eng. Lit. today draw their salaries for denying what everyone who knows poetry knows: that it gets at *truth* in many ways and by means of many strategies, rhetorical and linguistic: but if it does not arrive some-how the poem has failed, failed to discover the inevitability of itself.

In abolishing the truth, and in abolishing the poet himself as an individual who seeks it, the professors and theorists have of course in mind the importance of their own role as creators of the 'virtual reality' of literature, which they offer their students and the public. The fill the gap that they have made themselves. But a poet like Thom Gunn shows, if any demonstration was needed, just how wrong they are. As poet he is both individual and truth-seeker – the three roles fused into one. 'Who would true valour see/ Let him come hither', as Bunyan's hymn says. Gunn's indi-viduality is manifested not only in the truth of what he writes but in the ways – highly crafted as they are – in which he seems to come closer and closer to writing it. In realising himself as a poem he realises truth both universal and unique.

This of course happens all the time with good poetry, but in Gunn's case the process is peculiarly visible: not the matter in hand, but how that matter seeks to know itself. In his collected poems we can see the whole process coming clean, as it were, in a fascinating way. In *Fighting Terms* (1954) he seemed to exist as an uncertain individual inside the certainty of the poem he has created, an impression that receives a natural confirmation, which none the less only art could give it, when, in the Auto-biography section of *Jack Straw's Castle* (1976), he looks back on the uncertain young man who was trying to be so certain.

> The sniff of the real, that's
> what I'd want to get
> how it felt
> to sit on Parliament

> Hill on a May evening
> studying for exams   skinny
> seventeen   dissatisfied
>   yet sniffing such
> a potent air, smell of
> grass in heat from the day's sun

The poem seems at first to lose itself, deliberately, even self-indulgently, in those vividly commonplace memories of adolescence which everyone has, and indulges from time to time. 'The sniff of the real' is truth, but not a truth specific to this individual. It is what we all have and we all recognise, admirably conjured up as it is in the devices of the poem. But then comes the thing that is specific to the poem, its hard little unique talisman, which, taken in memory's hand, suddenly provides the answer, the specific truth about the kind of picture memory cannot avoid making.

> a green dry prospect
> distant babble of children
> and beyond, distinct at
> the end of the glow
> St Paul's like a stone thimble
> longing so hard to make
> inclusions that the longing
> has become   in memory
> an inclusion

The inclusions that the poem makes in itself, as perfectly as in a poem, are those recognitions 'robed as destinies' which Larkin understood in 'Church Going'. The truth of the mind is the inevitability with which it cannot but make a 'picture', make 'inclusions'; and this truth is finally recognised as the being of the poem. We cannot, as it were, step outside the inevitable shapes of our own mental image and process. And this is not falsity but the root of being, recognised enormously in the 'inclusion' of the cathedral: investigated meticulously in the fulfilment of a poem.

So the poet who once seemed outside his own poems, making them like vigorously decorated armour – byrnies for sad captains – becomes himself at last, in his last two collections. It is interesting to compare the process with Yeats' realisation that the point of poetry, as he could fashion it, was to make it continually into a new kind of self – a naked self. 'It is myself that I remake'. Yeats also wrote of 'withering into the truth', after he had 'swayed my leaves and flowers in the sun' as a young man. But that image, and that way of looking at it, in no way suits Gunn. In a curious sense his early poems not only used their severities and formalities, those uncontemporary skills in metre and rhyme, to strengthen the uncertainty – possibly also the sexual instability and bewilderment – of the young poet, but were even able to suggest that the poet did not *wish* to be at home, that he had not yet learned or cared to be there. Poems like 'On the Move', about birds and motorcyclists, took their inspiration from 'the gust of birds/ That spurts across the field', and the Boys, with their 'donned impersonality'.

> In gleaming jackets trophied with the dust,
> They strap in doubt – by hiding it, robust –
> And almost hear a meaning in their noise.

Strapping in doubt – a complex phrase – means that weakness is converted into a kind of strength, and also prevented from seeming to appear in the poem. Yet the clarity of the poem, and its impassively triumphant air of being in full panoply, is brilliantly called in question by the very tendencies and characteristics it seeks to secure itself against: that uncertain scholarly youth who sat his exams and read Lamartine lying in the grass of Parliament Hill. Clarity itself is threatened by movement, which makes for

> an uncertain violence
> Under the dust thrown by a baffled sense
> Or the dull thunder of approximate words.

These words are not approximate – very much the opposite – but in creating this paradox the poem seems almost wishing that they were, so that they too could vanish in movement, like 'those dying generations at their song'.

> For birds and saints complete their purposes.
> At worst, one is in motion; and at best,
> Reaching no absolute, in which to rest,
> One is always nearer by not keeping still.

Movement and expression in 'On the Move' are often reminiscent of Larkin's 'Church Going', an approximately coeaval poem, and one that moves with its own clear certainty, presented as the poet's fumbling or musing difficulty in knowing what he feels. 'On the Move' is the opposite: the poet seems quite sure of it all, but in an odd way he isn't.

The notion of what is secure has always fascinated Gunn, and provided him both with this kind of dramatic undertext in the poem and with a degree of thoroughly sharp and 'unpoetic' self-insight. Yeats turned day-dreams, vacillations and weaknesses into the stuff of his own legend. Gunn has the air of keeping them out, while at the same time being fully conscious of what they mean. There are ways of letting the reader see this, in the earlier collections, without revealing it directly. Sometimes the early poems try to be, and are, in the old sense, 'impersonal', and they they are often remarkably bad. 'Jesus and His Mother', 'Julian the Apostate', 'Autumn Chapter in a Novel', 'The Silver Age' – these are the sort of poems which the movement, or more particularly Larkin, were apt to deride as '*école de* Sidney Keyes'. Gunn has always, or at least up till recently, written poems much like them – well-made, rational, cultivated, but by now dead feeling poems – which have not done his reputation much good, except, perhaps, in America, where campus poets and poetry are more respectful of them than they would be in England. The Day-Lewis legacy of cultured verse has had a bad press here for some time now, a fact in which there is none the less nothing to be proud of. But Thom Gunn is not a poet who really seemed at home with that legacy, or able to give it his own or a new being. The particular truths towards which he was working were not amenable either to his knowledge of art and literature ('Rastignac at 45') or even to the Yeatsian heroic metaphors – the heroes and the captains – whom he made his more special property.

But if these poems have not held up well (quite the worst of them is 'Readings in French', a perky little critique of Mallarmé, Poe, Proust etc. which should probably not have been reprinted) a poem like 'My Sad Captains' reads even more impressively and satisfyingly now than when it first came out. In a very different way the humour has lasted well too.

> I think of all the toughs through history
> And thank heaven they lived, continually.
> I praise the overdogs, from Alexander
> To those who would not play with Stephen Spender.

At this distance of time that variation on one of Spender's most memorable poems seems in no way derisive, but rather a kind of praetorian salute. Overdogs get a bad press now too in poetry, as bad a one as does culture, and it is good to hear their stature recognised. But it was not until he had settled in America, and been to the west coast, that Gunn found his real milieu, and the topics he was most at home in. This was, in its way, for him the process of 'Withering into the truth', and it has been continued up to his most recent and most memorable collection, *The Man With Night Sweats* (1992).

The changes began to be annunciated as far back as *My Sad Captains*, for instance in the significantly named 'Waking in a Newly Built House', a house putatively in California, in which Gunn felt at home. In it

> Calmly, perception rests on the things,
> and is aware of them only in
> their precise definition, their fine
> lack of even potential meanings.

That set a scene that was by no means empty, or lacking in the best and simplest sorts of human warmth and celebration, American things which cats and dogs can understand. Gunn seemed suddenly to have discovered not only Walt Whitman but William Carlos Williams. This had already shown itself in some superb examples from what are here 'Poems from the 1960s', like 'The Goddess', a celebration about spring and water, soldiers and prostitutes; and which then becomes fully domesticated, as it were, in marvellous poems like 'Yoko' (a black dog), 'The Waitress', 'The Girls Next Door', and the new high rise girders along which

> Indians pad like cats
> With wrenches in their pockets, and hard hats.

(I remember becoming very attached to that poem when reviewing *Jack Straw's Castle* for *Agenda* back in 1976).

But there is a difference between truth in poetry and the 'terrible truthfulness' with which a reviewer hailed *The Man with Night Sweats* two years ago. 'Terrible truthfulness' is not a poetic concept but merely a media one: and because the subject of many of these poems is Aids, the poetry, as real poetry, would not necessarily be any truer for that. Anyone can be truthful, terribly or otherwise: what matters is that 'a sniff of the real' has got into the subject, because a real poet is treating it, and recording 'the small but clustering duties of the sick'. The poems are without either indignation, or terror, but they have a great deal of observation and a great deal of feeling.

401

About ten days ago or so
After we saw you dead
You came back in a dream.
I'm all right now you said.

And it *was* you, although
You were fleshed out again:
You hugged us all round then,
And gave your welcoming beam.

How like you to be kind,
Seeking to reassure.
And, yes, how like my mind
To make itself secure.

I find that as moving as Geoffrey Hill's more subdued admission that he cannot help writing chiefly for himself a poem which is in sorrow for a concentration camp victim. But its neighbour in the collection, 'Still Life', tells a truth of a different sort: about the face of a terminal victim.

He still found breath, and yet
It was an obscure knack.
I shall not soon forget
The angle of his head,
Arrested and reared back
On the crisp field of bed,

Back from what he could neither
Accept, as one opposed,
Nor, as a life-long breather,
Consentingly let go,
The tube his mouth enclosed
In an astonished O.

In a review of *The Man with Night Sweats* in the *TLS*, Hugh Haughton remarked of Thom Gunn that he had been 'strangely neglected in England'. Having helped to award him the first Forward Poetry Prize last year I very much hope that neglect, if it existed, will not longer continue. I think Haughton's comment refers to the fact that Gunn has never fitted into any recognised category where contemporary poetry is concerned, in England, America, or anywhere else. Critics of the fifties assigned him to the 'movement', which in spite of the Larkinian echoes and resemblances which I noted, quite fails to suggest where his originality and potential lay. Such categorising was particularly misleading where Gunn was concerned; and about as intelligent as labelling Roy Campbell (or Larkin himself) poets with a Fascist mentality. Gunn was in his own way just as wholly an original as they were; and a poet, moreover, with a gift for development as striking as that of Yeats, and much more natural.

Possibly Gunn himself contributed in some degree himself to the confusion about him, and therefore the neglect, which Haughton noticed. Poetry is always intimate with sex; and the nature and mythology of Gunn's sexuality – what John Cowper Powys would call its 'life illusion' – was originally ambiguous and oddly indeterminate. When he 'came out', in America, his verse did not adopt any of the appropriate localised styles and rituals: it remained obstinately itself and on its own. It still does. When his poems were bad, as they sometimes were, they were bad wholly in their own way: the Jack Straw poems were quite unlike anything else done by the Beat generation, and never carried any of its hypnotic, ready-made reassurances. Their exactness must have been disconcerting to a generation which had abandoned exactness, together with any other intellectual disciplines. Their exactness, on the question of Aids, is now triumphant. But it was always there – casting a cold but friendly eye on the new people Gunn had elected to live among. 'Three', for instance, is an ordinary poem about nude bathing in California, but full of sharp unexpected insights: the naturalness of the hippy child who runs about and greets the poet before running back to where 'the parents sit/ At watch, who had to learn their nakedness'. Gunn had learnt his the enterprising way, and for him the best way. Nakedness is the state of death; and great poetry is seldom 'positive', in the way the media today is always telling us everything from politics to poetry ought to be. Great poetry is more often one of the voices of death.

EZRA POUND

Gists from Uncollected Prose

Chosen by William Cookson

Richard of St. Victor who was half a neo-platonist, tells us that by naming over all the beautiful things we can think of, we may draw back upon our minds some vestige of the unrememberable beauties of paradise. If we are not given to mystical devotions we may suspect that the function of poetry is, in part, to draw back upon our mind a paradise, if you like, or equally, one's less detestable hours and the outrageous hopes of one's youth.

'The Approach to Paris VI', *The New Age*, 13 October 1913.

*

'She was so fine and she was so healthy that you could have cracked a flea on either of her breasts,' said the old sea captain bragging about the loves of his youth. It seems a shame that the only man who could have made any real use of that glorious phrase in literature, is dead.

'John Synge and the Habits of Criticism', *The Egoist*, 2 February 1914.

*

... when Ireland turned against Synge it ceased to be of any more importance than any other unclassified slum of Cardiff or Birmingham.

A man of genius cannot help where he is born, and Ireland has no claim upon Synge. It did not produce him. And we for our part have no need to accept Ireland on Synge's account. A nation's claim to a man depends not upon the locality of his birth, but upon their ability to receive him.

'The Non-existence of Ireland', *The New Age*, 25 February 1915.

*

From my own personal point of view, as an artist, it is infinitely preferable that there should be internationalism *of any sort* than that there should be nationalism. Civilization has everything to gain by internationalism, by tunnels, by aerial posts...It seems to me that every poor man who joins a national movement of *any* sort acts against his own interest.

*

There are, the astronomers tell us, several millions of suns, with an equal number of solar systems attached, but these Christian matoids still go on believing that they have had a private wireless from the boss of the conglomeration, and to them alone has been revealed the particular set of taboos that most puts His godly back up.
'Studies in Contemporary Mentality XVIII', *The New Age*, 3 January 1918.

*

Nietzsche has done no harm to France because France is accustomed to treating thought as thought, and has not the mania for putting *all* thoughts into action.
. . .
The Hun must get the word 'Macht' out of his occiput. He needs a course in Confucius, the one 'founder' who cannot be made the basis of devastating crusades. He must learn 'fraternal deference', a formula which does not allow itself to be translated into an over-concern with your neighbours' affairs.
'What America Has to Live Down', *The New Age*, 19 September 1918.

*

All religions are evil because all religions try to enforce a certain number of fairly sound or fairly accurate or 'beneficial' propositions by other propositions which are sheer bluff, unsoundness, will-to-power, or personal or type predilections, regardless of the temperament or nature of others.
'Pastiche The Regional 1', *The New Age*, 21 August 1919.

*

Provincialism of time is as damned as provincialism of place;
'Pastiche. The Regional VIII', *The New Age*, 28 August 1919.

*

One need never be surprised at an atavism; yet atavism is almost the last phenomenon which even 'great' historians recognize; nowhere have I seen it pointed out that Napoleon was the completion, the last and hugest example, of the common Renaissance type of Italian condottiere; a Corsican provincial with energy and a demoded ideal, his 'contribution' was to do the thing in larger France instead of an Italian city republic.
'Pastiche. The Regional – XVIII', *The New Age*, 20 November 1919.

*

Lasting literature is perhaps always the literature which tries to build simply and undisguisedly the image of its subject matter.
'Some Notes on Francisco de Quevedo Villegas', *Hermes*, March 1921.

*

Adolphe is, an, almost, pathetic hysteric; . . . he is, so far as I can make out, a tool of *almost* the worst Huns.[1]
'From Italy', *The New English Weekly*, 24 May 1934.

*

People treated by Freudians, etc. get steadily more and more interested in their own footling interiors, and become progressively less interesting to anyone else. Never, after treatment, do they seem to do anything of the least use or interest.
They are at the nadir from Spinoza's sane and hearty; the more perfect a thing is the more it acts and the less it suffers.
'Private Worlds', *The New English Weekly*, 2 May 1935.

*

---

[1] Compare Canto 86, ' "hysteric presiding over it all" '39'. Ed.

True, I have never advocated the travesties of Fascism presented in alien newspapers or by the antics of Sir O. Mosley. On the other hand I have no objection to being called a communist. I mean I couldn't pass a test for non-communism that would satisfy any member of the British Labour Party.

I decline, however, and very firmly, to accept a purely muscovite tyrannous man-crushing variety of collectivism that jettisons the last 300 years of Europe's CULTURAL and, if you like, communal, heritage.

. . .

I don't expect Englishmen to sympathize with my politics. It is Jeffersonian and democratic, but includes 'responsibility', an element that has for a long time been degraded out of what has been labelled democracy.

'Organically Speaking', *The New English Weekly*, 26 December 1935.

*

The STATE has credit. There is no need for any state to pay rent on its own credit to groups of private individuals.

'Demarcations', *British Union Quarterly*, January/April 1937.

*

In national economy the WHOLE people must be able to buy what the WHOLE people produces. That is the first postulate in totalitarian economics.

I AM FOR ANY PARTY THAT FIGHTS OR PERMITS ME TO FIGHT ECONOMIC ILLITERACY.

'Intellectual Money', *British Union Quarterly*, April-June 1937.

*

I dislike the term 'theology' it having ever appeared to me that men start talking of God when they dare not face anything nearer, and when they chiefly want to pass the buck and get out of immediate obligations or duties. . . . Let us, for 'God's sake' or 'Heaven's sake' or in the name of the TIEN or the *'summa sapienza e il primo amore'*, recognize that so far as human intellect is concerned this desire to get the 'theology right' is a commendable desire to relate ALL parts and components of one's thought to a

CENTRAL CONCEPT. The best minds in the race have been in total accord as to the UNKNOWABILITY of the real central whatever. And when logic attempts to deduce particular *shoulds* and *should nots* from the UNKNOWABLE it generally paralyses all thought and all action, or gives it up and muddles along amid leftovers and superstitions.

'The «Criterion» Passes', *British Union Quarterly*, April/June 1939.

*

The real Greek heritage is neither the Swinburnian swish or the 18th century formalism but the laconism, and the dissociation of verbal meanings.

Edge, February 1957.

*

Even the Victorian era with its formula: Greece for the arts, Rome for the law, the Hebrews for religion was trying to preserve elements, the main elements of different cultures, not, à la UNESCO, trying to melt out all distinctions and reduce the whole to a dull paste of common inhumanity. (? and/or nucleosity.)

Agenda, July-August 1959.

(1979)

SOURCES

Texts and Dates

Part 1: The Founders

Ezra Pound 'From Canto 115'
Vol.4 No.2 October-November, 1965 (Special Issue in Honour of Ezra Pound's Eightieth Birthday).

'Canto 115'
Vol.17 Nos 3-4 – Vol.18 No.1 (3 issues) Autumn-Winter 1979/80 (21st Anniversary Ezra Pound Special Issue).

'Notes'
Vol.8 Nos 3-4 Autumn-Winter 1970 (Special Issue in Honour of Ezra Pound's Eighty-Fifth Birthday).

David Jones 'A, a, a, Domine Deus'
Vol.5 Nos 1-3 Spring-Summer 1967 (First David Jones Special Issue).

'The Sleeping Lord'
Vol.5 Nos 1-3 Spring-Summer 1967 (First David Jones Special Issue).

Basil Bunting 'On the Fly-leaf of Pound's Cantos'
Vol.4 No.2 October-November, 1965 (Special Issue in Honour of Ezra Pound's Eightieth Birthday).

'Birthday Greeting'
Vol.4 Nos 5-6 Autumn 1966 (Basil Bunting Feature).

'Stones trip Coquets burn'
Vol.8 Nos 3-4 Autumn-Winter 1970 (Special Issue in Honour of Ezra Pound's 85th Birthday).

'All the cants they peddle'   Vol.12 No.2 Summer 1974.

'Per Che No Spero'
Vol.16 No.1 Spring 1978 (Basil Bunting Special Issue).

'Snow's on the fellside, look! How deep'
Vol.16 No.1 Spring 1978 (Bunting Issue).

Hugh MacDiarmid 'When the Birds Come Back to Rhiannon'
Vol.2 No.5 September-October 1961.

'Bracken Hills in Autumn'
Vol.5 No.4 – Vol.6 No.1 Autumn-Winter 1967/68 (Hugh MacDiarmid and Scottish Poetry Double Issue).

'The Day before the Twelfth'
Vol.12 No.4 – Vol.13 No.1 Winter-Spring 1975 (Fifteenth Anniversary Special Issue).

William Carlos Williams 'The Painting'   Vol.1 No.10 April 1960.

'Iris'   Vol.3 No.1 August-September, 1963.

from 'Asphodel, That Greeny Flower'
Vol.3 No.2 October-November 1963 (William Carlos Williams Special Issue).

Louis Zukofsky: Extracts from a Special Issue, edited by Charles Tomlinson   Vol.6 No.6 December 1964.

Part 2   A Sheaf of Poems

Michael Alexander 'Of Green Fields' & 'Thomas Hardy'
Vol.4 No.1 April-May 1965.

'Do You Remember That?'   Vol.13 No.2 Summer 1975.

Anne Beresford 'Eurydice in Hades'
Vol.9 Nos 2-3 Spring-Summer 1971.

'The Condemned'   Vol.12 No.4 – Vol.13 No.1 Winter-Spring 1975.

'The Comforter'   (from *The Curving Shore*, Agenda Editions, 1975)

'August'   (also from *The Curving Shore*, 1975).

'Ancestors'   Vol.30 No.3 Autumn 1992.

Heather Buck 'At the Window' & 'Child's Play'
Vol.14 No.2 Summer 1976

'Psyche'   Vol.26 No.1 Spring 1988.

Stanley Burnshaw 'A Poem for Peter Dale'
Vol.26 No.2 Summer 1988 (Peter Dale Fiftieth Birthday Issue).

John Cayley 'Elsewhere'   Vol.26 No.1 Spring 1988.

'Against Nature'   Vol.26 No.3 Autumn 1988.

Humphrey Clucas 'In Darkness'
Vol.21 No.4 – Vol.22 No.1 Winter-Spring 1983/4.

William Cookson *Spell*
Vol.21 No.3 Autumn 1983, Vol.21 No.4 – Vol.22 No.1 Winter-Spring 1983/4; Vol.22 No.2 Summer 1984 and Vol.22 Nos 3-4 Autumn-Winter 1984/5.

Peter Dale 'Last Respects'   Vol.3 No.5 September 1964.

'Old Poet on a Rainy Day'
Vol.11 No.4 – Vol.12 No.1 Autumn-Winter 1973/4 (2nd David Jones Special Issue).

'Thinking of Writing a Letter'   Vol.7 No.2 Spring 1969 (revised 1993).

'Old Haunt'   Vol.10 No.4 – Vol.11 No.1 Autumn-Winter 1972/3.

'Shades'   Vol.12 No.4 – Vol.13 No.1 Winter-Spring 1975
(Fifteenth Anniversary Issue).

'Storm'   (from *One Another*, Agenda Editions/Carcanet, 1978).

'Memorial'   Vol.22 Nos 3-4 Autumn-Winter 1984/5.

'Upland'   Vol.26 No.2 Summer 1988
(Peter Dale Fiftieth Birthday Issue).

'Journey'   Vol.31 No.2 Summer 1993.

Donald Davie 'In the Stopping Train'
Vol.11 No.4 – Vol.12 No.1 Autumn-Winter 1973/4
(2nd David Jones Special Issue).

Peter Dent 'Momentum'   Vol.4 Nos 5-6 Autumn 1966.

'Hesitation'   (from *Proxima Centauri*, Agenda Editions, 1972).

Ronald Duncan No.1 is from Vol.1 No.4 April 1959, and No.2 from Vol.1 No.9 December 1959.

Thom Gunn 'Touch'   Vol.4 Nos 5-6 Autumn 1966.

Donald Hall 'In the Kitchen of the Old House'
Vol.2 Nos 11-12 March-April 1963.

Michael Hamburger 'Travelling I'   Vol.7 No.2 Spring 1969.

'A Walk in the Cotswolds'   Vol.27 No.2 Summer 1989.

Ian Hamilton 'Birthday Poem'   Vol.3 No.5 September 1964.

'At Evening', 'Again', 'Soliloquy', 'The Garden'
Vol.31 No.2 Summer 1993.

Seamus Heaney From 'Station Island'   Vol.22 No.2 Summer 1984.

David Heidenstam 'The land stands silent...'
Vol.26 No.1 Spring 1988.

A.L. Hendricks 'The Tree-Lady'   Vol.26 No.1 Spring 1988.

Geoffrey Hill *Soliloquies*   Vol.4 No.1 April-May 1965.

From 'The Songbook' of Sebastian Arrurruz   Vol.4 Nos 5-6 Autumn 1966.

'Copla'*   Vol.23 Nos 3-4 Autumn-Winter 1985/6.
*(This Copla first appeared in *Stand* 14/1, 1972).

'Lachrimae'   Vol.12 No.4 – Vol.13 No.1 Winter-Spring 1975.
(Fifteenth Anniversary Issue).

'Terribilis est locus iste'   Vol.13 No.3 Autumn 1975.

Five Sonnets from 'An Apology for the Revival of Christian Architecture in England'   Vol.15 Nos 2-3 Summer-Autumn 1977.

'Ritornelli' & 'Sobieski's Shield'   Vol.30 Nos 1-2 Spring-Summer 1992
(Geoffrey Hill's Sixtieth Birthday Issue).

'Of Coming-into-being and passing-Away', 'Psalms of Assize' & 'Sorrel'
Vol.31 No.3 Autumn 1993.

Roland John 'Memory'   Vol.12 No.4 – Vol.13 No.1
Winter-Spring 1975 (15th Anniversary Issue).

Peter Levi 'Didactic Poem'   Vol.2 Nos 11-12 March-April 1963.

'For Denis Bethell'   Vol.19 No.4 – Vol.20 No.1 Winter-Spring 1982.

Eddie Linden 'The Miner'   Vol.22 Nos 3-4 Autumn-Winter 1984/5.

Edward Lowbury 'Learning to Walk Again'
Vol.22 Nos 3-4 Autumn-Winter 1984/5.

Patricia McCarthy 'Circe'   Vol.21 No.3 Autumn 1983.

'Last Rites'   Vol.22 Nos 3-4 Autumn-Winter 1985/6.

'Visiting the Horses at Midnight, Midwinter'
Vol.31 No.3 Autumn 1993.

Jean MacVean 'Return'   Vol.27 No.2 Summer 1989.

Eve Machin 'Sea Phantom' & 'On your Journey towards the Dead'
Vol.31 No.2 Summer 1993.

Sylvia Mann 'For Three Lords'   Vol.13 No.2 Summer 1975.

Virginia Maskell 'Heat touching heat'   Vol.1 No.4 April 1959.

'The Sunday Hours'   Vol.2 No.6 February-March 1962.

Alan Massey Three Extracts from 'Leechcraft'
Vol.12 No.2 Summer 1974.

W.S. Milne 'In Memoriam Hugh MacDiarmid'
Vol.19 Nos 2-3 Summer-Autumn 1981.

'Hesperus'   Vol.31 No.3 Autumn 1993.

George Oppen 'Psalm'   Vol.4 Nos 3-4 Summer 1966.

Penelope Palmer 'To My Grandmother'
Vol.3 No.1 August-September 1963.

'The Chapel'   (from *The Lamp*, Agenda Editions, 1981).

'Green Beads'   Vol.6 No.2 Spring 1968.

'The Cornflowers'   Vol.14 No.4 – Vol.15 No.1 Winter-Spring 1977.

Rachel Pelham Burn 'Fragment from Sleep'
Vol.19 No.4 – Vol.20 No.1 Winter-Spring 1982.

Kathleen Raine 'Fire' & 'Charity'   Vol.26 No.1 Spring 1988.

Theodore Roethke 'The Rose'
Vol.3 No.4 April 1964 (A Feature on Roethke).

Peter Russell 'Russell's Rest'
Vol.30 No.4 – Vol.31 No.1 Winter-Spring 1993 (Tom Scott Special Issue).

N.K. Sandars 'S.F.'   Vol.9 Nos 2-3 Spring-Summer 1971.

Tom Scott 'Cursus Mundi'
Vol.30 No.4 – Vol.31 No.1 Winter-Spring 1993.

'The Annunciation'   Vol.4 Nos 5-6 Autumn 1966.

From 'The Ship', 'Lament for Eurydice' & 'Let Go Who Will'
Vol.30 No.4 – Vol.31 No.1 Winter-Spring 1993 (Tom Scott Issue).

C.H. Sisson 'Numbers'   Vol.3 No.3 December-January 1963/4.

'In Flood'   Vol.17 No.1 Spring 1979
(Geoffrey Hill Special Issue – the first one *Agenda* did).

'On Living Rather Long'   Vol.30 No.3 Autumn 1992.

W.D. Snodgrass 'Owls'   Vol.11 Nos 2-3 Spring-Summer 1973.

R.S. Thomas 'Two Versions on a Theme'   Vol.4 No.1 April-May 1965.

Charles Tomlinson 'Winter Journey'
Vol.23 Nos 3-4 Autumn-Winter 1985/6.

Peter Whigham 'The Orchard Is Not Cut Down'
Vol.1 No.2 February 1959.

Julie Whitby 'After "The Road in Louveciennes"'
Vol.21 No.3 Autumn 1983.

Caroline Wright 'Leaves'   Vol.18 No.2 Summer 1980.

'Time and Place' & 'Dead of Night'
Vol.19 Nos 2-3 Summer-Autumn 1981.

Part 3   Translations

Peter Whigham Five Translations from Sappho
Vol.4 Nos 5-6 Autumn 1966.

Peter Jay Three Translations from Ibycus   Vol.4 Nos 5-6 Autumn 1966.

Basil Bunting 'Eheu Fugaces' (from Horace)
Vol.8 Nos 3-4 Autumn-Winter 1970
(Special Issue in Honour of Ezra Pound's 85th Birthday).

Peter Whigham Catullus 31   Vol.1 No.12 July 1960.

Arthur Cooper Wang Wei & P'ei Ti   Vol.12 No.2 Summer 1974.

'Flower or not Flower'   Vol.16 No.2 Summer 1978.

Michael Alexander 'The Ruin'   Vol.2 No.6 February-March 1962.

Alan Massey from Arnaut Daniel   Vol.21 No.2 Summer 1983.

Peter Dale Dante's 'Sestina'
Vol.17 Nos 3-4 – Vol.18 No.1 Autumn-Winter-Spring 1979/80 (3 issues)
(Twenty-first Anniversary Ezra Pound Issue).

W.D. Snodgrass 'Miorita'
Vol.12 No.3 Autumn 1974 (Romanian Poetry Supplement).

Tom Scott 'Ballat o the Hingit' and 'Ballat o the Leddies o Langsyne'
Vol.30 No.4 – Vol.31 No.1 Winter-Spring 1993 (Tom Scott Issue).

Peter Dale 'Ballade' (from Villon)   Vol.9 Nos 2-3 Spring-Summer 1971.

Michael Hamburger / Hölderlin 'But when the heavenly'
Vol.27 No.2 Summer 1989.

Peter Russell/Mandelstam 'When the urban moon...'
Vol.1 No.1 (the first issue!) January 1959.

'Tristia'   Vol.1 No.4 April 1959.

'Leningrad 1930'   Vol.1 No.10 April 1960.

Cocteau / Neame Leoun   Vol.2 Nos 2-3 December-January 1960/61.

Ungaretti Two Poems / MacDiarmid versions   Vol.8 No.2 Spring 1970.

David Rokeah Two Poems   Vol.17 No.2 Summer 1979.

Pound / Montanari 'L'ultima Ora'   Vol.3 No.5 September 1964.

Part 4   Two Landmarks of Prose

T.S. Eliot 'Scylla and Charybis'   Vol.23 Nos 1-2 Spring-Summer 1985.
(T.S. Eliot Special Issue).

Donald Davie 'Can Literary History Be Permitted'
Vol.30 No.3 Autumn 1992.

Part 5   Essays

Moelwyn Merchant 'The Coke *Cantos*'
Vol.17 Nos 3-4 – Vol.18 No.1 Autumn-Winter-Spring 1979/80
(21st Anniversary Ezra Pound Issue).

Tom Scott 'The Poet as Scapegoat'   Vol.7 No.2 Spring 1969.

Henry Swabey 'The Just Price'
Vol.23 Nos 3-4 Autumn-Winter 1985/86.

Robert Lowell 'A Tribute' & **Marianne Moore** 'A Note'
Vol.4 No.2 October-November 1965. (Ezra Pound 80th Birthday Issue)

Stuart Piggott 'David Jones and the Past of Man'
Vol.5 Nos 1-3 Spring-Summer 1967 (David Jones Special Issue);
reprinted in the Second David Jones issue (Vol.11 No.4 – Vol.12 No.1
Autumn-Winter 1973/4).

Saunders Lewis 'A Note'   Vol.5 Nos 1-3 Spring-Summer 1967
(David Jones Special Issue).

Kathleen Raine 'Tom Scott and the Bardic Heritage'
Vol.30 No.4 – Vol.31 No.1 Winter-Spring 1993 (Tom Scott Special Issue).

Heather Buck 'Geoffrey Hill'   Vol.30 Nos 1-2 Spring-Summer 1992
(Geoffrey Hill Sixtieth Birthday Issue).

Alan Massey 'Geoffrey Hill'   Vol.23 Nos 3-4 Autumn-Winter 1985/6.

Part 6   A Reconsideration

Jonathan Barker 'A Land that Is Lonelier than Ruin'
Vol.21 No.1 Spring 1983 (revised 1993).

Part 7   Two Memoirs

Basil Bunting 'Yeats Recollected'   Vol.12 No.2 Summer 1974.

Norman Rea '9.9.42 Hill, Geoffrey W.'
Vol.30 Nos 1-2 Spring-Summer 1992
(Geoffrey Hill Sixtieth Birthday Issue).

Part 8   A Closing Miscellany

W.H. Auden 'On Technique'
Vol.10 No.4 – Vol.11 No.1 Autumn-Winter 1972/3
(Special Issue on Rhythm).

Basil Bunting 'Hugh MacDiarmid Lost'
Vol.16 Nos 3-4 Autumn-Winter 1978/9.

Geoffrey Hill ' "The Age Demanded" (Again)'
Vol.26 No.3 Autumn 1988.

Peter Levi 'Penelope Palmer'   Vol.20 No.2 Summer 1982.

John Bayley 'Death and the Captain'   Vol.31 No.3 Autumn 1993.

Ezra Pound 'Gists from Uncollected Prose'
Vol.17 Nos 3-4 – Vol.18 No.1 (3 issues) Autumn-Winter-Spring 1979/80.
(21st Anniversary Ezra Pound Issue). The final Gist, 'Even the Victorian
era with its formula . . .' comes from Vol.1 No.6 July-August 1959. This is
added now and was not included in the 21st Anniverary *Agenda*.

INDEX OF AUTHORS

Alexander, Michael   65-6, 233-4
Auden, W.H.   391
Barker, Jonathan   351-62
Bayley, John   397-403
Bedford, William   67
Beresford, Anne   68-72
Buck, Heather   73-5, 343-4
Bunting, Basil   34-7, 229, 365-75, 392
Burnshaw, Stanley   76
Cayley, John   77-84
Clucas, Humphrey   85
Cookson, William   86-91
Cooper, Arthur   231-2
Dale, Peter   92-9, 237-8, 245-6
Davie, Donald   100-7, 300-5
Dent, Peter   108
Duncan, Ronald   109-10
Eliot, T.S.   285-99
Gunn, Thom   111-2
Hall, Donald   113-4
Hamburger, Michael   115-7, 247-51, 278
Hamilton, Ian   118-20
Heaney, Seamus   121-3
Heidenstam, David   124
Hendriks, A.L.   125
Hill, Geoffrey   126-49, 393-4
Jay, Peter   227-8
John, Roland   150
Jones, David   8-33
Levi, Peter   151-6, 395-6
Lewis, Saunders   336-7
Linden, Eddie   157
Lowbury, Edward   158
Lowell, Robert   331
McCarthy, Patricia   159-63
MacDiarmid, Hugh   38-44, 279

MacVean, Jean   164-7
Machin, Eve   168
Mann, Sylvia   169
Maskell, Virginia   170
Massey, Alan   171-80, 235-6, 345-7
Mead, Ruth and Matthew   280
Merchant, Moelwyn   309-17
Milne, W.S.   181-2
Moore, Marianne   331
Oppen, George   183
Neame, Alan   255-77
Palmer, Penelope   184-7
Pelham Burn, Rachel   188
Piggott, Stuart   332-5
Pound, Ezra   3-7, 281, 404-8
Raine, Kathleen   189-91, 338-42
Rea, Norman   376-88
Roethke, Theodore   192-5
Rokeah, David   280
Russell, Peter   196, 252-3
Sandars, N.K.   197-8
Scott, Tom   199-204, 243-5, 318-27
Sisson, C.H.   205-9
Snodgrass, W.D.   210, 239-42
Swabey, Henry   328-30
Thomas, R.S.   211-2
Tomlinson, Charles   55-7, 213-5
Whigham, Peter   216, 225-6, 230
Whitby, Julie   217
Williams, William Carlos   45-54
Wright, Caroline   218-22
Zukofsky, Louis   58-62

AGENDA

Issues published since AGENDA – AN ANTHOLOGY and future plans

A TRIBUTE TO KATHLEEN RAINE including 40 New Poems and an Interview. In the same issue: **A FEATURE ON W.H. AUDEN** with essays by Grey Gowrie, Glyn Maxwell and Peter Mudford. Heather Buck on T.S. Eliot's *Four Quartets*. Poems, reviews.

333 pages   Vol.31 No.4   Winter-Spring 1994

GERMAN POETRY SPECIAL ISSUE including *De Jure Belli ac Pacis*, a sequence of 8 poems by Geoffrey Hill. An Anthology of twentieth century German Poems in translation edited by Richard Dove. Advisory Editor: Michael Hamburger. Also Friedrich Hölderlin/ Michael Hamburger – Tributes by John Bayley, Raymond Hargreaves and Kathleen Raine.

144 pages   Vol.32 No.2   Summer 1994

A TRIBUTE TO PETER RUSSELL 14 New Poems by him (Seven from Quintilius). Also, an Anthology of 93 New Poems with work by John Burnside, Donald Davie, Heather Buck, Peter Levi, Tom Scott, R.S. Thomas and many others. A review supplement.

328 pages   Vol.32 Nos.3-4   Autumn-Winter 1994/5

THE SEVENTIES RECONSIDERED with essays on W.S. Graham, Peter Dale and Alan Massey. A Feature on Small Presses. Poems by Jon Silkin and others. Alan Wall on David Jones.

168 pages   Vol.33 No.1   Spring 1995

CHARLES TOMLINSON: INTERNATIONAL ISSUE including a New Sequence by Tomlinson and an Interview. Guest Editor: Richard Swigg.

160 pages   Vol.33 No.2   Summer 1995

IRISH POETRY DOUBLE ISSUE with new work by Seamus Heaney, Thomas Kinsella, Derek Mahon, John Montague, Brendan Kennelly, Desmond O'Grady, Theo Dorgan, Kerry Hardie, Mary O'Malley, Eiléan Ní Chuilleanáin and many more. Essays on John Montague, Thomas Kinsella, Derek Mahon, Seamus Heaney and W.B. Yeats. Guest Editor: Patricia McCarthy.

320 pages   Vol.33 Nos.3-4   Autumn-Winter 1996

A TRIBUTE TO W.D. SNODGRASS including new poems by him and essays on his work by James Fenton, Philip Hoy and others. *Lenses*, a long poem, by Alan Wall and poems by R.S. Thomas, Michael Hamburger, Donald Hall, Peter Porter and Jean MacVean. Kathleen Raine on Ted Hughes's Coleridge and Kieron Winn on 'New Generation Poets'.

192 pages   Vol.34 No.1   Spring 1996

A TRIBUTE TO GEOFFREY HILL with new poems by him and essays by David Gervais, Jeffrey Wainwright, Peter Walker, Alan Wall and Peter Walton. Geoffrey Hill on T.S. Eliot's *Varieties of Metaphysical Poetry*. Poems, reviews.

176 pages   Vol.34 No.2   Summer 1996

DANTE, POUND AND THE CONTEMPORARY POET. A double number including new versions of Dante by John Burnside, Peter Dale, Thom Gunn, John Montague, Alan Neame, Charles Tomlinson and others. Essays reconsidering *La Divina Commedia* and Pound's *Cantos*, including Ronald Bush on recently discovered drafts of cantos that Pound wrote in Italian during the Second World War that shed new light on the composition of *The Pisan Cantos* and A.David Moody, 'Dante as the Young Pound's Virgil: an Introduction to some early Drafts and Fragments'.

320 pages   Vol.34 Nos.3-4   Autumn-Winter 1996/7

Issues for 1997 and beyond: Spanish Poetry, guest editor: Jordi Doce; Japanese Poetry; Greek Poetry; an Issue on Culture; Regular Anthologies of new Poems with Review Sections.

AGENDA EDITIONS
Books from our list

DAVID JONES *The Roman Quarry*. AGENDA is proud to be the publisher of this substantial collection of the posthumous writings of the author Hugh MacDiarmid described as 'the greatest living poet in the British Isles'.

284 pages   Price £9.90

TOM SCOTT *Collected Shorter Poems* 'It is astonishing that such a powerful and original poetic voice should have been so neglected. Tom Scott is a poet of the highest order'. Harold Pinter.

208 pages   £12

DANTE *The Divine Comedy* Laurence Binyon's translation, together with Rossetti's version of *La Vita Nuova*. 'The venerable Binyon has...produced the most interesting English version of Dante that I have seen or expect to see'. Ezra Pound.

662 pages   £9.90

KATHLEEN RAINE *On a Deserted Shore* A new edition of one of the very few great sequences of the 20th century.

56 pages   Price £6

PETER DALE *One Another* A Sequence of 62 Sonnets. 'Dale is a love poet of the greatest tenderness' Glyn Pursglove. 'Poetry...quite worthy to be mentioned in the same breath as that published in its decade by Philip Larkin, Geoffrey Hill and F.T. Prince...' W.G. Shepherd.

75 pages   Price £6

ANNE BERESFORD *Landscape with Figures* 'The finest of mystic poets, her work is pitched on the very edge of perception: celebratory, frightening, elusive – meditative and unique'. David Storey.

72 pages   Price £6

PENELOPE PALMER *The Lamp* 'This is a book for grown-ups, not for professors. God knows what poetry ought to be, but if it is like these poems it will still be the most beautiful and serious use of the breath of mankind'. Peter Levi.

48 pages   Price £6

WILLIAM COOKSON *Vestiges 1955-1995* 'A lovely book with a clear voice and nothing wasted, dream tempered by reality, reality by dream, the diction exact without fuss'. Charles Tomlinson. 'Many memorable phrases' – R.S. Thomas. Cover paintings by Julie Ann Noad

40 pages   Price £6

JEAN MacVEAN *The True and Holy History of the Sangrail* after Sir Thomas Malory. Cover designed by Josef Herman.

32 pages   Price £4.50

ALAN MASSEY *The Fire Garden* A Selection of Poems and Translations. 'Alan Massey is a prodigiously talented poet, and deserves to be much better known than he is'. Philip Hoy.

80 pages   Price £6

ROLAND JOHN *Believing Words Are Real* 'In clear, sharp, classical language Roland John solemnises pain'. Brian Merrikin Hill.

56 pages   Price £6

MICHAEL ALEXANDER *Twelve Poems* 'Every one...is austerely concerned...with what is undoubtedly the central business of the Post-Romantic lyric, the intimation of "transcendence" or "the moment outside time"' – Donald Davie.

24 pages   Price £3

WILLIAM BEDFORD *Journeys* 'The key to Bedford's poetry is the unflinching openness in his dealings with readers'. Anthony Selbourne.

64 pages   Price £6

JOHN CAYLEY *Ink Bamboo* A First Collection of original poems and translations from the Chinese.

120 pages To be published jointly with Bellew Publishing
Autumn 1996   Price £6

Forthcoming: Anne Beresford, *Selected Poems*, with a Foreword by David Storey.

A subscription to AGENDA costs £20 for one year (4 issues).
A complete list of back issues, and books in print, is available on request.
AGENDA, 5 Cranbourne Court, Albert Bridge Road, London, SW11 4PE
Tel. & Fax. 0171-228 0700.